Women Workers in India

Women Workers in India

Edited by

Ravi Prakash Yadav
Department of Industrial Relations and Personnel Management,
T.M. Bhagalpur University, Bhagalpur

Kumar Chandradeep
Department of English, College of Commerce, Patna

Barsa
Researcher in Social Scientist

New Century Publications
New Delhi, India

NEW CENTURY PUBLICATIONS
4800/24, Bharat Ram Road,
Ansari Road, Daryaganj,
New Delhi – 110 002 (India)

Tel.: 011-2324 7798, 4358 7398, 6539 6605
Fax: 011-4101 7798
E-mail: indiatax@vsnl.com • info@newcenturypublications.com
www.newcenturypublications.com

Editorial office:
LG–7, Aakarshan Bhawan,
4754-57/23, Ansari Road, Daryaganj,
New Delhi – 110 002

Tel.: 011-4356 0919

First Published: **2012**

ISBN: **978-81-7708-295-1**

Published by New Century Publications and printed at Salasar Imaging Systems, New Delhi.

Designs: Patch Creative Unit, New Delhi.

PRINTED IN INDIA

DEDICATED TO

The Divine Memory

of

The Great Sufi Saint of Bihar

'Hazrat Makhdum Shah Muhammad Muneım Pak—(1671-1771)'
Whose holy Shrine, situated at Mitan Ghat (Patna City)

"The holy dargah of Hazrat Muneim Pak at Mitan Ghat, Patna City has been a live testimony of communal harmony and spiritual learning since the 18th Century. Pachna village of Shekhpura district is the birth place of this great sage. You had your basic education and initiation done under the guidance of Huzrat Deewan Syed Khaliluddin of Badh, Patna. Thereafter, you received higher education at a traditional university near Jama Mosque in Delhi for a long period of time. During this period, you had the rare opportunity of getting spiritual and philosophical learning under the great Sufi Saint Hazrat Khwaja Farhad Dehalvi and his equally worthy successor Shah Asadullah before shouldering the leadership of Sufi Spiritualism.

Before 12 years of your ultimate departure, you received a divine spark and eventually decided to make the Jama Mosque premises of Hazrat Mulla Mitan, the Guru of Shahzada Azim as your work place. This place is now renowned as "Munymiya" due to your consistent effort in the sufi chain. The singular credit for popularising this holy place goes to your highness. Your range of successors has already crossed eleven illustrious generations and the current 12th generation is treading the same path of spiritualism as shown by your holiness rising above the petty barriers of caste, community and creed.

FOREWORD

Women are an integral part of the society. The status and employment of women have often been argued as an indicator of the level of development of societies. India has about 40 crore workers, out of which about 12.30 crore are women. Over 95 percent women workers are in the unorganized sector and only 5 percent in the organised sector. They constitute the most "vulnerable group" in the Indian economy.

Dr. Ravi Prakash Yadav, Faculty Member of University Department of Industrial Relations and Personnel Management, T.M. Bhagalpur University, Bhagalpur, Dr. Kumar Chandradeep, Faculty Member of P.G. Department of English, College of Commerce, Patna and Mrs. Barsa deserve kudos and appreciation for their invaluable academic enterprise in editing the book "Women Workers in India". This book will prove to be a milestone in the field of "women studies" in India. The book contains 16 academic and research papers contributed by scholars in the field belonging to reputed universities and centres of academic excellence in India. Many of these papers dealing with women workers in the informal sector and organized sector, gender discrimination in employment, entrepreneurship, women self-help groups, economic empowerment and legal protection for women workers, have thrown light on the intricacies of the process.

This book will generate meaningful debate and discussion on this topical subject affecting the lives of the millions of women workers in India. I congratulate Dr. Yadav, Dr. Chandradeep and Mrs. Barsa for their commendable effort in bringing out an extremely useful book, based on the analysis of facts and data. This book will prove to be of utmost importance for the post-graduate students, research scholars, teachers, labour organisations, social workers, governmental and non-governmental organisations of India.

Harinarayan Singh
Minister,
Department of Human Resource Development,
Patna, Bihar

About the Book

The problems of women workers in general—and in the unorganised sector in particular—deserve special attention and focus in view of their marginalised position within the class of workers. The position of women workers in rural India is considerably lower than that of women in general. The bottom layer is constituted by women belonging to the lowest social status groups. A number of national and international studies have documented the sex-typing of jobs and occupations by women. Occupational segregation represents a form of discrimination.

Discrimination on the lines of gender is not always overt. It appears in very subtle forms such as in the nature of work performed, skills required to perform the work and the valuation of these skills and the technology used by men and women. One problem more specific to women is that they are subject to various forms of harassment at the workplace. Verbal and physical violence against women has been an age-old method of subjugating them.

Female and child domestic workers constitute a large portion of migrant worker population. Working in the unregulated domain of a private home, mostly without the protection of national labour legislations, allows for female domestic workers to be maltreated by their employers with impunity.

This volume contains 16 well-researched papers by scholars in the field of women studies. These scholarly papers explain and examine the various aspects of working conditions of women workers in India.

About the Editors

Dr. Ravi Prakash Yadav is a faculty member of the University Department of Industrial Relations and Personnel Management, T.M. Bhagalpur University, Bhagalpur (Bihar). He has more than 35 articles to his credit published in various journals, edited books and magazines. He has presented more than 17 papers in national and international seminars and conferences. He has authored 4 books, viz. *Bal Shram: Samasaya Avam Samadhan; Bharat May Mahila Shramik; Globalisation and the Indian Economy* and *Lengik Hinsa Avam Mahila Sashaktikaran.*

Dr. Kumar Chandradeep is a faculty member of the Department of English, College of Commerce, Patna. He has to his credit a number of research papers and book reviews. He has attended and presented papers at various seminars and conferences, both national and international. He has authored two books, viz. *Walter de la Mare: Poetry and Novels: An Evaluation* and *Indian Drama in English.* He is one of the editors of *Cyber Literature, Patliputra Journal of English Studies* and *Vimarsh.*

Mrs. Barsa is an active researcher in social sciences. She has to her credit a number of academic papers. She has participated and presented papers in national and international seminars.

Contents

Contributors and Their Affiliations

Vibhuti Patel	Professor and Head, University Department of Economics, S.N.D.T. Women's University, Mumbai.
Anupama	Reader in Economics, Department of Post-graduate Studies, Punjabi University Regional Centre, Bathinda, Punjab.
Neru Gupta	Head, Department of Commerce, S.S.D Girls College, Bathinda, Punjab.
Sarita Agrawal	Reader, Department of Business Economics, Faculty of Commerce, M.S. University of Baroda, Baroda.
Jyoti Achanta	Lecturer, Department of Business Economics, Faculty of Commerce, The M.S. University, Baroda, Gujarat.
Raginideep	HIG-13, Block-1, Sector-7, Bahadurpur Housing Colony, Bhuthnath Road, Patna.
P. Anita	Lecturer, Department of Economics, Fatima College (Autonomous), The Mary Land, Madurai, Tamil Nadu.
Puja Roy	Flat No.-16, Comfort Enclave, First Cross, First Main, B.D.A Layout, Ganga Nagar, Bangalore.
Harvinder Kaur	Professor of Economics, Department of Correspondence Courses, Punjabi University, Patiala, Punjab.
Monika Rani	Department of Correspondence Courses, Punjabi University, Patiala.
Minaxi Pathak	Professor, Department of Family Resource Management, Faculty of Home Science, AAU, Jorhat, Assam.
Nandita Bhattacharyya	Department of Family Resource Management, Faculty of Home Science, AAU, Jorhat, Assam.
H.L. Kaila	Faculty Member, Department of Psychology, S.N.D.T. Women's University, Mumbai.

A. Sangamithra	Faculty Member, Department of Economics, Bharathiar University, Coimbatore, Tamil Nadu.
S.K. Karpagavalle	Research Scholar, Department of Economics, Bhavathair University, Coimbatore, Tamil Nadu.
Kaistha Sunita	Reader, Jesus and Mary College, University of Delhi.
Amar Nath Singh	Professor, Department of Social Work, Mahatma Gandhi Kashi Vidyapeeth, Varanasi, U.P.
Bindu Arora	Reader, Department of Management Studies, Kanya Gurukul, 47, Sewak Ashram Road, Dehradun.
Patiraj Kumari	Reader, Department of Management Studies, Kanya Gurukul, Dehradun.
Yasmeen Ansari	Assistant Professor, Department of Management Studies, Bharat Institute of Technology, Meerut.
Atanu Sengupta	Reader, Department of Economics, Burdwan University, Burdwan, West Bengal.
Soumyendra Kishore Datta	Professor, Department of Economics, Burdwan University, Burdwan, West Bengal.
Susanta Mondal	Lecturer, Department of Economics, Bolpur College, Birbhum, West Bengal.
Tejpreet Kang	Associate Professor, Department of Human Development, College of Home Science, Punjab Agriculture University, Ludhiana, Punjab.
Vandana Kumari	Department of Human Development, College of Home Science, Punjab Agriculture University, Ludhiana, Punjab.
Rekha Kumari	College of Home Science, Punjab Agriculture University, Ludhiana, Punjab.
Dhruvalata D Bhatt	Faculty Member, Department of Banking and Insurance, Faculty of Commerce, The M.S. University of Baroda, Vadodara.

V. Girija Devi	Reader in Home Science, Government College for Women, Thiruvanathapuram, Kerala.
Kameshwar Pandit	Lecturer, Post-graduate Department of Personnel Management and Industrial Relations, Patna University, Patna.
Prabhakar Jha	Senior Reader, University Department of Personnel Management and Industrial Relations, Darbhanga House, Patna University, Patna, Bihar.
Randhir Prasad Singh	Bihar State Electricity Board, Patna.
Ravi Prakash Yadav	Faculty Member, University Department of Industrial Relations and Personnel Management, T.M. Bhagalpur University, Bhagalapur.
Kumar Chandradeep	Faculty Member, P.G. Department of English, College of Commerce, Patna.
Barsa	L-20, Ganga Apartment, University Professor's Colony, Bhagalpur.

Editors' Note

The problems of women workers in general and in the unorganised sector in particular deserve special emphasis and focus in view of their marginalised position within the class of workers. Even when women are not employed in the sense of contributing to the national output, a considerable share of their time is consumed by socially productive and reproductive labour. This is what is called the *double burden of work* that distinguishes women from men. For women workers in the informal economy the double burden of combining the tasks of production and reproduction is even more arduous because they are already engaged in activities that require long hours to obtain a subsistence wage.

It is quite clear that the position of women workers in rural India is considerably lower than that of women in general. But the bottom layer is constituted by women belonging to the lowest social status groups. Urban women workers in general are better off than even rural men workers. But this advantage is somewhat dented when we look at the status of urban women belonging to Scheduled Castes (SCs) and Scheduled Tribes (STs). However, rural women workers in general seem to be more disadvantaged than even the urban SCs/STs women workers.

A number of national and international studies have documented the sex-typing of jobs and occupations by women. Occupational segregation represents a form of discrimination when large segments of the labour force are in essence restricted from entering many occupations. Sexual division of labour has implications for the wages earned, permanency in the job and the possibilities for upward mobility in the industry.

Discrimination on the lines of gender is not always overt. It appears in very subtle forms such as in the nature of work performed, the skills required to perform the work and the valuation of these skills and the technology used by men and women.

Female and child domestic workers constitute a large portion of today's migrant worker population. Sadly, they also join the category of migrant workers, most being at the risk of exploitation and human rights abuse. Working in the unregulated domain of a private home, mostly without the protection of national labour legislation, allows for female domestic workers to be maltreated by their employers with impunity. Women are often subjected to long working hours and excessively arduous tasks. They may be strictly confined to their places of work. They are frequently the victims of sexual harassment and, in the very worst cases, rape and torture. Thus, women as well as children working as domestic servants are often forced to work in sub-human conditions with no job security, no benefits and no dignity. The increasing demand for domestic workers in all big cities and towns of the country played a major role in the migration of women from rural or tribal areas. Most of them are from poor families and are illiterate. Due to the lack of education and skill they become easy victims of exploitation.

One problem more specific to women is that they are subject to various forms of harassment in the workplace. Verbal and physical violence against women has been an age-old method of subjugating women. This is used in the workplace to further strengthen the sexual division of labour and keep women at the bottom of the work hierarchy. Such harassment leads to stress and reduces the productivity of the workers. It can also be used to curb upward mobility and inhibit growth of women-operated enterprises.

The overall picture that emerges is one of greater disadvantage for women workers in general and those belonging to rural as well as SCs/STs in particular. Apart from such inherited disadvantages as lower social position, a number of other factors also contribute to such a picture. These are their limited asset position, access to resources, and low level of education and skill. Education, and consequently some ability to acquire formal skills, could be a moderating force but this aspect presents a dismal picture.

We place on record our deep sense of gratitude to all the scholars for their respective contributions to this volume.

Bhagalpur

Ravi Prakash Yadav
Kumar Chandradeep
Barsa

Acknowledgements

The editors wish to record their deep sense of gratitude to their learned teachers for their creative guidance. Editors are equally grateful to the faculty members of University Department of Industrial Relations and Personnel Management, T.M. Bhagalpur University and College of Commerce, Patna for their co-operation and moral support.

Editors are grateful to all the contributors for their academic contributions and prompt response.

Editors are immensely thankful to late Justice R.P. Mandal, Patna High Court, Dr. Ranjan Yadav, M.P., Dr. R.K. Yadav 'Ravi', Ex-M.P. and Former Vice-Chancellor, Justice K.K. Mandal, Patna High Court, Sri Nand Kishore Yadav, Health Minister, Government of Bihar, M.M. Rahman, Runa Ghosh Singh, K.C. Khurana, Anil Yadav, Mukesh Roy, Ramesh Yadav, Professor Syed Shah Shamimuddin, Syed Shahabuddin and Syed Shakeel Azimi for their encouragement and sincere co-operation. Editors take this opportunity to extend their sincere thanks to Sri Ram Deo Prasad, Chairman, BSCLC, Patna for his encouragement and support.

Editors are immensely grateful to Honourable Hari Narayan Singh, H.R.D. Minister, Government of Bihar for so kindly writing a 'Foreword' for this book. It would be gross omission, if editors forget to thank their family members—this work would not have possible without the inspirations of their most loving parents, Smt. Shobha Yadav, Sri Rajendra Prasad Yadav, Smt. Meera Yadav, Dr. Ramendra Kumar Yadav 'Ravi', and Dr. Birendra Prasad Yadav, who have fostered interest in socio-economic issues rights from the beginning of their academic career.

Last but not the least, editors wish to express their thanks to Shri Sandeep Sury of New Century Publications, New Delhi and his publication team for their keen interest and timely publication of this book. The editors sincerely appreciate their efforts in this regard.

Editors' Note

1

Women Workers in Informal Sector

Vibhuti Patel

Introduction

Women all around the world have been doing paid, underpaid and largely unpaid work in homes, factories, fields, forests and mines. Over and above 3Cs—cooking, cleaning and caring—large number of women do activities such as collection of fuel, fodder and water, animal husbandry, kitchen gardening, raising poultry that augment family resources. If women would not do this work, these goods would have to be purchased from the market.

Our Census defines work as an activity done by a person that brings remuneration, income, payment, salary, wages and honorarium. All able bodied persons in the age group of 15-59 are part of the labour force. According to Census, those who are employed for 183 days in a year for 8 hours per day are main workers. Those who get paid work for 4 hours a day for continuously 186 days a year are considered to be marginal workers. The rest are classified as non-workers.

Visible and Invisible Work

Women's household work is invisible as it is performed inside four walls of their house and their work is not recognized and remunerated. Invisibility of women's household work is the outcome of definition of work in economics that defines 'work' as any type of physical and mental activity undertaken in anticipation of economic returns. Women's household work remains invisible as it is ignored in estimating national income. National income is defined as the sum total of all production. 'Production' is defined as the creation of utility, like place utility, time utility and service utility. Women are continuously producing one or more of these utilities. Yet, it is not included in the national income. Production by women in the household has 'use value' but not 'exchange value' as it is not traded in the market. Women's production in the household is ignored as there is no price tag attached to it.

Women in the Organized Sector

Women constitute only 14 percent of the total employment in the organized sector. It is concentrated in Maharashtra, Delhi, West Bengal, Uttar Pradesh and Tamil Nadu. In the urban areas, FEAR in tertiary sector increased from 37.6 percent in 1983 to 52.9 percent in 1999 (Economic Survey, 2002, GOI).

Here, women workers and employees get relatively better wages, standard working hours, and the protection of labour laws. But, here too they are threatened due to recommendation of the Second Labour Commission that has given increased freedom to the employers to hire and fire workers at their whims and fancies.

Women in the Informal Sector

Poor women's labour force participation has been adversely affected due to changes in age-structure, urbanisation, level and nature of economic development, infrastructure, government policies, labour laws, nature of work, structure of family, culture and tradition affecting autonomy and control, fertility levels and child-bearing practices, nature of housework, women's property rights, education, age at marriage, migration, access to technology, and segmentation in the labour market. Nature of wage differentials (WD) is such that for identical tasks, women are paid less and they are confined to relatively inferior tasks or casual work. Causes of WD are, namely, patriarchal attitude and myths about women's low productivity. Effects of WD have been subordination of women, son preference, man being treated as a "bread winner" and a head of the household (HoH). Affirmative action to remove these prejudices is the need of hour. Both the state and the social action groups need to join hands to provide gender justice in the labour market.

Poor Women in the Urban Labour Force

Marked feature of a neo liberal policy is an enlightened self-interest activated through market forces in the era of economic globalisation. Globalisation rides on the back of cheap labour of women and children.

Landscape of urban informal sector in dozens of South Asian countries (India, Pakistan, Bangladesh, Sri Lanka, Nepal) and South East Asian (Thailand, Indonesia, Philippines, Malaysia) countries, Indochina (Laos, Kampuchea and Vietnam) and China is flooded with sweatshops, ghetto labour markets and stigmatised migrant workers.

ASEAN countries have recently discussed establishment of Special Economic Zones (SEZs) that would ensure flexibility of the labour force to attract Foreign Direct Investment (FDI).

During the 1980s, employment of adult women decreased and employment of adolescent girls and child labour increased. They were given less skilled and underpaid jobs. Budgetary cuts for *balwadis* and crèches enhanced the burden of poor working women. FTZs and EPZs thrive on young women's super-exploitation. The employers also overlook occupational health hazards.

Girl Child Labour in the Urban Areas

In 1986-87, 32.6 percent of rural and 29.4 percent of urban girls were never enrolled in schools due to paid and unpaid work they had to do in homes, fields, factories, plantations and in the informal sector. Sexual abuse at the work place is a hidden burden that a girl worker endures. The child labour policies, however, do not spell out anything specific to girl child workers. There is no implementation of prohibition of girls working in hazardous occupations as per Child Labour (Prohibition and Regulation) Act, 1986. About 6 percent of males and females in rural areas and about 3 percent males and 2 percent females in age group 5-14 in urban areas were found to be working during 1993-94.

"Women carry a disproportionately greater burden of work than men and since women are responsible for a greater share of non-SNA (system of National Accounts) work in the care economy, they enter the labour market already overburdened with work" (Report of Gender Diagnosis and Budgeting in India, National Institute of Public Finance and Policy, New Delhi).

Conventional understanding has been that women are last to be hired at the time of economic expansion and first to be fired at the time of economic crisis. Women become major victims of rationalisation, mechanisation and automation. When structural changes take place, women are not selected for skill upgradation, if they don't assert collectively.

But, new international division of labour has changed the dynamics, as the focus is on induction of young, moderately educated girls who would do minute and monotonous jobs with concentration and dexterity e.g., pharmaceuticals, computers, electronic, and garments.

Factors Affecting Women's Entry in Labour Market

Factors hindering the gainful employment of women in the labour market include, age structure, urbanisation, level and nature of economic development, infrastructure, government policies, labour laws, nature of work, structure of family, culture and tradition affecting autonomy and control, fertility levels and childbearing practices, nature of housework, women's property rights, education, age at marriage, migration and access to technology.

Nearly 1/3rd of Indian women and 1/6th of Indian girls are part of the labour force. In the low productivity segments of the economy, the choices before the girls have been child-marriage, child-prostitution or child-labour (CM, CP, and CL). Grooming of girls in different parts of the country determines whether they would be part of the SS side of the CM, CP or CL or grow as empowered women. Studies on this process from the political economy perspective are handful but they throw light only on the areas of active intervention by the state, civil society and social movements. National Campaign against Child Labour has carved out a phase-wise programme of rehabilitation of child-labour and integrating them into the formal/non-formal educational institutions. Homes for street-children have been established in cities like Delhi, Bangalore, Bombay, Ahmedabad, and Kolkata. Public interest litigation cases against inhuman conditions in the rescue homes by social organisations have forced the iron wall of secrecy to fall. Employers with modern outlook have realised that without healthy and educated\skilled labour force, they cannot attain high productivity.

However, in spite of this awareness, condition of girl child labour is deplorable. In match industry in Sivakasi, out of 45,000 children, 90 percent are girls. [1] Highest number of girl children is sold either as child-brides or as bonded labourers or as child-sex workers in the drought-prone areas. [2] Brutalisation of girl-victims of CM-CP-CL is more pronounced because their male counterparts have to face control of their labour and sexuality while girl children have to bear multiple burdens of control of sexuality, fertility and labour and consequences of teenage pregnancy. Sociological studies examining material basis of this phenomenon have helped to sensitize the professional bodies to make the state intervention more effective. [3]

Table 1.1 reveals that the enrolment ratio is much lower in the BIMARU states, which are known as the lowest literacy (for women and girls) states. States known for child prostitution, right from the colonial days to the present, have been Himachal Pradesh, Rajasthan, Gujarat (tribal belt), West

Bengal, North-Eastern states, Orissa, Kerala (Malabar region) and Goa. Percentage of girl children involved in the agrarian and non-agrarian economic activities has been above 5 percent in Gujarat, Maharashtra, Tamil Nadu, Karnataka and Andhra Pradesh.

Table 1.1: Work Participation Rate, Enrolment and Discontinuation of Girls' Education in Rural India

States	*WPR*	*Enrolment*	*Discontinuation*
Kerala	0.5	98.0	2.0
Himachal Pradesh	0.6	90.0	2.2
Uttar Pradesh	0.8	53.4	5.6
North East Region	1.0	76.3	4.1
Rajasthan	1.1	41.9	6.6
Bihar	1.2	51.2	4.1
Haryana	2.3	72.3	4.6
West Bengal	2.3	65.1	6.5
Punjab	3.0	84.4	6.1
Madhya Pradesh	4.1	55.8	9.0
Orissa	4.2	63.4	9.3
Gujarat	5.0	74.5	9.5
Maharashtra	5.8	82.	8.4
Tamil Nadu	7.5	84.3	14.8
Karnataka	7.8	75.1	9.1
Andhra Pradesh	10.3	73.8	12.1
Rural India	**3.5**	**64.8**	**7.6**

Source: NCAER, 1994.

In the segments of the economy where the adult population enjoys food security and better quality of life as well as commitment towards women's development, the girl children can easily avoid the vicious circle of CM-CP-CL. Girls from the female headed households (i.e. households which are headed by unmarried, divorced, widowed and deserted women) are the most vulnerable in this regard. [4] In the last two decades of women's empowerment, they have been guided through the collective efforts of the women's movement.

In the 1980s, women constituted 14-17 percent of the total work force and within a decade, it has risen to 22 percent. Due to globalisation, work participation of women and young girls has increased drastically in the industrial sector. Recruitment of women in the electronic, garment, diamond, gems and jewellery, dairy, food processing, horticulture and floriculture sectors have multiplied. Availability of home-based work for women has opened more avenues for women of all class and background to use their abilities, skills and education more productively. Home-based work ensures flexitime, secured environment and freedom from travelling and also allowing the women to take care of domestic responsibilities such as child-care, nursing of the old, sick and disabled members of the family.

Supply and Demand for Female Labour in Developed and Developing Countries

Today, women worldwide are better educated and hold more high-level professional jobs than ever before. Yet, they rarely break through the so-called "glass ceiling" which separates them from top-level management and professional positions (ILO, 1997). Despite recent progress, the glass ceiling remains relatively intact. Women hold less than 5 percent of the top jobs in corporations. Even when they manage to rise to the top, female executives nearly always earn less than men. The higher the position, the more glaring is the gender gap. Moreover, the old contention that there is insufficient number of qualified women to fill more top jobs is out of date. Though gender differences still exist in terms of choice of profession, women are increasingly taking up scientific and technological fields for study. With few exceptions such as engineering, women are approaching men in educational attainment in most of the fields.

In many industrialized countries, education has played an important role in providing women with access to better and higher-level jobs. Women have graduated in large numbers in areas such as medicine, law, accountancy and business studies, which have previously been dominated by male students. Growing employment opportunities and employers' willingness to recruit women have stimulated demand for courses in these areas. Although women still earn less than men for every level of educational qualification in most countries, the wage gap for highly educated women is much smaller (ILO, 1998, p. 145). Improvement in pay scales that women workers have achieved in recent years, at least in some European countries and the United States, has resulted due to changes in the pattern of occupational segregation.

Educational attainment also appears to have helped women to maintain continuity of employment. One of the major risks that women face is the loss of occupational status when they withdraw from the labour market to have children or attend to other family responsibilities. Female employees in higher-level jobs in large organizations, especially in the public sector where "equal opportunity" policies often exist, are much more likely to be able to draw on various defensive measures to help them retain their position in the labour market. However, the risk of occupational downgrading following an absence from the job market is compounded if job training relies on informal work experience instead of recognized transferable skills. Indeed, under-representation of women in training systems—such as workplace-based training, lifelong learning, training programmes for the unemployed, training for new technology-might actually be reinforcing occupational segregation by sex (ILO, 1998, Chapter 6).

The proportion of women has increased in administrative and managerial work, but the nature of women's career paths block their progress to top positions. At lower management levels, women are typically placed in non-strategic sectors and in personnel and administrative positions, rather than in professional and line management jobs leading to the top. Often, such initial disadvantages are compounded by exclusion from networks, both formal and informal, which are so essential for advancement within enterprises. Women are seldom found in product development and corporate finance, and thus there is a need for an explicit gender mainstreaming strategy to advance women in these areas. Participation in decision-making proves to be one of the most resistant areas for gender equality.

Economic theory states that historically there has been a U-shaped relationship between women's labour force participation (WLFP) and economic development. For very poor countries, WLFP is high and women work mainly in the farm or non-farm family enterprises. Development initially moves women out of the labour force because of rise in male market opportunities and prejudice against blue collar work. With further development, with high rate of women's education, WLFP once rises in white collar jobs.

94 percent of women workers are in the informal sector. There is pronounced declining trend in the importance of the self employed women in both, rural and urban areas. Erosion of credit/loan facilities due to structural adjustment programme is a major reason for women being weeded out of the market. Safety net of social sector budget is also weak. Women workers in the informal sector are governed by the law of jungle.

Though certain activities might lend themselves more readily to "informalization", no intrinsic set of characteristics-other than responsiveness to economic opportunity and the fluidity of its borders-defines what informal activities are. Since 1972, when the term was first officially used by the ILO, there has been considerable debate on the definition and characteristics of the informal sector. The official international definition includes (a) unregistered enterprises below a certain size; (b) paid and unpaid workers in informal enterprises; (c) casual workers without fixed employers. Standards for enterprises to be considered informal, such as maximum number of paid workers and whether domestic servants and the agricultural sector are included in the informal sector, vary between countries. Also, in any given country, the legal and regulatory framework defines what is a registered/formal or an unregistered/informal enterprise.

Considered a defining feature of underdevelopment in the 1960s and 1970s, the informal sector was expected to wither away with economic growth. Contrary to those expectations however, throughout much of the developing world it has become the locus of employment growth since the 1980s. In an environment where austerity policies are dictated by structural adjustment programmes, by changing forms of production and by increased competition, the formal sector simply has failed to generate sufficient employment for the growing labour force. As the informal sector has grown in size, it has progressively become harder to associate the dichotomy between formal and informal sectors with that between traditional and modern.

On the one hand, the informal sector works as a huge "labour sponge" which mops up the labour force excess in the formal sector (ILO, 1991). Many of the informal sector establishments, owned mostly by self-employed producers with little capital, technology or skills, follow a subsistence logic. Lacking access to organized markets, credit, formal education and training institutions, and public services and amenities, such enterprises provide very low and irregular incomes and employment (Tokman, 1990). On the other hand, with its resurgence in the altered conditions of the 1980s, the informal sector has also become a part of economic restructuring, providing both flexibility and an opportunity to lower costs for formal sector establishments (Sassen, 1998). Far from being archaic, it has become an integral part of the formal sector.

Given the extensive heterogeneity of the informal sector, it is possible to delineate three distinct types of informal activity in terms of their level of productivity and the nature of their linkage to the formal economy. The first type is the "own-account" production of the self-employed urban and rural poor. Their level of productivity is very low and links to the formal economy are, if any, marginal. The second type includes relatively more productive workers engaged in wage-labour in a capitalistic setting with close links to the formal sector. It is common for this part of the informal sector to subcontract to the formal sector, enabling the latter to lower costs and acquire flexibility in the face of demand volatility. Also within this group are financially hard-pressed firms, for whom operating informally is a means of survival. Finally, the third type is constituted by independent professionals providing highly priced, customized services and products to satisfy the demands of the swiftly expanding, high-income population.

Partly because they are under-represented in the formal sector, women comprise the majority of informal sector workers in most countries, especially in the first two segments. Informal activities in the first segment generate little value added, and incomes are so meagre that almost no savings materialize which are worth reinvesting to improve productivity or enlarge the scale of operation. They are a means of subsistence livelihood, rather than a form of entrepreneurial activity, and need rather than profit is the motivating factor (Joshi, 1997). With few marketable skills to their credit, women from poor households flock into this type of informal activities to generate whatever level of income they possibly can. They operate in a highly competitive environment characterized by ease of entry and exit, high rates of both start-up and failure, and for many, relatively short life cycles of economic activity. A large number of women also work at home, performing piece-rate work for manufacturing enterprises. This is more likely to fall under the second type of informal activities, where the increased demand for contingent female labour is associated with the restructuring of production and technological changes discussed above (Pollack and Judisman, 1997).

In many countries, national regulatory frameworks have

been biased in favour of big business and public-sector enterprises. Small firms have often resorted to illegality to survive (De Soto, 1986). Barriers to entering full legality can take many forms and may rest in different elements of the work process: the status of labour, the conditions of work or the form of management (Castells and others, 1989). Even though some excessive bureaucratic requirements can rightly be blamed for setting up unnecessary barriers, government regulations are required to protect the general interests of the community. Thus, it might not always be easy to strike the right balance between regulatory measures that are essential for public health and safety, and those that erect unnecessary obstacles for the operations of informal sector units. The dilemma is to design a policy stance in favour of a dynamic informal sector capable of generating more jobs, higher incomes, but one that is also supportive of better conditions and more widespread protection for those attempting to earn a livelihood in it.

Of particular concern is, of course, the widespread non-compliance with labour legislation and basic labour standards within the informal sector. The precarious existence of the informal enterprises and the difficult nature of labour organization in this sector are the ultimate sources of the problem. Until such enterprises are able to operate in a more stable environment not much progress on this score can be expected (ILO, 1991). Moreover, the recent erosion in standards of protection for formal-sector workers has only made it more difficult to improve working conditions in the informal sector.

Women constitute only 14 percent of the total employment in the organized sector. It is concentrated in Maharashtra, Delhi, West Bengal, Uttar Pradesh and Tamil Nadu. In the urban areas, FEAR in tertiary sector has increased, from 37.6 percent in 1983 to 52.9 percent in 1999 (Economic Survey, 2002, GOI). Here, women workers and employees get relatively better wages, standard working hours, and the protection of labour laws. Women employees, workers and officers in the public sector enterprises constitute the largest segment of the organized sector employment. But due to rationalization, automation and mechanization, women in the organized sector are also encouraged to opt for voluntary retirement.

Wage Differentials in Female Activities

Female-male pay differentials (or the so-called "gender wage gap") can be an important indicator of women's disadvantaged position in labour markets. In economies of all types, women typically earn two thirds of male incomes on average. Moreover, only a part of this gap in earnings can be explained by differences in educational attainment and job experience between women and men which suggest that discrimination on the basis of sex could be widespread.

There is mixed evidence about whether or where the gender wage gap has shown a tendency to diminish with women's increased participation in paid work. In some industrialized countries, such as the United States of America, the gap appears to have narrowed. In others, such as Japan, it has widened. Similarly, in developing economies, trends vary. Women's wages, relative to men's, seem to have risen slightly in some developing countries, such as El Salvador and Sri Lanka, while in other developing countries or areas, such as Hong Kong SAR, Myanmar, Singapore and Taiwan Province of China, the wage gap has widened. Also, it is not clear if or to what extent this modest change reflects the general improvements in women's level of education relative to men's). There have been improvements in women's educational attainments relative to men in all regions, with improvements in the ratio of female to male years of education achieved first (between 1960 and 1975) in the high-performing Asian countries, and later (1970 onwards, from a high base) in Latin America and (from 1975 onwards, from a very low base) in South Asia .

Even though the evidence is sparse, trade expansion and liberalization with FDI flows are likely to affect gender wage gaps in two ways: (a) through differential impact on the demand for female and male labour; and (b) through increase in bargaining power relative to organized workers in industries that are directly affected by the export of capital. FDI flows might be expected to drive up the wages of women workers because they tend to stimulate demand for female labour. By contrast, the increased ability of businesses to relocate all or some segments of their production across national borders puts a downward pressure on the wages of workers in the affected industries. The little existing research suggests that the latter effect has been stronger.

Evidence shows that the signing of the North American Free Trade Agreement (NAFTA) and concomitant threat of moving offshore helped manufacturing employers in the United States of America to successfully resist the demands for wage increases. Likewise, FDIs by MNCs tend to move away from the newly industrialized economies, where wages and working conditions have improved, to less developed countries such as India, Mauritius, Sri Lanka, and more recently Bangladesh, China and Viet Nam. Women's wages relative to men's might thus be unlikely to rise if women are more heavily concentrated than men in industries where capital is "footloose" (i.e., where the threat by businesses to move offshore is highly credible).

Indeed, that is likely to be the case in many low-wage sites in developing countries which attract FDI. Not surprisingly, wage differentials are especially marked in those developing countries or areas which pursue export-led industrialization or have EPZs. The divergent trend in the gender wage gap in Taiwan Province of China and the Republic of Korea might also be instructive. The gender wage gap has been steadily widening in the former since 1981, while marginally narrowing in the latter. In Taiwan Province of China, capital is more "footloose" than in the Republic of Korea. There is considerably less inward and outward FDI in the Republic of Korea in comparison with Taiwan Province of China (Seguino, forthcoming).

By contrast, in some developed economies, such as the United States, the forces of globalization appear to have adversely affected men's wages more than women's. Over the last two decades, trade liberalization and capital mobility have eroded well paying blue-collar wages in concentrated industries where men were the well entrenched insiders. Increased international competition, which reduces the bargaining power of male workers in such industries, may be one explanation for the decreasing gender wage gap. Three quarters of the decrease in the wage gap in the United States since late 1970s is estimated to stem from the decline in male real wages (Lawrence and Bernstein, 1994). At least in some countries, the narrowing of the gender wage gap reflects in part a "downward harmonization" between men and women.

Other factors could also have influenced gender wage differentials over the past decades. As discussed in detail below, there have been significant changes in the patterns of occupational segregation by sex around the world. Although women still earn less than men at every level of education, increasing numbers of women in higher-level jobs, especially in developed countries, have effectively improved women's aggregate labour-market income relative to men.

Other important factors, depending on the region and the country, have been the following: the type of wage settlement (female-male pay differentials tend to be lower in countries with centralized collective bargaining); the earnings gap is relatively small in Australia, Germany, Norway and Sweden, countries where there is centralized collective bargaining which emphasizes egalitarian wage policies in general. In Canada and the United States, the earnings gap is relatively larger because wage bargaining is decentralized, market-oriented and enterprise-level (Lim, 1996; Kucera, 1998). The size of enterprise (within the same country, large enterprises tend to pay higher wages to and are more likely to hire women); technological change; the pattern of industrial development; and societal values about gender inequality.

Determinants of Wage Differentials

Nature of wage differentials (WD)-for identical tasks women are paid less. And women are confined to relatively inferior tasks, casual work. Women employees get differential opportunities, differential treatment and differential treatment. Causes of WD are gender gaps in education, skills, opportunities due to patriarchal attitude and myths about women's inferiority. Absence of affirmative action by the state and trade unions also perpetuate wage differentials.

Effects of WD are subordination of women in the workplace, family, community and public life, son preference, man is treated as a "bread winner" and Head of the Household (HoH).

Despite the rapid and global increase in female paid employment in recent years, occupational segregation by sex remains a worldwide phenomenon not always adverse for women; it can be an important indicator of women's disadvantaged position in labour markets. Indeed, higher levels of occupational segregation are generally associated with poorer labour-market conditions for women: lower pay, lower status, and more limited career opportunities, among others. It can also be a source of labour market rigidity and thus economic inefficiency.

Women are more likely to be working in "men's jobs" than the opposite. But, as a rule, women are employed in a narrower range of occupations than men. Male-dominated, non-agricultural occupations are over seven times as numerous as female-dominated occupations. They dominate in clerical and secretarial jobs and in low-end service occupations (as shop assistants, waitresses, maids, hairdressers, dressmakers), and as professionals they are most likely to be teachers or nurses. These "female occupations" generally pay less and have lesser status and advancement prospects.

A distinction is usually made between two different forms of occupational segregation. One, called "horizontal segregation", refers to the distribution of men and women across occupations (e.g., women as maids and men as truck drivers); while the other, termed "vertical segregation", refers to the distribution of men and women in the job hierarchy in terms of status within an occupation (e.g. production workers versus production supervisors). Neither form of occupational segregation correlates well with the level of socio-economic development across countries. Both vary by region, however, which suggests that social, historical and cultural factors might be important in determining the extent of occupational segregation by sex. In his work on occupational segregation by sex, Anker (1998) distinguishes five "regions": OECD countries, transition economies, the Middle East and North Africa, Asia and the Pacific, and other developing countries and areas.

The level of horizontal segregation is lowest in the Asia and Pacific region and highest in the Middle East/North Africa. It is also relatively high in other developing regions, while of average magnitude in the OECD and transition economies in Eastern Europe. There are also large and significant differences in occupational segregation by sex across OECD sub-regions. North America has the lowest level, while Scandinavia as a sub-region has the highest. The reason for the high level of segregation in the latter seems to be related to the way in which the welfare state developed in Scandinavia, where the comprehensive monetization of the "care economy" has created occupations that have remained "female" (Anker and Melkas, 1998, p. 9). Vertical segregation, by contrast, is higher in Asia and the Pacific than in other parts of the world. Export-led industrial development has apparently opened up many industrial occupations to women (thereby significantly reducing horizontal segregation)—without, however, decreasing gender inequalities within occupations in terms of pay, authority and career advancement possibilities (vertical segregation).

In the past two decades, the horizontal form of occupational segregation by sex has fallen considerably around the world. It appears to have fallen the most in countries where it was relatively high, and to have remained unchanged in countries where it was relatively low. The greatest sustained fall has occurred in several small developing and a few OECD countries. The rest of the OECD and transition countries, as well as large East Asian, Middle Eastern and North African countries, seem to have experienced little change, while in China and Hong Kong Special Administrative Region of China there have been increases. In countries and regions where it has decreased, the reason is integration of men and women within occupations, rather than a shift in the occupational structure of employment. The expansion of "feminine" occupations has apparently been sufficient to absorb the marked increase in the female non-agricultural labour force. As the number of women entering the non-agricultural labour force has risen, many women have taken up jobs that were traditionally "men's", thereby reducing the occupational segregation by sex.

Occupational segregation by sex is often justified on the grounds that women have specific attributes which make them more suitable than men for particular types of work. It is argued that traditionally "female" occupations involve caring types of work, manual dexterity and experience at typical household activities, all of which women are expected to possess. Similarly, subservience and docility, the other characteristics commonly associated with female workers, are thought to shape gender employment patterns.

Women's work and wage structure can be categorized into seven sub-divisions.

- Wage and salaried employment.
- Self-employment outside the household for profit.
- Self-employment in cultivation and household industry for

profit.

- Self-employment in cultivation for own consumption.
- Subsistence activities in allied sectors like dairy, poultry, fishing.
- Collection of fuel, fodder, water and forest produce for sale as well as self-consumption.
- Food production, preservation, domestic work for market and non-market purposes.

Wage structure is skewed in favour of organized/statutory sector, male workers and industrialized countries. Public sector offers better wage rates than the private sector. As compared to agrarian sector, wage rates in industrial sector are better. In comparison with rural areas, urban areas ensure better wages.

Notes

1. Neera Burra *Born to Work-Child Labour in India*, Oxford University Press, Delhi, 1997.
2. Girl Child- A Status Report, UNICEF, SAARC Decade for a Girl Child (1990-2000 A.D.), Delhi.
3. Jean D'cunha *Prostitution* Joint Women's Programme, Delhi, 1990.
4. (a). Pradeep Kumar Panda: "Female Headship, Poverty and Child Welfare- A Study of Rural Orissa", Economic and Political Weekly, October 25, 1997, WS-73. (b) John Hoddinott and Lawrence Haddad "Does Female Income Share Influence Household Expenditures? Evidence from Cote D' Ivoire", Oxford Bulletin of Economics and Statistics, Vol. 57, No.1, 1995, pp. 305-9049.

References

D. Dwyer and J. Bruce (eds.). (1988). *A Home Divided: Women and Income in the Third World*, Standard University Press, Stanford

Government of India (1974). *Towards Equality—Report of the Committee on the Status of Women in India*, Department of Social Welfare, Ministry of Education and Social Welfare, New Delhi.

ILO (1978). *Women's Participation in the Economic Activity of Asian Countries*, ILO, Geneva.

Jhabwala, R. and R.K. Subramanya (eds.). (2000). *The Unorganized Sector: Work Security and Social Protection*, Sage Publications, New Delhi.

Mira Seth. (2000). *Women and Development: The Indian Experiences*, Sage Publications, New Delhi.

MHRD, Government of India, (1987). *Shram Shakti: Report of the National Commission on Self-Employed Women and Women Workers in the Informal Sector*, Ministry of Human Resource Development, New Delhi.

S. Purushothaman (1988). *The Empowerment of Women in India: Grassroots Women's Network and the State*, Sage Publications, New Delhi.

S. Narasimhan (1999). *Empowering Women: An Alternative Strategy from Rural India*, Sage Publications, New Delhi.

T.S. Papola and A.N. Sharma (eds.). (1999). *Gender and Employment in India*, Vikas, New Delhi.

Yong, K. et al. (eds.). (1987). *Serving Two Masters*, Routledge and Kegan Paul, London.

2

Women Workers in Unorganized Manufacturing Sector of Punjab

Anupama and Neru Gupta

Introduction

The status of women in any society does not have an economic interpretation only. Its threads are closely interwoven with those of culture, society, state and above all with the lives of the people. So, the economic status finds its roots in the patriarchal society. The process of economic development alone can not bring a positive change in the working patterns of the women. They are still being employed in low paid and less secure jobs. In present economic world, if we witness an increase in female participation in work force then we will also witness a larger increase in their participation in the informal sector jobs vis-à-vis the formal sector jobs. Thus, in the fast growing globalised world, the women are more likely to be employed in low paid, less secure jobs (Anker and Hein, 1986; Lee and Nagraj, 1995; Chen and Heintz, 2006). That is why 'feminisation of workforce', coincides as well with 'feminisation of poverty' (Chen and Heintz, 2006).

Many a time it is blamed that lower wages have nothing to do with the gender than to the productivity and as women are low productive workers so they are paid low wages but a few studies like that of Elson (1999) and Mehra and Gammage (1999) have shown that the gender gap in earnings exists even for same level of education, age and job tenure of women as compared to men. Several empirical cross-sectional studies have shown that individual wages differ with gender composition of occupations (Groshen, 1991; MacPherson and

Hirsch, 1995). Oliveira (2001) found a significant positive relationship of male workers with wages and a strong negative relationship with female workers in Brazil from 1981 to 1999. Finding reasons in the sociological patterns behind low productivity of women may lead us not to justify their lower wages but to the concern that due to their access to low human capabilities, which may not have been their choice have led them to choose low-skilled and low paid jobs. For these women the family responsibilities never diminish even if they go out for earnings (Heyzer and Sen, 1994; Kalpagam, 2001).

Actually, due to these household responsibilities the women are not able to take up jobs on a full time and regular basis. So, if the women offer themselves to low paid, low-skilled and part time jobs then it may be a 'forced choice' rather than a preferential one (Anupama, 2007). But there very alarming long run consequences of the lower earnings of the women as people are less interested in investing in their human capital due to lower returns. There seems to be a vicious circle- 'women are less productive due to lower human capabilities. So, they are paid less. Due to lower returns people are less interested to spend on education and training of their daughters. So, due to low level of education the women workers are less productive'. In light of these concerns, present paper tries to find the relationship among female work participation, productivity and wages in the unorganized manufacturing sector of Punjab.

Punjab economy has been a vibrating economy since green revolution in the mid sixties. This 'bread basket' of India boasts its high income levels on basis of agriculture. Though, economic development in Punjab is mainly led by agriculture, thousands of small manufacturing units across the state are also growing. Actually, the industrial structure of Punjab is dominated by small scale and unorganized manufacturing units. Though Punjab economy has performed fairly well in case of per capita income, yet the social indicators are far from the satisfactory level, keeping in view the income level of the state. That is why this state was ranked at 12th position among 32 states and union territories regarding human development index, despite its being one of states with the highest per capita income (Planning Commission, 2002).

This state has performed miserably regarding male-female ratio, due to its cultural bias in favour of a male child. Wide spread sex-determination tests leading to female-foeticide have further aggravated the problem. This has led to use of the term DEMARU (Daughter Eliminating Male Aspiring Rage for Ultrasound) for this economically well-off, non BIMARU state (Bose, 2007). Since gender equity is an essential building block in sustainable development (UN, 2006), it is quite relevant to analyze the gender disparity in employment in this particular state.

Data Sources and Methodology

For measuring gender discrimination in the unorganized sector of Punjab the segregation indices such as the Index of Dissimilarity and Size Adjusted Index have been calculated. These indices are scalar summaries of complex segregation curves that represent the sex-composition of all occupations.

The simple ID can be calculated by using the following equation-

$$ID = \frac{1}{2}\sum_{j=1}^{n} |(f_j / f - m_j / m)| \times 100$$

where, f_j and m_j denote the number of female and male employees in the jth occupation and f and m are total female and male employment, respectively. The index denotes the percentage of total employment that would have to be relocated between occupations to achieve zero gender segregation. This index is a measure of difference between the integrated and actual distribution of employment by gender. Though, this index is easy to calculate and interpret, it is not free from the flaws. ID can easily change due to change in occupational structure, even though the proportion of women in the occupational categories remains the same. To control this drawback a modified index i.e. Size Standardized Dissimilarity Index (Ds) is used. This index is not affected by the shape of occupational distribution as it standardizes each occupation to the same size. Thus, this index eliminates the dependence of the occupational structure. The Size Standardized Dissimilarity Index can be expressed by the following equation-

$$D_s = \frac{1}{2}\sum_{j=1}^{n} | [\frac{f_j / T_j}{\sum_{j=1}^{n} f_j / T_j}] - [\frac{m_j / T_j}{\sum_{j=1}^{n} m_j / T_j}] | \times 100$$

Here, T_j is total number of men and women in j^{th} occupation.

Using unit level NSSO data, above indices are measured on 2-digit to 5-digit occupational level (using National Industrial Classification-1998) for each district separately. The indexes are calculated at various levels of occupations, as there is a general proposition that a higher level of aggregation of occupations underestimates segregation indexes (Anker, 1997). For analyzing the impact of structural and economic factors on the occupational sex-segregation, the district level variables of income index, work participation rate, literacy rate, sex ratio, gender related development index and per worker emoluments are analyzed through a correlation matrix. The data for these variables (except per worker emoluments, which is calculated from NSSO data on unorganized manufacturing sector) is taken from Punjab Human Development Report, 2004 (Government of Punjab, 2004), Punjab Statistical Abstract and Primary Census Abstract (CD-ROM Vol. 1, Census of India, 2001).

Gender Discrimination in Employment in Unorganized Manufacturing Sector of Punjab

A look at the Tables 2.1a and 2.1b clearly shows that in majority of the cases as the occupations are disaggregated to various levels of industrial classification, the degree of segregation increases.

Table 2.1a: Scalar Indices of Occupational Sex Segregation in Punjab (2000-01)

District	ID							
	2-digit		3-digit		4-digit		5-digit	
	R	U	R	U	R	U	R	U
Amritsar	83.0	59.7	83.0	66.6	83.0	69.0	83.0	74.5
Bathinda	41.3	65.5	41.3	66.5	43.9	69.3	43.9	70.9
Faridkot	85.6	71.2	85.6	74.0	85.6	75.1	85.6	75.2
Fatehgarh Sahib	77.8	77.4	77.8	77.4	77.8	80.9	77.8	86.6
Ferozepur	21.5	63.1	21.5	64.8	21.5	66.3	21.5	68.1
Gurdaspur	56.6	66.9	57.0	78.7	57.6	84.8	58.1	86.3
Hoshiarpur	37.5	82.4	38.4	82.4	43.6	86.9	51.2	87.6
Jallandhar	61.4	57.9	77.4	62.1	82.0	68.4	82.4	73.0
Kapurthala	72.5	75.4	76.8	76.2	78.0	76.2	80.0	79.9
Ludhiana	49.2	40.8	51.1	44.0	52.2	48.6	53.3	57.6
Mansa	91.7	78.5	91.7	84.1	93.6	84.5	93.6	84.5
Moga	65.4	81.8	66.3	82.5	66.3	82.5	68.2	82.5
Muktsar	55.8	68.6	55.8	70.9	61.4	72.0	62.1	72.0
Nawanshar	74.6	99.5	74.6	99.5	78.5	99.5	79.0	99.5
Patiala	67.9	57.5	67.9	63.9	72.6	73.6	72.6	78.7
Roopnagar	59.7	59.7	63.1	61.7	67.3	70.8	67.3	72.4
Sangrur	84.7	85.0	84.7	85.9	84.7	86.4	84.7	87.0
Punjab	46.4	48.9	46.8	54.2	48.6	59.3	50.0	66.5

Contd...

District	Ds							
	2-digit		3-digit		4-digit		5-digit	
	R	U	R	U	R	U	R	U
Amritsar	89.7	76.3	93.3	77.5	93.4	79.4	93.2	86.1
Bathinda	72.7	77.9	75.8	84.4	75.2	85.6	74.3	88.0
Faridkot	71.9	79.7	75.5	87.7	78.2	93.0	78.2	95.0
Fatehgarh Sahib	87.1	73.4	89.6	78.6	89.6	83.3	90.4	88.3
Ferozepur	78.2	80.7	80.9	87.3	81.4	91.0	84.8	91.5
Gurdaspur	75.6	75.0	74.4	80.2	83.2	88.5	91.3	92.4
Hoshiarpur	57.2	87.7	72.6	89.4	74.5	96.5	82.4	97.0
Jallandhar	72.6	61.7	81.7	77.8	84.6	78.2	87.4	84.4
Kapurthala	82.3	78.2	83.2	84.0	86.2	86.2	88.3	90.4
Ludhiana	81.6	56.2	91.0	69.3	93.2	78.4	94.3	86.2
Mansa	80.2	76.8	86.9	82.0	83.7	86.8	89.1	88.0
Moga	77.1	81.3	85.0	90.8	86.3	90.5	88.3	92.0
Muktsar	84.3	62.5	87.8	78.0	80.9	79.8	76.7	82.4
Nawanshar	79.2	97.2	85.1	97.9	86.8	98.3	86.6	98.7
Patiala	84.9	63.8	87.8	76.0	87.1	82.5	87.5	87.6
Roopnagar	81.3	69.2	81.1	78.3	81.4	83.1	81.4	87.3
Sangrur	90.0	85.0	89.5	84.6	91.8	87.5	93.1	91.0
Punjab	63.3	49.3	79.1	60.0	84.0	68.4	85.2	81.7

Source: Calculated from unit level data, 56th Round, NSSO (2002), CD-ROM- Sch.2.2

This confirms the general proposition that a higher level of occupation underestimates segregation indexes (Anker, 1997). Table 2.1a shows the gender discrimination for the year 2000-01. It can be observed from this table that the value of ID for all districts taken together is 46.47 percent in rural areas at 2-digit level occupations and increases to 50.03 percent at 5-digit level occupations, while for urban areas it increases from 48.94 to 66.51 percent. Interestingly, the value of segregation jumps to a very high level when it is measured through Size Standardized Dissimilarity Index (Ds). This value jumps from 50.03 percent (at 5-digit level) in case of ID to 85.28 percent in case of Ds for rural Punjab and from 66.51 to 81.74 for urban Punjab.

Besides, it is interesting to note that the value of segregation is higher in rural areas as compared to urban areas if calculated through ID and opposite is the case if it is calculated through Ds. Following the 5-digit level occupational sex-segregation, it is being found that Punjab has very high degree of the segregation in each district. It is more than 75 percent (except in rural Bathinda, where it is marginally lower at 74.36 percent) in every district, which means that at least 75 percent of total workers need to be relocated to achieve zero gender segregation in Punjab. A comparison with segregation indices in 2005-06 shows (Table 2.1b) that sex-segregation in unorganized manufacturing sector of Punjab has increased as compared to 2000-01.

However, rural-urban break-up shows different patterns at different levels of industrial classification. At 2-digit level the value of ID as well as Ds in rural Punjab shows that the segregation has increased, while in urban Punjab, it has actually declined in 2005-06 as compared to 2000-01. However, going to higher order of classification (at 5-digit level), it is clear from the Table 2.1b, that the values of ID as well as Ds in urban areas have increased indicating that sex-segregation has increased in urban unorganized manufacturing.

Table 2.1b: Scalar Indices of Occupational Sex Segregation in Punjab (2005-06)

District	*ID*							
	2-digit		3-digit		4-digit		*5-digit*	
	R	U	R	U	R	U	R	*U*
Amritsar	63.5	47.1	63.5	51.7	63.5	60.4	63.5	*65.0*
Bathinda	74.3	58.4	74.3	59.0	74.3	64.5	74.3	*70.9*
Faridkot	33.6	84.9	33.6	84.9	85.7	84.9	85.7	*84.9*
Fatehgarh Sahib	71.4	53.0	71.4	55.5	71.4	55.5	71.4	*55.5*
Ferozepur	38.5	43.7	38.5	50.1	46.3	54.2	46.3	*54.2*
Gurdaspur	65.4	59.9	72.6	61.3	73.4	70.0	74.4	*73.2*
Hoshiarpur	32.5	76.3	39.6	78.6	40.6	78.6	49.8	*80.1*
Jallandhar	54.1	60.8	71.4	62.7	74.7	70.2	75.8	*73.8*
Kapurthala	54.1	85.8	70.8	85.8	79.1	90.8	79.1	*93.8*
Ludhiana	43.6	57.7	54.5	65.8	54.5	69.0	54.5	*73.8*
Mansa	45.1	72.5	74.6	72.5	75.7	72.5	75.7	*72.5*
Moga	80.0	#	91.1	#	91.1	#	91.8	#
Muktsar	16.6	82.6	16.6	82.6	16.6	82.6	16.6	*82.6*
Nawanshar	62.1	80.0	62.1	80.0	62.1	80.0	62.1	*80.0*
Patiala	86.0	69.2	86.0	69.7	88.0	71.5	88.0	*72.8*
Roopnagar	74.3	59.4	74.3	67.3	76.9	67.3	76.9	*67.3*
Sangrur	83.7	77.3	83.7	79.6	86.2	79.8	86.2	*83.8*
Punjab	*61.9*	*38.9*	*65.1*	*53.3*	*69.0*	*59.9*	*70.4*	*67.5*

Contd...

District	*Ds*							
	2-digit		3-digit		4-digit		*5-digit*	
	R	U	R	U	R	U	R	*U*
Amritsar	85.7	60.6	89.4	67.5	89.6	80.3	90.5	*84.1*
Bathinda	88.6	76.3	90.6	73.4	91.4	76.0	92.1	*82.4*
Faridkot	78.0	84.9	78.0	84.9	71.7	84.9	71.7	*84.9*
Fatehgarh Sahib	92.8	73.9	92.8	80.2	94.2	82.2	94.2	*86.4*
Ferozepur	58.1	56.4	66.2	66.3	70.7	78.3	70.7	*78.3*
Gurdaspur	77.2	56.8	79.9	65.2	81.4	76.7	84.7	*84.8*
Hoshiarpur	65.1	89.9	64.3	93.8	68.3	94.7	70.5	*98.0*
Jallandhar	82.4	63.5	91.8	72.8	93.4	85.4	94.4	*89.6*
Kapurthala	83.8	89.8	89.5	91.0	93.2	91.8	93.2	*94.6*
Ludhiana	76.0	73.4	92.0	76.7	92.0	82.2	92.0	*88.6*
Mansa	63.1	76.2	69.6	76.2	74.0	82.7	74.0	*84.8*
Moga	66.6	#	76.9	#	82.3	#	85.9	#
Muktsar	39.7	87.1	39.7	91.0	39.7	91.8	39.7	*91.8*
Nawanshar	73.0	93.0	73.0	94.3	72.8	94.3	72.8	*94.3*
Patiala	83.0	81.0	86.7	86.1	89.7	93.0	91.2	*94.0*
Roopnagar	80.2	83.7	81.1	87.4	86.7	88.1	86.7	*89.7*
Sangrur	84.9	73.5	86.3	88.8	90.0	89.1	90.5	*92.6*
Punjab	*65.8*	*40.2*	*72.9*	*62.0*	*79.8*	*68.6*	*85.0*	*84.2*

Source: Calculated from unit level data, 62nd Round, NSSO (2008), CD-ROM- Sch.2.2
share of females is zero percent so the values of ID and DS are indeterminate.

In rural areas, the 5-digit level ID has indicated an increase in segregation, while the 5-digit level Ds has shown a marginal decline, though the value of segregation is very high (85.06 percent). Table 2.1b indicates that in 2005-06, about 85 percent workers (85.06 percent in rural areas and 84.28 percent in urban areas) need to be relocated to achieve gender equality in the labour market for the unorganized manufacturing sector.

Further, in Table 2.2 an attempt has been made to establish a correlation of occupational sex-segregation (at the 5-digit level) with the district level gender sensitive variables of GDI and sex ratio as well as non-gender sensitive variables such as Income Index, Work Participation Rate, Literacy rate and per worker emoluments in the unorganized manufacturing sector of Punjab. Since, Ds is better than ID and highest level of classification of occupations gives the clearest picture of segregation, Ds (at the 5-digit level) is being taken as the covariate.

Table 2.2: Correlation Co-efficient of Sex-Segregation and other Variables (Punjab-2000-01)

Variables	*Segregation Index*	
	Rural	*Urban*
Sex-Ratio	-0.113	*0.419***
Work-Participation Rate	-0.335*	*0.214*
Literacy Rate	0.235	*0.177*
Income Index	0.209	*0.102*
Gender Related Development Index	-0.571***	*-0.219*
Per worker Emoluments	*0.607****	*-0.371**

Source: Calculated from unit level data, 56th Round, NSSO (2002), CD-ROM- Sch.2.2 and Govt of Punjab, 2004

***1 percent level of significance

**5 percent level of significance

*10 percent level of significance

In rural Punjab, it is being observed that the gender sensitive variables of Sex-ratio and GDI in each district are negatively correlated with occupational sex-segregation in unorganized manufacturing sector. Though, the relationship with sex-ratio is very weak, the negative correlation coefficient with GDI is 0.571 and is significant at 1 percent level of significance. This shows that as the degree of occupational sex-segregation declines, disparities among males and females regarding attainment of education, income and life expectancy are also reduced leading to increased value of GDI.

Among non-gender sensitive variables, it is observed that in rural areas, there is a significant (at 10 percent level) negative correlation with Work Participation rate in each district, showing that as occupational sex-segregation declines the work participation rate increases. Weak positive relationships are found with income index and literacy rate in each district. Since income index is the average adjusted income from all occupations in each district, its impact on a particular occupation is weakened.

So, for more appropriate relationship between income and sex-segregation the effect of income in that particular sector only should have been taken. That is why, we have calculated the correlation of occupational sex-segregation in unorganized manufacturing sector with the wages in this particular sector as well. Interestingly, in rural areas, a positive correlation is being found with per worker emoluments in the unorganized manufacturing sector. Since, both the segregation index and per worker emoluments belong to the same sector, it gives more important result, showing that as per worker emoluments in the unorganized manufacturing units of rural Punjab increases, the occupational sex-segregation increases. This means with increased wages, men replace women in this particular sector and the women are pushed towards low paid jobs. Thus, we can say that as wages increase, women become under-represented in the informal jobs as well.

These covariates in urban Punjab give different relationship with occupational segregation. The positive relationship of segregation index with sex ratio and WPR shows that as the competition between males and females in the labour market becomes harder, women are pushed into the corner which raises the segregation level in the economy. While on the other hand a negative relationship emerges with per worker emoluments indicating that at higher level of wages segregation falls. This is entirely contrary to the results obtained in rural areas. Two possible explanations may emerge from this result in urban areas: firstly, at higher wages since employment falls, more and more men are out of jobs (as in urban areas, women employment is already as low as 5.64 percent in total employment in unorganized manufacturing sector of Punjab), leading to a fall in sex-segregation. Secondly, it seems that at higher wages employers are more interested in meek, submissive and less disturbing labour force. Lastly, like rural areas, the relationship of occupational segregation in urban areas with GDI is found to be negative.

Quality of Female Employment

It is generally found that women are more likely to be employed in low quality jobs. They will occupy more of the part time jobs while men being placed in the full-time jobs. Table 2.3a shows the share of female workers in various types of employment in unorganized manufacturing sector of Punjab during 2000-01. It is being observed that while women comprised 20.27 percent of total employment in unorganized manufacturing sector of rural Punjab, they were only 12.72 percent of total hired workers, 13.97 percent of full time workers and as high as 87.86 percent of part-time workers. In urban areas, the situation was even worse as women share in total employment was 5.64 percent, 81.33 percent of part time jobs, 4.41 percent of full-time jobs and 1.61 percent of the hired workers. During 2000-01, within the informal sector women were more employed in part-time jobs while men filled the full-time jobs. However, of total working owners in the unorganized manufacturing sector of Punjab, women's share was 30.11 percent in rural and 12.15 percent in urban areas.

Table 2.3a: Share of Female Workers in Various Types of Employment in Punjab (2000-01)

District	Total Employment	Part Time Employment	Full Time Employment	Working Owners	*Hired Workers*
			Rural		
Amritsar	17.6	72.73	15.74	18.73	*3.18*
Bathinda	16.88	96	9.89	31.51	*6.83*
Faridkot	4.17	--	4.17	18.87	*0*
Fatehgarh	14.29	--	14.29	18.75	*0*
Ferozepur	26.52	100	26.41	7.32	*29.53*
Gurdaspur	36.37	95.05	21.88	83.33	*35.61*
Hoshiarpur	27.36	63.54	13.00	27.95	*21.67*
Jallandhar	8.35	80	5.65	13.85	*0*
Kapurthala	7.42	47.06	4.25	14.55	*0*
Ludhiana	8.42	100	7.48	8	*9.92*
Mansa	33.20	98.81	1.16	36.76	*0*
Moga	11.20	100	10.48	17.5	*0*
Muktsar	9.00	100	7.14	32.73	*4.88*
Nawanshar	11.97	100	0.96	17.39	*0*
Patiala	10.15	--	10.15	20	*0*
Roopnagar	11.50	100	5.66	17.33	*0*
Sangrur	36.72	100	36.14	46.42	*0*
Punjab	*20.27*	*87.86*	*13.97*	*30.11*	*12.72*

Contd...

District	Total Employment	Part Time Employment	Full Time Employment	Working Owners	*Hired Workers*
			Urban		
Amritsar	5.15	88.46	4.76	10.44	*0.70*
Bathinda	11.95	76.36	5.48	14.46	*7.83*
Faridkot	7.98	--	8.10	3.38	*12.62*
Fatehgarh	2.41	33.33	1.68	5.97	*0.19*
Ferozepur	5.63	0.00	5.25	7.81	*1.60*
Gurdaspur	3.93	79.55	2.64	12.61	*0.93*
Hoshiarpur	14.10	90.48	8.90	14.54	*14.71*
Jallandhar	7.79	85.23	4.14	16.97	*1.10*
Kapurthala	6.39	78.43	2.09	5.92	*0.00*
Ludhiana	3.29	53.94	3.03	9.00	*1.36*
Mansa	7.07	86.67	1.62	10.29	*0.00*
Moga	7.53	100.0	5.71	14.17	*1.45*
Muktsar	8.51	83.33	6.59	21.43	*4.00*
Nawanshar	1.18	71.43	0.00	3.25	*0.00*
Patiala	7.13	80.0	7.50	14.27	*0.00*
Roopnagar	5.39	0.00	5.41	46.92	*6.67*
Sangrur	12.23	100.0	13.81	20.92	*0.00*
Punjab	*5.64*	*81.33*	*4.41*	*12.15*	*1.61*

By the year 2005-06, the share of women in total employment increased in both rural and urban areas. In rural areas, it increases to 24.78 percent from 20.27 percent in 2000-01. Similarly, in urban unorganized manufacturing, the share of female workers in total employment increases to 11.10 percent as compared to 5.64 percent in 2000-01. It is note worthy that this increase in share of female workers in total employment is in positive direction as far as quality of employment is concerned. A comparison of Table 2.3a and 2.3b indicates that in rural as well as urban areas, the share of female workers in full time employment and working owners has increased while it has declined in part-time employment.

In case of hired workers, the participation of females has declined in rural areas and marginally increased in urban areas showing that female workers in the unorganized manufacturing units of Punjab still work as unpaid family workers. Though, the trends of female employment are in the positive direction, yet still the decent work deficit is very large as their share in part time workers is very high vis-à-vis full-time and hired workers.

A district level analysis has shown that out of 17 districts, three districts during 2000-01 and two in 2005-06 didn't employ any worker on part-time basis and six districts in rural areas (Ferozepur, Ludhiana, Moga, Nawanshahr, Roopnagar and Sangrur) in 2000-01 and two in urban areas (Moga and Sangrur) employ women only in their part-time jobs in the unorganized manufacturing sector.

In 2005-06 two districts (Ludhiana and Mansa) employ women only in the part time jobs. In 2000-01, ten districts in rural areas and five in urban areas did not employ any women worker as a hired labour. Number of such districts increased to 11 in rural areas and 9 in urban areas. This shows that during both the time periods, whatever jobs for women exist remain unpaid in these districts. However, the share of women in total working owners is far greater than their share in total employment in almost every district with a few exceptions.

Table2.3b: Share of Female Workers in Various Types of Employment in Punjab (2005-06)

District	Total Employment	Part Time Employment	Full Time Employment	Working Owners	Hired Workers
	Rural				
Amritsar	25.00	66.67	12.24	25.00	0.00
Bathinda	36.21	66.67	33.02	39.74	0.00
Faridkot	9.41	75.00	2.60	18.18	0.00
Fatehgarh	61.11	---	61.11	61.11	---
Ferozepur	9.18	62.50	4.44	12.07	0.00
Gurdaspur	27.49	77.01	23.49	47.79	12.35
Hoshiarpur	25.74	75.00	17.24	25.00	10.81
Jallandhar	23.53	75.00	22.52	33.82	0.00
Kapurthala	42.86	83.33	36.11	45.45	0.00
Ludhiana	8.33	100.00	10.77	14.58	0.00
Mansa	41.54	100.00	48.08	59.09	22.22
Moga	2.88	4.55	1.37	6.45	0.00
Muktsar	23.08	83.33	5.00	10.53	0.00
Nawanshar	55.26	80.00	46.43	54.05	---
Patiala	23.08	---	23.08	31.91	0.00
Roopnagar	11.36	83.33	2.44	17.14	0.00
Sangrur	18.08	90.00	13.77	22.86	1.72
Punjab	24.78	60.21	20.87	35.55	8.51

Contd...

District	Total Employment	Part Time Employment	Full Time Employment	Working Owners	Hired Workers
	Urban				
Amritsar	20.00	78.79	16.29	23.45	17.5
Bathinda	12.00	86.67	1.82	6.67	0.00
Faridkot	3.64	33.33	1.92	8.33	0.00
Fatehgarh b	7.35	20.00	6.35	13.51	0.00
Ferozepur	5.77	33.33	3.45	8.60	0.00
Gurdaspur	28.36	71.88	21.05	38.74	7.14
Hoshiarpur	16.56	72.72	14.38	22.09	13.04
Jallandhar	14.64	57.14	11.79	24.00	1.49
Kapurthala	10.09	20.00	9.62	22.73	1.67
Ludhiana	3.82	86.11	2.06	8.54	0.53
Mansa	15.00	62.5	7.69	15.15	0.00
Moga	0.00	0.00	0.00	0.00	0.00
Muktsar	2.13	--	2.13	4.35	0.00
Nawanshar	31.82	20.00	35.29	21.43	25.00
Patiala	14.34	20.00	35.29	23.90	0.00
Roopnagar	10.00	66.67	6.83	17.95	1.72
Sangrur	17.60	83.33	15.43	30.48	0.00
Punjab	11.10	65.68	8.41	18.84	2.85

Source: Same as Table 2.1b.

It is due to the fact that majority of the enterprises under unorganized manufacturing are own account enterprises (OAMEs), which are mainly run by the family members, who may be working on part time basis or unpaid family labour. In such family enterprises a woman member easily fits in.

Actually, the districts, in which certain industries, that have employability for female workers are located, have shown higher percentage of female workers. I've used the words 'employability for females', instead of usual term 'female dominated occupations' because during both the time periods, except one occupation (in rural areas), none of the occupations in unorganized manufacturing sector of Punjab comply with the latter term.

Thus, to sum up we can say that the degree of occupational sex-segregation is very high in unorganized manufacturing sector in every district of Punjab. Women in Punjab are found under-represented in positive qualities of occupations (e.g. full time jobs, paid jobs etc) and are over-represented in the negative qualities of employment (e.g. part time jobs etc). However, unlike the Indian unorganized manufacturing sector, women in Punjab have a greater share in total working owners as compared to their share in total employment in the unorganized manufacturing sector. But, it is also found from the unit level data that most of the women working owners are working on part time basis, as compared to it majority of the full-time working owners are males.

This shows that either women may be working along with their unpaid household duties or they may be doing two or more jobs at the same time due to insufficiency of income from this particular occupation. Data shows that a big percentage of women workers are employed in the lowest paid occupation, particularly in urban unorganized manufacturing sector of Punjab. Among the covariates, it is found that economic development in each district (represented by the income index) and literacy rate have weak impact on segregation and moreover an increased value of these variables increases the segregation. A negative relationship of segregation with the GDI shows that a more integrated labour market can lead to the decline in disparities regarding achievement of these variables among men and women. Thus, gender equality in employment may be considered a key to investment in human capital for females and so to their economic and social empowerment.

References

Anker, Richard (1997), 'Theories of Occupational Segregation by Sex: An Overview', *International Labour Review*, Vol. 36, No. 3.

Anker, Richard and Hein, Catherine (1986), *Inequalities in Urban Employment in the Third World*, Macmillan, London.

Anupama (2007), 'Gender Discrimination in Quality of Employment and Wages in Unorganized Manufacturing Sector of India', paper presented at seminar on 'Gender Issues and Empowerment of Women', Indian Statistical Institute, Kolkata, 1-2, February.

Blau, Francine D. and Khan, L. (1992), 'The Gender Earnings Gap: Some International Comparisons', *American Economic Review,* Vol. 82, No. 2.

Bose, Ashish (2007), 'Eradicating Female Foeticide in India: Crucial Role of DEMARU States', key note address at seminar on 'Gender Issues and Empowerment of Women', Indian Statistical Institute, Kolkata, 1-2, February.

Chen, Martha, Vanek, J and Heintz, J. (2006), "Informality, Gender and Poverty: A Global Picture", *Economic and Political Weekly*, Vol. XLI, No. 21.

Elson, Daine (1999), "Labour Markets as Gendered Institutions: Equality, Efficiency and Empowerment Issues" *World Development*, Vol. 27, No. 3.

Government of Punjab (2004), *Human Development Report 2004 Punjab,* Government of Punjab.

Groshen, Erica L. (1991), The Structure of the Female/Male Wage Differential: Is it Who You Are, What You Do or Where You Work?, *Journal Of Human Resources*, Vol. 26, No. 3.

Hakim, C. (1993), 'Segregated and Integrated Occupations: A New Approach to Analysing Social Change', *European Sociological Review*, Vol. 9 No. 3.

Heyzer, N. and G. Sen (eds.) (1994), *Gender, Economic Growth and Poverty: Market Growth and State Planning in Asia and the Pacific,* International Books, Utrecht.

Kalpagam, U. (2001), 'Globalisation, Liberalisation and Women Workers in the Informal Sector' in A. Kundu and A. N. Sharma (eds) *Informal Sector in India: Perspectives and Policies,* Institute for Human Development and Institute for Applied Manpower Research, New Delhi.

Lee, K.H. and Nagraj, Shyamala (1995), 'Male-Female Earning Differentials in Malaysia', The Journal of Development Studies, Vol. 31 No.3

MacPherson, David A. and Barry T. Hirsch (1995), 'Wages and Gender Composition: Why Do Women's Jobs Pay Less?', *Journal of Labour Economics*, Vol. 13, No. 3.

Mehra, Rekha and Gammage, Sarah (1999), "Trends, Counter-Trends and Gaps in Women's Employment", *World Development*, Vol. 27, No. 3.

NSSO (2002), Unit Level Data on Unorganized Manufacturing Sector of India, 56th Round (July 2000-June 2001), Schedule 2.2, CD-ROM, Government of India, New Delhi.

Oliveira, Ana Maria H. C. (2001), 'Occupational Gender Segregation and Effects on Wages in Brazil', XXIV General Population Conference, IUSSP, June.

Planning Commission (2002), *National Human Development Report, 2001*, Government of India, New Delhi.

Population Research Centre (PRC), International Institute of Population Sciences (IIPS) and Centre for Rural Research and Industrial Development (CRRID) (1995), *National Family Health Survey: MCH and Family Planning, Punjab 1993,* Bombay.

UN (2006), *The Millennium Development Goals report 2006*, UN Publications, New York.

3

Growth, Urbanization and Women

Sarita Agrawal, Jyoti Achanta and Raginideep

Introduction

Any definition of economic development includes an element covering the degree of participation by the population at large. Women are potential contributors to the production and development and human development is impossible without gender equality (HDR, 1995). It ought to inevitably improve the status of women and equality among the genders. Similarly, equality for women promotes economic growth through more effective utilization of existing resources thereby speeding up the pace of development as economic development has an impact on the socio-political structure of the society such as it is influenced by it (HDR, 1995).

The last decade of the twentieth century has seen a visible shift in the focus of development planning from a mere expansion of production of goods and services and the consequent growth in per capita income to planning for enhancement of human well-being.

The notion of human well being itself is more broadly conceived to include, not only consumption of goods and services but also the accessibility of all sections of the population, especially the deprived and those who are living below the normative minimal poverty line, to the basic necessities of a Productive and socially meaningful life. Such a conceptualization of well being encompasses individual attainments in areas of education and knowledge; health and longevity; as well as in the quality of overall social and physical environment of people. A specific focus on these aspects of development is necessary, as experience shows that economic prosperity measured in terms of per capita income does not always ensure enrichment in quality of life reflected in broader dimensions of well-being like in indicators on longevity, literacy or, for that matter, environmental sustainability.

Attainments in these dimensions of well being are desirable in themselves, hence, they are socially valued. They are also desirable because of their instrumental value in sustaining the development process and enlarging available opportunities and choices for people. While equality in development outcomes may not be a feasible goal of equity and social justice, such an approach to human well-being emphasises equality in opportunities for all in the process of development (NHDR, 2002).

The full benefits of development can only be realised with people's participation and effective use of its human resources. Development analysis cannot be divorced from gender categories and the participation of women cannot be isolated from the total framework of development. The ultimate goal of social justice can only be achieved with equal opportunities to all irrespective of the gender since discrimination against women is incompatible with human dignity and the welfare of the family and of the society; prevents their participation on equal terms with men and is an obstacle to the full development of the potentialities of women in the service of their countries and humanity (UN, 1967). This paper examines the process of development in India from a gender perspective. The paper is divided into four sections. Section I deals with the introduction and changes in the concept of development in the present times and need for women's participation in the process of economic development.

Gender Empowerment Index, the index of gender equality that measures the attainments in human development indicators for females as a proportion of that of males during the eighties shows an improvement in India but only marginally. At the national level, it increased from 62 percent in the early eighties to 67.6 percent in the early nineties. This implies that on an average the attainments of women on human development indicators were only two-thirds of those of men. At the State level, gender equality was the highest for Kerala followed by Manipur, Meghalaya, Himachal Pradesh and Nagaland during the same period. Goa and the Union Territories had gender equality higher than the national level. In the nineties, Himachal Pradesh had the highest equality, whereas Bihar was at the bottom and witnessed a decline in absolute terms over the earlier period.

Demographic Features

One important factor that has a bearing on female to male in the demographic features of a country is the sex ratio. The sex ratio in India has been constantly declining over the years. Though it has slightly improved from 927 to 933 per thousand of male population during 2001. Also, there are wide variations in the sex ratios with Kerala (1036) at the top and the union territory of Chandigarh having the lowest.

Not only the overall sex ratio but also the juvenile sex i.e. sex ratio in the age group 0-9 years, is a cause of concern. It can be directly associated with pattern of mortality among children by sex (NHDR, 2002). A reduction in this ratio would mean higher female mortality compared to males, that indicate discrimination against girl child in availability and access to food, nutrition; health care and, perhaps or even medical support services. In other words this would also mean that there would be more women dying at an early age. The proportion of women not expected to live beyond the age of 40 years. Except in some states such as Kerala, Tamil Nadu, etc., the proportion of women not expected to survive beyond the age of 40 years is high compared to men. Even at the All India level, the proportion of women not expected to live beyond the age of 40 years is more than 19 percent compared to 16.9 percent males.

Between 1981 and 1991, juvenile sex ratio declined from

958 to 946. The decline was in the age group of 0-4 years, and also in 5-9 years. At the national level, difference between rural and urban areas was marginal, though it widened marginally in 1991 compared to 1981.

The ratio was more unfavourable for females in age group 5-9 years than that prevailing in age group 0-4 years for both the decades. However, the inter-State variations were quite striking. The sex ratio was relatively more favourable for females in the states of South, Northeast and East. It was adverse in the States of Haryana, Punjab, Rajasthan, Uttar Pradesh and Delhi. For many of the States both in rural as well as urban areas, the sex ratio was lower in age group 5-9 years than in age group 0-4 years though the differences declined over the period. The preliminary results from Census 2001 for sex ratio in age group 0-6 years was 927 females for thousand males, with a similar pattern at State level.

Among the factors that explain these patterns in the sex ratios, it indicates that while female mortality was 10.5 percent higher than male mortality in the age group 0-4 years, it was higher by 19 percent in the age group 5-9 years in 1981. These differences in male and female age specific mortality rates were relatively high for rural areas as compared to the urban areas. In 1991, mortality differences narrowed down. However, there are significant differences in the female-male mortality at the regional level. For a few States, such as Bihar, Haryana (in 1981), Madhya Pradesh, Punjab (in 1991), Rajasthan and Uttar Pradesh the female mortality was higher compared to the males in both the age groups.

The old age dependency rate, i.e., the number of persons in the age group of 60 years and above, per 1000 persons in the age group 15-59 years Any increase in the old age dependency rate would mean an increase in the number of the elderly people. Deteriorating physical, or may be even professional capabilities and with reduction in work participation rates makes them dependent on the working age group for their economic support. This could have serious implications for the well-being of the elders at household level (NHDR, 2002). The old age dependency ratio in India has increased marginally from about 12.04 percent in 1981 to 12.19 percent in 1991, being higher for females compared to the males. That means more women are dependent on their families compared to the males.

A survey conducted by the NSS on the elderly in 1995-96 estimated that 30 percent of the males and 70 percent of the females were economically completely dependent on others. This incidence of old age dependence was significantly high in case of females in West Bengal, Punjab, Assam, Haryana and Gujarat and marginally more for males in Karnataka, Punjab, and Andhra Pradesh compared to the All India average.

Another survey also conducted by NSS in 1995-96 reveals that nearly 54 percent of the elderly in urban areas and only 37 percent of the elderly in rural areas owned some financial assets. Looking at the sex wise distribution of the financial assets shows that the proportion of females possessing financial assets was significantly less compared to the males. While the gender disparity in the possession of financial assets was 3.2:1 in rural areas it was 1.5:1 in the urban areas.

Elders are often forced to work in the absence of adequate social security or post retirement benefits or when they cannot depend on the traditional family support systems. Most of this work is confined to the informal sector, which makes the economic vulnerability of the elderly even greater. The Census of India 1991 shows that the work participation rate was as high as 60 percent for the males while in case of females it was 16 percent. As against 65 percent of the elderly males and 19 percent of the elderly females working in rural areas, the corresponding figures were 43 percent and 6 percent respectively in the urban areas. In the coming years with the aging of the population as is the case in India, more so in case of elderly women, makes it necessary to suitably reflect the economic, social and physical concerns of the older people in public policies, programmes and interventions as also in the mobilisation of the civil society (NHDR, 2002).

Literacy Rates

Education is an investment in people that allows them to develop, expand and make full use of their capacities to work and live in dignity (NHDR, 2002).

A commitment of the Constitution of India is to provide free and compulsory primary education to all its citizens. During 1991-2001, literacy rates for overall population improved from 52.01 percent in 1991 to 65.38 percent in 2001. In case of males, the literacy rate improved by almost 13 percent but in case of females, there was an improvement of nearly 15 percent. Hence, increase in women's literacy was more than that of the males. Over a period of two decades from 1981 to 2001, the overall literacy rate in India has risen from 43.5 to 65.3 percent. In case of males, the literacy rate increased from 56.3 percent to 75.8 percent while in case of females from 29.7 percent to 54.1 percent showing a substantial rise in the literacy rate of the women. Hence, gaps in access to education have declined over the years in India. Female adult literacy and school enrolment has increased by almost two thirds since India became independent. However, there still remains a differential of nearly 22 percent points.

Women and Work

The level of employment, its composition and the growth in employment opportunities is an important indicator of the process of development in any economy. It is also an indicator that, in most cases, directly captures the economic attainments and hence the level of well-being of individuals (NHDR, 2002).

Although women have been contributing fully to the economic life of the community in every sphere, the full significance of their contribution has hardly ever been recognised or rewarded adequately. Women's place and work generally been considered to be in the home, their sphere of activity-domestic work and bringing up the family. Even when they participate in economic activity and contribute to the family's earnings, they are expected to be homemakers, too (Asaf Ali, 1975).

Studies carried out to understand the labour force participation of women have shown that the participation of women in the labour market activities has been not only low but also declining. Besides, it varies from one state to another depending on GDP, industrialisation, etc. The decline in the employment growth for females has been significantly higher than that for males. In fact, in both rural and urban areas, it has declined nearly by half.

The structural reforms programme was adopted in the country during the early 1990s. The country is now in the second generation of reforms. The adoption of structural changes has affected the employment opportunities for the entire working class but more so for women.

Women and Political Participation

Another measure of women's empowerment in the society is their participation in active politics. Development has to lead to empowerment to all sections of the society and coexist with empowerment. Women's participation covers a range of activities including movements, protests and support meetings on all issues connected with labour, dowry, rape, domestic violence, price-rise, food adulteration and deforestation, as also movements for the promotion of peace despite that rapid growth of informal political activities by women, their role in the formal political structure has virtually remained unchanged. This has resulted in a serious debate on the concepts and indicators for political participation. Even after more than five decades of independence women's participation and their role in political life still remains a distant dream (NHDR, 2002).

The participation of women in active politics has remained almost negligible despite the fact that the Constitution of India grants equal rights to women. Representation of women in the First Lok Sabha was 4.4 percent, in the second Lok Sabha 5.4 percent, in the third Lok Sabha 6.7 percent, in the fourth Lok Sabha 5.9 percent, in the fifth Lok Sabha 4.2 percent, in the sixth Lok Sabha 3.4 percent, in the seventh Lok Sabha 5.1 percent, in the eighth Lok Sabha 7.9 percent, in the ninth Lok Sabha 5.3 percent, in the tenth Lok Sabha 6.6 percent and eleventh Lok Sabha it is still in the single digit. The situation is quite similar even at the state level.

This under representation of women in politics indicates the male dominance in decision-making in the country. It implies that the requirements of women and their priorities receive the least attention. Patriarchal forces have worked in favour of men and against women. Consequently, women are still left on the periphery of the political process and political participation remains elusive to most of them in spite of their voting and election, and also capture of some seats of power and influence. Political participation seeks to organise the lives of members of human society and insure that the participation by women is not underestimated by being branded 'non political' and women concerns treated as social in nature.

Growth and Urbanisation

The process of economic growth is also marked by several socio-economic changes. Urbanisation is another important fall out of the process of economic growth. Historically, cities have been the driving forces in economic and social development. As centres of industry and commerce, cities have been centres of wealth and political power and contribute significantly to the country's GDP [WRI, 1996]. The world is undergoing transition towards urbanization. It is estimated that in 1975 one third of the world population lived in the urban areas and by 2025, this proportion will rise to two-third. This Process of urbanization is radically changing the socio-economic structure of the world economy. The change is much more rapid in the less developed economies where the rate of urbanization is much faster compared to that in the developed countries. According to a World Bank estimate nearly 80 percent of the economic growth will take place in the urban areas more particularly in the developing economies where the rate of urbanization is higher. During 1970-1995, the rate of growth of urban population in India has been 3.3 percent. During the next two decades, this process of urbanization is expected to slow down to 2.8 percent [HDR, 1998].

The process of urbanization in any economy is followed by human development reflected in improvement in living standards, rise in literacy rate, better health, etc. It also has a positive effect on the empowerment of women. The coefficient of correlation value calculated for rates of urbanisation and Gender Empowerment index value for 15 major states of India gives a Karl Pearson's correlation value of 0.76 indicating a very high correlation. Those states that have high rate of urbanisation also have high GEI. This is also shown in the scatter diagram.

However, urbanization also has negative impacts. These include a vast range of problems such as environmental degradation, rise in slums, water, and air pollution, etc. For many of the regions, urbanization goes in tandem with urban poverty not only in absolute terms but also in relative terms. Over crowding, air pollution, uncollected garbage and other deficiencies in the physical environment frequently represent the most obvious manifestations of urban environmental health problems (WRI, 1996). It also leads to growing social tensions that adversely affect the mental health of the human beings. Rise in crime and violence, etc., are also the fall out of urbanization that adversely affect the mental health of the human beings. There is no denying the fact that women are more vulnerable to violence compared to men. Socially and economically they constitute a disadvantaged group.

Uneven Urbanisation

The urban population worldwide has been rising though

much of it is in the less developed countries. In the developed countries, rapid urbanisation occurred a century ago and a vast majority of the population lives in urban areas.

The urban population in India has been rising at a rapid rate although rates of urbanisation vary across the states. There are significant differences in the rates of urbanisation.

As per 1991 census, 25.7 percent of the population lived in urban areas. There are interstate variations in the rates of urbanisation. Maharashtra, Gujarat and Tamil Nadu have witnessed the highest rates of urbanisation in the country being almost 39 percent and 35 percent respectively. On the other hand, it has been extremely low in the states like Assam, Bihar and Orissa. Not only are the rates of urbanisation different in different states but there are also differences in the concentration of urbanisation and much of the mobility is from the small and intermediate size cities to large metropolis. During 1951, the proportion of population in class I cities with a population of 1 lakh or more was nearly 45 percent This has continuously been rising and as per 1991 figures, there were 300 urban centres with the population of 1 lakh and more that accounted for 65 percent of the total urban population.

Also, there have been variations in the growth of urban areas. The proportion of population in smaller urban areas has been declining. This does not directly have an impact on the rate of urbanisation. But the process of urbanisation moves in favour of larger cities. This is giving rise to a new class of "international cities" that are the nerve centres of an increasingly globalising economies (Sassen, 1994). As transnational spaces for economic activity these international cities have more in common with each other rather than the cities in their own regions.

The process of globalisation has been initiated in many of the countries of the world. This has led to aggravation of distribution of income. In 1960, the richest 20 percent of the world's population had income 30 times more than the poorest 20 percent. By 1990, the richest 20 percent were getting 60 times more. This comparison is based on the distribution between rich and poor countries. Adding the maldistribution within countries, the richest 20 percent of the world's people get at least 150 times more than the poorest 20 percent.

Historically, poverty has been concentrated in rural areas. Yet, as migration from rural to urban areas is taking place, poverty is gradually being transferred from the rural areas as an urban phenomenon. This urbanization of poverty has implications for the urban environment and quality of life. The urban poor bear the greatest burden of urban environmental risks. This is because of the situations in which they are forced to live in slums. Through out the cities of the developing world, around 30-60 percent of the city's population lives in sub standard houses (WRI, 1997). The overcrowding increases the risks of air borne infections and accidents.

Related to this is the problem of availability of physical infrastructure facilities to people in the urban areas. Lack of availability of safe drinking water and sanitation facilities at times lead to spread of various diseases. Access to drinking water, sanitation, health services and educational opportunities is often high in the urban areas that has an impact on human life reflected in higher life expectancy and lower infant mortality rates, etc. However, these benefits are not available to the poorer sections in the urban areas. At times the poor are not served with potable water and sanitation facilities and garbage collection. In 1994, at least 220 million people still lacked a source of potable water near their homes. The proportion of the urban population covered by sanitation facilities is even smaller. More than 420 million urban people did not have access to even the simplest latrines.

Studies show that in some cases local governments are unable to pay for extending services to these regions. In others, they are reluctant to do so. The lack of these services at times increases the risk of intestinal infections and other communicable diseases. In Manila for instance, mortality rates in the slums are 3 times higher in the slums than in the rest of the city; rates of tuberculosis are 9 times higher (UNDP, 1990). Some of the worst problems in terms of human suffering occur in the poorest cities of the world. As of 1995, there were 131 persons per lakh persons suffering from tuberculosis, which is higher than the average for the countries with low HDI being 94 per lakh population. Similarly, the number of malaria cases per lakh population in India has been 243 as of 1994 being higher than many other less developed countries.

Deteriorating Health

The World Health Organisation defines health as a state of complete physical, mental and social well being, and not merely as the absence of infirmities. For a large majority of people in India, these conditions do not exist. More so for women, given the skewed distribution of resources within households and communities, that makes not just access to health, but often, basic survival itself an arduous struggle. For most individuals the choice to live a healthy life—free from illness and ailments—and a reasonable life span, are crucial attributes in the notion of personal well being. Similarly, for a society, a transition from high incidence of morbidity and mortality to a state where people generally enjoy long and disease free lives is considered a desirable and valued social change. It is only natural, then, that indicators on health and longevity, as well as indicators that variously capture demographic concerns of a society are important constituents in the framework for evaluating the development process under the human development approach.

Studies show that in India, women's nutrition levels are lower than men's. More women die before the age of 35 than do men. Lack of adequate diet for women creates serious problems, before and during pregnancy. Dietary surveys have shown that the intake of women of the low income groups is deficient by 500 to 600 calories. The corresponding findings for pregnant and lactating women reveal daily deficiency of

1100 calories and 1000 calories respectively. Women belonging to a lower socio-economic group gain around 3 to 5 kgs during pregnancy as against 10 kgs in the developed countries. 88 percent of pregnant women aged between 15 and 49 suffer from anaemia (1975-1991) (HDR 1997). Statistics reveal that in India only 3.06 percent of all female deaths are pregnancy related. Approximately one third of the deaths take place in the age group 0-14 years and one third in the age group of 45 +. It is the accidents and injuries that appear to be the major cause in the reproductive age group. This shows clearly that even within the reproductive age group, pregnancy related deaths are not the main reason for mortality.

The medical attention received by mothers by untrained professionals is as high as 62.7 percent, those attended by training professionals were 18.1 percent and 19.2 percent by institutional care in 1983. A rounded figure of deliveries by trained birth attendants is 30-35 percent in 1982 according to GOI estimates. An emphasis on "mothers health" by the Government of India has also meant that very little research has been done on other aspects of women's health such as the morbidity patterns amongst adult women, occupational hazards for working women at home as well as outside, effects of violence, especially domestic, stress and environmental degradation.

However, discrimination against the girl child starts even before birth in the form of sex determination tests, which often result in the abortion of the female foetuses. A survey carried out in Bombay in 1984, revealed that out of 8,000 abortions 7,999 were of female foetuses. Other health indicators for the status of women's health is the sex ratio (927 per 1000 in 1991) life expectancy (at birth years, for males is 52.6 as compared to 51.6 percent for females (1976-1981) (GOI 1982) and maternal mortality which have given a pessimistic prognosis over the years. Both morbidity and mortality patterns are greater among women of almost all age groups, especially the younger age groups as compared to men.

Despite this, studies show that in India, women use health facilities to a lesser extent than men. Vital factors corresponding to the health of the people is their access to sanitation facilities and safe drinking water. Only 29 percent of the population in the country has access to proper sanitation facilities and 81 percent of the population has access to clean drinking water (1990-1995; HDR, 1997).

People face the risk of biological and chemical contamination which is an important cause of e rampant cholera, typhoid, fluorosis and diarrhoea in a number of villages estimated to be 39 percent of the total villages in the country (1986).

Growing Social Tensions and Women's Health

There is no denying the fact that there has been a collapse of the value system and marginalisation of social life in general but more so in the urban areas that is indirectly affecting the security and mental health of the people. Closely related to this insecurity is the growing social tension that threatens social community cohesion (HDR, 1999). In addition, the contribution of urban social environment to deterioration in mental health is also increasingly being recognised. However, the recognition of this aspect has been very low in general and almost negligible in many of the developing countries in particular, which are still in war with several economic problems such as wide spread unemployment and poverty at their end. If the number of patients admitted in the mental hospital is taken as an indicator of mental health of the people in a country, statistics show that there has been deterioration in the mental health of the people in the countries across the world. In addition, the social problems such as family tensions and problems, growing number of divorces, unemployment, etc. are leading to frustrations in the urban areas which is reflected in the suicides committed which also shows a growing trend world over.

Urbanisation and Growing Crime and Violence

Violence is a means to keep the oppressed under terror and control .To a woman it is a violation of her rights over her body, her integrity and her dignity. Violence is a structural feature of the severely unequal relationship between man and woman. This perpetuates the sub-ordination of women. Crime and Violence are a means to keep the oppressed under terror and control. To a woman it is a violation of her rights over her body, her integrity and her dignity. Violence is a structural feature of the severely unequal relationship between man and woman. This perpetuates the sub-ordination of women.

The nature and the extent of violence directed at women vary according to class, region, culture and the strata of the society across the country.

However, it impacts women in all age groups and is deeply embedded within the family context of the women. The women are often subjected to violence from their husbands and from relatives in their natal as well as marital homes. The violence against women includes not only physical aggression but sexual, psychological and emotional abuse as well, all of which may not be easy to capture in terms of data as such incidences are often not reported or, if reported, the cases may not be registered for various reasons.

The data on suicide by women manages to capture some aspects of the psychological and emotional abuse, particularly when women who are subjected to such violence see in the act of killing themselves, the ultimate escape from their miseries. It is worthwhile to mention that the number of suicides by the males is much higher compared to the females and also the rate of increase in suicide cases has been higher in case of males. One major reason cited in some studies for this is the growing incidence of unemployment. In 1997 the rate of suicides in some of the States such as Kerala, Karnataka, West Bengal, Tamil Nadu, Goa, Maharashtra and the Union Territories of Pondicherry, Andaman and Nicobar Islands, Dadra and Nagar Haveli and Tripura were well above the national average.

Clearly, development whether captured through conventional indicators or through human development indicators, does not necessarily imply better social environment, in terms of less crime and violence, for women in particular. Throughout her life cycle, a women's dignity, self-esteem and emotional well-being are compromised by some less overt, but widespread form of discrimination such as personal confinement and restriction on mobility, particularly in rural areas; almost complete marginalisation in the decision making process at the household level; responsibility for household work including, looking after younger siblings; sexual abuse by the family members, even incest; childhood/forced marriage and verbal abuse. Most of these are not even recognised as a form of violence and are often condoned or justified on grounds of religious, cultural and traditional social norms or on grounds of attracting social stigma and thus jeopardising the social status of the concerned family (NHDR, 2002).

Any attempt, therefore, at assessing the level of development, even when the conventional and the human development indicators are impressive, cannot be complete unless an assessment is also made of the social environment, particularly with regard to the extent of crime and violence that an average individual faces in that society. It is all the more important as it has been often seen that the more prosperous or developed regions are not necessarily the safest for all segments of population. In India too, the more prosperous places are the ones where incidence of crime, in some form, is perhaps the highest—where organised crime and extortion is an unfortunate reality (NHDR, 2002).

There is no denying the fact that there has been a growing crime during the recent times. Crime is increasing in scope, intensity and sophistication. The data for most of the countries show that there has been a phenomenal rise in homicide, thefts, assaults, burglary, robberies, frauds, rapes, etc., irrespective of the level of development of the country. On the contrary, it has been found that in highly industrialized countries like USA, the crime rate is much higher than that in some of the less developed countries. This has resulted into growing socio-psychological tensions. It also threatens the safety of citizens around the world and hampers countries in their social, economic and cultural development. It is also estimated that a highly corrupt country is likely to achieve aggregate investment level of almost 5 percent less and lose half a percent point of GDP growth than a relatively incorrupt country.

Though violence and the threat of it is universal, it is not to deny that certain sections of women, who are socially and economically disadvantaged, and poor working women, minority women and so on, are more vulnerable to acts of violence than others. Sectarian politics and sectarian violence have in many ways strengthened gendered inequities. Globalisation has provided the environment for growing internationalization of criminal activities (WRI, 1997) and criminals are reaping the benefits of globalisation. Multinational criminal syndicates have significantly broadened the range of their activities from drug trafficking to money laundering. According to an estimate, as many as 4 million illegal migrants are moved every year generating gross earnings of around US$ 5-7 billion. Drug related crimes increased from 4 per 100,000 people in Belarus in 1990 to 28 in 1997. The sexual traffic king in women and girls to Western Europe alone has been estimated to be around US$ 7 billion business. And at the root of this is the growing organized crime, estimated around US$ 1.5 trillion per year. Globalisation has given new characteristics to conflicts by feeding them, involving new actors and blurring political and business interests. In the power vacuum of the post- cold war era, military companies and mercenary armies began offering training to governments and corporations.

The public policies and civil society interventions to bring about an improvement in domestic and work environment of women have to be seen essentially in terms of strengthening such process that are conducive to bringing about attitudinal shifts in individuals, particularly among the men, and evolving social norms supportive of gender specific concerns.

One important aspect that has been emphasised in the UNDP Human Development Report 2002 and also the National Human Development Report by the Planning commission is the issue of governance for sustainable human development. "A development that, while being sustainable in terms of resources over generations and across space recognizes, the legitimate claim of each person in a society to be an active and a productive participant in the development process. Augmentation in a country's resources and its material means is but one of the essential steps towards achieving human development. Equally important, if not more, is the process of transforming these means into valued outcomes. A critical element in this process of transformation of the available means—the natural endowments and the acquired—into socially desired outcomes, is the quality of governance".

It touches upon almost all aspects of the individual's and social life. Moreover, as public and private resources are being utilised, particularly in the developing countries, to support strategies for human development, there is a concern that every effort should yield better results. This can be made possible only when the processes supporting these are more efficient and effective in achieving the objectives. "While good governance can help secure human well-being and sustained development, it is equally important to recognize that poor governance could well erode the individual capabilities, as well as institutional and community capacities to meet even the basic needs of sustenance for large segments of the population. This is particularly so for the poor, the disadvantaged and the marginalised sections of the society, more so, in the developing world".

By now it has been accepted in the literature that human deprivation and inequalities are not merely for economic reasons; rather they go hand-in-hand with social and political factors rooted in poor governance. In the case of India, one can find any number of regions in the country, or States within a region or even districts within a State, where development outcomes, in terms of social indicators, reflect a mismatch between the available resources and the potential of the local community. "Empowerment of women, the marginal and the excluded has been demonstrated, in many cases, to be among the important means to establish countervailing forces in the society for checking deterioration in governance standards and personal exploitation by others. The vested interests in any system always have stakes in maintaining the status quo of such institutions and their practices, which are beneficial to them. The only way to break these informal but deliberate and often stubborn arrangements is by equipping the marginalised of the society to fight for their legitimate rights".

This calls for legislative initiatives and policy formulation effectively implemented for instance, by undertaking reservation for women in the legislative bodies at all levels and better participation in decision making, but it also requires explicitly directing the public efforts to address the social, economic and political insecurities of vulnerable sections of the society. "It requires the dissemination of information and free access to all. Most of all it requires capacity building of the individuals through human development strategies involving the access to education, basic health care facilities and opportunities of livelihood".

Concluding Observations

The process of economic growth via its fallouts such as urbanisation has helped in improving the empowerment of women, which is reflected in improvement in literacy rate, their labour force participation. Not that the rural women's economic participation in work is low, but that they work on family farms and enterprises, work which is unpaid; their contribution to work is not recognised. In urban areas, women's direct participation in labour market activities has improved and hence recognition to their contribution to paid work. However, their political participation remains low indication their absence in the process of decision making.

In short, there is an improvement in women's economic participation but political structure keeps women out of the decision making. Hence, social values seem to be super imposed on the political structure. Even the higher unemployment rates among women are an indication of subordination of women in the labour market activities being looked down upon as secondary.

In this sense, women seem to be the victims during the process of economic change. Precisely, they are considered as reserve army of labour—first to be fired during recessionary situations and the last to be hired. At the same time, urbanisation has brought forth many other problems for human kind in general and women in particular. It has led to growing crime and violence against the human kind and women precisely.

The real wealth of a nation is its people. The purpose of development is to create an enabling environment for people to enjoy long, healthy and creative life. Globalisation has given new dimensions to social and cultural changes. But it can safely be argued that much of the institutional environment that creates a better link between economic growth and human development is simply missing. The challenge of globalisation is not to stop the expansion of global markets but rather, to find the rules and institutions for stronger governance—national, regional and global—to preserve the advantages of global markets and competition.

References

Abraham, K.G., and Mckersie, R.B., (eds.) (1990), *New Developments in the Labour Markets: Towards a new Institutional Paradigm,* MIT Press, Cambridge, Massachusetts,

London.

Agrawal. S (1995) Employment of women in India, *Journal of Indian school of political economy*, Vol. 7, No. 1, January-March 1995).

Agrawal S. (1997) Gender inequality in education. *Labour and Development* Vol. 3 No. 2 July-December.

Agrawal S. and Patel, J.R. (2000), *Gendered Development in India: Regional Perspectives*, Paper presented at International Women's Conference organised by TNAI, New Delhi and Mc Master University, Canada at New Delhi during Februay 27-March, 3.

Asaf Ali, A.(1975), The relation between paid and unpaid work, A source of inequality*: The Case of India. In Women in the Labour force and at Home,* IILR, series 22, Geneva.

Bang, R.A. and A. Bang. (1991) Why women hide them: Rural women's viewpoints on reproductive tract infections. *Manushi* 69:27–30.

Bardhan, Kalpana. (1985) Women's work, welfare and status: Forces of tradition and change in India. *Economic and Political Weekly* 20(51): 2261–2267.

Basu, Alaka Malwade. (1989) Is discrimination in food really necessary for explaining sex differentials in childhood mortality? *Population Studies* 43(2): 193–210.

Basu, Alaka Malwade. (1993) Cultural influences on the timing of first births in India: Large differences that add up to little difference. *Population Studies* 47:88–93.

Benaria, L. (1979), Reproduction, Production and the Sexual division of Labour, *Cambridge Journal of Economics*, Vol. 3, No. 3, September 1979.

Benton, L.A.(1989), Homework and Industrial Development: Gender roles and restructuring in the Spanish Shoe Industry, *World Development*, Vol. 17, No. 2, February.

Bhatia, J.C. and John Cleland. (1995) On self-reported symptoms of gynaecological morbidity and their treatment in South India. *Studies in Family Planning* 26(4): 203–216.

Braverman, H., (1974), *Labour and Monopoly Capital: The Degradation of Work in the Twentieth century*, Monthly Review Press, London.

Central Statistical Organisation. (1999) *Selected Socio-Economic Statistics, India 1998*. New Delhi: Department of Statistics and

Programme Implementation, Government of India.

Centre for Monitoring Indian Economy. (1991). *Basic Statistics Relating to the Indian Economy*, Vol 2: States. Bombay: Centre for Monitoring Indian Economy.

Centre for Monitoring Indian Economy. (1993) *Basic Statistics Relating to the Indian Economy*, Vol 2: States. Bombay: Centre for Monitoring Indian Economy.

Cherian Joseph and Prasad K.V. E., (eds.), (1995) *Women, Work and Equity: The reality of Gender*, National Labour Institute, NOIDA.

Clairmont, F.F., (1996), *The Rise and Fall of Economic Liberalism, the making of the economic Gulag*, The Other India Press, Third World Network, Mapusa, Goa.

Das Gupta, Monica. (1987) Selective discrimination against female children in rural Punjab, India. *Population and Development Review* 13(1): 77–101.

Desai, Sonalde and Devaki Jain. (1994) Maternal employment and changes in family dynamics: The social context of women's work in rural South India. *Population and Development Review* 20(1): 115-136.

Dholakia, R.H.(1985), On estimating Women's contribution to National Product, *Man Power Journal*, Vol. XXI, No. 3, October-December.

Draze Jean and Sen A.K. (1996) *Economic Development and Social Responsibility*, OUP, New Delhi.

Dyson, Tim and Mick Moore. (1983) On kinship structure, female autonomy and demographic behaviour in India. *Population and Development Review* 9(1): 35-60.

EPW Research Foundation. (1998) *National Accounts Statistics of India, 1950-51 to 1996-97*. Mumbai: EPW Research Foundation.

Ghosh, Shanti. (1987) The female child in India: A struggle for survival. *Bulletin of the Nutrition Foundation of India,* 8(4).

Government of India (1999) *Economic Survey*, Government of India, New Delhi.

Government of India, (2000), *Ninth Five Year Plan: Mid term appraisal*, New Delhi.

Government of India, (2002), *National Human Development Report*, Planning Commission, March.

International Institute for Population Sciences (2000) *National Family Health Survey India—1998-99*, National Reports,

Bombay.

International Institute for Population Sciences (IIPS) (1995) *National Family Health Survey (MCH and Family Planning), India 1992–93*. Bombay: IIPS.

Jaisingh, I. (1995) Violence Against Women: The Indian Perspective. In J. Peters and A. Wolper (eds.), *Women's Rights, Human Rights*. New York: Routledge.

Judy Lown, (1990), *Women and Industrialisation: Gender at Work in 19th Century England*, Polity Press, Cambridge.

Kahn-Hut, R., Daniels, A.K., and R. Colvard (1982), *Women and Work: Problems and Perspectives,* Oxford University Press, New York.

Kreps, J.M. (1976), *Women and the American economy: A look to the 1980s,* Prentice Hall, New Jersey.

Krishnaraj, M.,(1995), *Feminist Approaches to Economic Theory*, Report of a Workshop held at Bangalore, August 5-6, Indian Association of Women's Studies, Mumbai.

Miller, A. L. (1995), *The Third World in Global Environmental Politics*, Lynne Rienne Publications, London.

MOHFW. Ministry of Health and Family Welfare (MOHFW). 1994. *Annual Report 1992-93*. New Delhi:

Mukherjee A. and Agnihotri V.K. (1993), *Environment and Development: Views from East and West.* Concept Publishing Co., New Delhi.

Pandey, Arvind, Minja Kim Choe, Norman Y. Luther, Damodar Sahu, and Jagdish Chand. (1998) *Infant and Child Mortality in India. National Family Health Survey Subject Reports No. 11*. Mumbai: International Institute for Population Sciences; and Honolulu: East-West Centre.

Paukert, liba (1980) The Economic Status of Women in the Transition to a market system: The Case of Czechoslovakia. *International Labour Review*, Vol. 130, No. 5-6.

Redcliffe M. (1984), *Development and the Environmental Crisis,* Mathuen and Company, New York.

Sachdeva Arvinder S (2002) Urbanisation in India: Past Trends and Future Projections, *The Asian Journal*, Vol. 9, No. 1, February, New Delhi.

Sen Amartya (2001), *Development as Freedom*, Oxford University Press, New Delhi.

Sen, Amartya (1990). Gender and Cooperative Conflicts. In Irene

Tinker (ed.), *Persistent Inequalities: Women and World Development*. New York: Oxford University Press.

Sen Gita, Adrienne Germain, and Lincoln C. Chen (eds.) (1994), *Population Policies Reconsidered: Health, Empowerment and Rights*. Harvard Series on Population and International Health. Boston: Harvard School of Public Health.

Sen, Gita and Srilatha Batliwala. (1997) *Empowering Women for Reproductive Rights: Moving Beyond Cairo*. Paper presented at the Seminar on Female Empowerment and Demographic Processes: Moving Beyond Cairo, IUSSP, Lund, Sweden, 21–24 April.

Sundaram K (2001) Employment -Unemployment in the Nineties, results from NSS 55th Round, *Economic and Political Weekly*, Volume XXXVI No. 11, March 17, 2001

Tilak Jandhyala B G (1994) *Education and Development in Asia*, Sage Publications New Delhi.

UNDP (1990), *Human Development Report*, Oxford University Press, New York.

UNDP (1992), *Human Development Report*, Oxford University Press, New York.

UNDP (1995), *Human Development Report*, Oxford University Press, New York.

UNDP (1998), *Human Development Report*, Oxford University Press, New Delhi.

United Nations (1984), Improving Concepts and Methods for statistics and Indicators on the Situation of Women, New York, 1984.

United Nations (1994), *Population and Women*: Proceedings of the UN Expert group meeting on Population and Women, Gaborone, Botswana, 22-26 June, United Nations, New York.

United Nations (1995), *Women's Education and fertility Behaviour*, New York.

United Nations General Assembly. 1991. Advancement of Women: Convention on the Elimination of All Forms of Discrimination Against Women, Report of the Secretary-General. New York: United Nations.

United Nations (1967), Declaration on the elimination of Discrimination against women, UN , requote from *Towards equality, Report of the National Committee on the Status of Women*, Government of India, New Delhi.

Visaria, Leela. (1999) Violence against women in India: Evidence from rural Gujarat. In International Centre for Research on Women (ICRW), *Domestic Violence in India: A Summary Report of Three Studies*. Washington, DC: ICRW.

World Resource Institute and others (1996), *World Resources: A guide to the Global Environment,* Oxford University Press, New York.

World Resource Institute and others (2000), *World Resources: A guide to the Global Environment*, Oxford University Press, New York.

Youssef, Nadia H. (1982) The Interrelationship Between the Division of Labour in the Household, Women's Roles and Their Impact on Fertility. In R. Anker, M. Buvinic and N.H. Youssef (eds.), *Women's Roles and Population Trends in the Third World*. London: Croom Helm. 216.

4

Women Labourers Engaged in Agricultural and Allied Activities

P. Anita and Puja Roy

The position of women and their status in any society is an index of its civilization. Women constitute 48.30 percent of the country's population accounting for 495.74 million as per the 2001 census. Without their involvement in the process of economic development, the development itself would be incomplete and lopsided.

The economic independence is regarded to be the prime basis for enhancing the status and position of women at home as well in society. In order to improve the status and position of women at home as well in society at large, it is indispensable to empower women economically. Feasibility and timely availability of credit to women would reduce their level of dependency thereby empowering them to assert more in household decision-making process. As the society is stratified on the basis of religion, caste and class in India, women cannot be viewed as a homogeneous group. The position of women and their demand for institutional credit remain tied to class, caste and religious affiliations. In order to comprehend the nature of these causal relationships, it is incumbent to understand the socio-economic characteristics of sample women labourers in the study area (Madurai District). The present article attempts to analyze the following objectives:

- To analyze the socio-economic and familial characteristics of the women labourers engaged in agriculture and allied activities in Madurai District.

- To find out the variation in monthly income between the women beneficiaries engaged in three different activities in Madurai District.
- To analyze the share of respondent's income from their activities towards family income.

The following hypotheses have been considered:

There is no significant increase in the income of the respondents engaged in animal husbandry, cropping and farm development activities after availing of credit.

A sample of 300 women beneficiaries (67 from animal husbandry, 218 from cropping and 15 from farm development activities) have been selected from the 13 blocks in Madurai district by adopting proportionate random sampling technique.

The field survey was conducted from September 2008 to January 2009.

For analysis of data and testing the hypothesis averages, percents and the statistical techniques like One-way ANOVA test and percent share analysis have been used.

Socio-economic and Familial Characteristics of the Women Beneficiaries

Age Distribution: The respondents have been classified into four age groups. Table 4.1 presents the distribution of the sample women respondents according to their age.

Table 4.1: Age-Wise Distribution of the Respondents

Age group (years)	Animal husbandry	Cropping	Farm Development
18 to 30	18 (26.90)	43 (19.72)	4 (26.66)
31 to 40	28 (41.80)	73 (33.49)	5 (33.33)
41 to 50	12 (17.90)	55 (25.23)	3 (20.00)
Above 50	9 (13.40)	47 (21.56)	3 (20.00)
Total	67 (100)	218 (100)	15 (100)

Source: Field survey.

Note: Figures in brackets are the percent to total.

It has been observed that out of 67 beneficiaries engaged in animal husbandry, 18 (26.90 percent) of them fall under the age group of 18 to 30 years, about 28 (41.80 percent) of them fall under the age group of 31 to 40 years, 12 (17.90 percent) of them and 9 (13.40 percent) of them fall under the age group of 41 to 50 years and above 50 years respectively.

In case of cropping it has been observed that out of 218 beneficiaries, 43 (19.72 percent) of them fall under the age group of 18 to 30 years, 73 (33.49 percent) come under the age group of 31 to 40 years, 55 (25.23 percent) of them and 47 (21.56 percent) of them fall under the age group of 41 to 50 years and above 50 years respectively.

Further, it has been observed that out of 15 beneficiaries engaged in farm development activity, 4 (26.66 percent) of them fall under the age group of 18 to 30 years, 5 (33.33 percent) of them fall under the age group of 31 to 40 years and 3 (20 percent) of them fall under the age group of 41 to 50 years and above 50 years each respectively. Thus, it could be concluded from the analysis that more than one third of the respondents engaged in these activities belong to the age group of 31 to 40 years in the study area.

Religion: Table 4.2 depicts the distribution of women respondents by their religion.

Table 4.2: Religion-Wise Distribution of the Respondents

Religion	Animal husbandry	Cropping	Farm Development
Hindus	53 (79.10)	175 (80.30)	12 (80.00)
Muslims	6 (8.96)	21 (9.60)	1 (6.70)
Christians	8 (11.94)	22 (10.10)	2 (13.30)
Total	67 (100)	218 (100)	15 (100)

Source: Field survey.

Note: Figures in brackets are the percent to total.

It is clearly apparent from the table that out of 67 respondents engaged in animal husbandry 53 (79.10 percent) sample respondents were Hindus, 8 (11.94 percent) of them belong to Christianity and 6 (8.96 percent) of them were Muslims. In case of women beneficiaries engaged in cropping, it has been observed that, out of 218 sample respondents 175 (80.30 percent) of them were Hindus, 22 (10.10 percent) of them were Christians and remaining 21 (9.60 percent) of them were Muslims whereas in farm development category out of 15 respondents, 12 (80 percent) of them belong to Hinduism, 2 (13.30 percent) belong to Christianity and 1 (6.70 percent) of them belong to Muslim religion. Thus, it could be concluded that majority of the respondents in the study area were Hindus.

Caste and Community: Caste is a sub-division in the traditional varna system in India. In the past, caste used to determine the nature of work/occupation of inhabitants including women. Women in upper caste were kept away from taking up self-employment. They were expected only to assist their husbands in their occupations. But, today modernization, westernization and education have modified the traditional role of women. The distribution of women respondents by caste has been presented in Table 4.3.

Table 4.3: Caste-Wise Distribution of the Respondents

Caste	Animal husbandry	Cropping	Farm Development
OC	9 (13.40)	44 (20.20)	2 (13.30)
BC	9 (13.40)	66 (30.30)	4 (26.70)
MBC	28 (41.80)	87 (39.90)	6 (40.00)
SC/ST	21 (31.30)	21 (9.60)	3 (20.00)
Total	67 (100)	218 (100)	15 (100)

Source: Field survey.

Note: Figures in brackets are the percent to total.

It is clearly exhibited from the table that out of 67 sample respondents engaged in animal husbandry, 28 (41.80 percent) of them belong to Most Backward Classes (MBC), 21 (31.30 percent) of them belong to Scheduled Caste/Scheduled Tribes

(SC/ST) and 9 (13.40 percent) of them belong to Backward Class (BC) and remaining 9 (13.40 percent) of them belong to Other Caste (OC). In cropping activity, out of 218 respondents, 87 (39.90 percent) of them belong to MBC, 66 (30.30 percent) of them belong to BC, 44 (20.20 percent) of them belong to OC and remaining 21 (9.60 percent) of them belong to SC/ST. Further, it has been found out that out of 15 women respondents engaged in farm development activity, 6 (40 percent) of them belong to MBC followed by 4 (26.70 percent) in BC, 3 (20 percent) of them belongs to SC/ST and 2 (13.30 percent) of them belongs to OC. Thus, it could be concluded that majority of the respondents in the study area belong to the Most Backward Class.

Education Level: Education helps women to have mobility, exposure, bargaining power, to operate bank accounts and to become self-confident and self-reliant. Table 4.4 presents the educational status of women beneficiaries engaged in animal husbandry, cropping and farm development activities.

Table 4.4: Distribution of the Respondents According to the Level of Education

Qualification	Animal husbandry	Cropping	Farm Development
Illiterates	18 (26.90)	98 (45.00)	6 (40.00)
Primary	19 (28.40)	55 (25.20)	3 (20.00)
Secondary	24 (35.80)	54 (24.80)	4 (26.70)
College/Diploma	6 (9.00)	11 (5.00)	2 (13.30)
Total	67 (100)	218 (100)	15 (100)

Source: Field survey.

Note: Figures in brackets are the percent to total.

It is apparent from the table that, with regard to the educational qualification of the sample women beneficiaries in animal husbandry, out of 67 respondents about 18 (26.90 percent) of them have been illiterates, 19 (28.40 percent) of them have studied up to primary level, 24 (35.80 percent) respondents have completed secondary level and only 6 (9 percent) of them have gone for collegiate and diploma courses. In cropping, 98 (45 percent) of them have been illiterates, 55 (25.20 percent) of them have studied up to primary level, 54 (24.80 percent) of them have passed secondary level and only 11 (5 percent) of them were degree/diploma holders. Among the women engaged in farm development activities about 6 (40 percent) of them were illiterates, 3 (20 percent) have studied up to primary level, 4 (26.70 percent) of them have passed secondary level and only 2 (13.30 percent) of them were degree/diploma holders. Thus, it could be concluded from the analysis that nearly 60 percent of the sample respondents were literates while only 40 percent of them were illiterates.

Marital Status of the Respondents: Marital Status of the women beneficiaries has been explicitly presented in Table 4.5.

Table 4.5: Distribution of the Respondents According to the Marital Status

Marital Status	Animal husbandry	Cropping	Farm Development
Married	61 (91.00)	208 (95.40)	14 (93.30)
Unmarried	3 (4.50)	-	-
Widows/Divorcees	3 (4.50)	10 (4.60)	1 (6.70)
Total	67 (100)	218 (100)	15 (100)

Source: Field survey.

Note: Figures in brackets are the percent to total.

It is revealed from the table that out of 67 respondents engaged in animal husbandry, 61 (91 percent) of them were married, 3 (4.50 percent) of them were unmarried, and remaining 3 (4.50 percent) of them were widows/divorcees. It has been further deduced that out of 218 respondents engaged in cropping activity, 208 (95.40 percent) of them were married and 10 (4.60 percent) of them were widows/divorcees.

Finally, in farm development activity out of 15 respondents, 14 (93.30 percent) of them were married and only 1 (6.70 percent) of the respondent has been in the category of widow and none of them were unmarried. Thus, it could be concluded that majority (more than 90 percent) of women respondents engaged in these activities were married in the study area.

Type of Family of the Respondents: Society is a web of social relationship and relationship begins within the family. Family is of two types namely; joint family and nuclear family. The distribution of women respondents according to their type of family has been presented in Table 4.6.

Table 4.6: Distribution of the Respondents According to the Type of Family

Type of Family	Animal husbandry	Cropping	Farm Development
Joint Family	30 (44.77)	80 (36.70)	6 (40.00)
Nuclear Family	37 (55.23)	138 (63.30)	9 (60.00)
Total	67 (100)	218 (100)	15 (100)

Source: Field survey.
Note: Figures in brackets are the percent to total.

It has been inferred from the table that, out of 67 respondents in animal husbandry, 37 (55.23 percent) of them had nuclear family and only 30 (44.77 percent) of them were members of the joint family. In case of cropping activity, out of 218 respondents, 138 (63.30 percent) of them have nuclear family and only 80 (36.70 percent) of them belonged to joint family. Among the 15 respondents engaged in farm development activities majority of 9 (60 percent) respondents were having nuclear family and about 6 (40 percent) of them were part of a joint family. Thus, it could be deduced from the analysis that more than 55 percent of women beneficiaries in the study area belong to the nuclear family.

Family Size of the Respondents: The distribution of

women respondents according to their family size has been presented in Table 4.7.

Table 4.7: Distribution of the Respondents According to the Size of Family

Size of Family	Animal husbandry	Cropping	Farm Development
3 and Below	34 (50.70)	115 (52.80)	12 (80.00)
4 to 5	26 (38.80)	61 (28.00)	1 (6.67)
5 above	7 (10.40)	42 (19.30)	2 (13.33)
Total	67 (100)	218 (100)	15 (100)

Source: Field survey.
Note: Figures in brackets are the percent to total.

It has been clearly deduced from the table that, out of 67 respondents in Animal husbandry, 34 (50.70 percent) of them have 3 members and below in the family, 26 (38.80 percent) of them have 4 to 5 members in the family and 7 (10.40 percent) of them have above 5 members in the family.

Further, it has been observed that, out of 218 respondents engaged in cropping activity, 115 (52.80 percent) of them have 3 members and below in the family, 61 (28 percent) and 42 (19.30 percent) of them have 4 to 5 and above 5 members in the family respectively.

While in farm development activity, it has been found that, 12 (80 percent) of them have 3 members and below in the family and 2 (13.33 percent) of them have above 5 members respectively. Thus, it could be concluded from the overall analysis that majority (more than 50 percent) of the respondents in the study area have 3 members and below in their family.

Number of Children: The distribution of beneficiaries by the number of children has been explicated in Table 4.8.

It is apparent from the table that out of 64 respondents in Animal husbandry, 30 (46.87 percent) of the respondents have children below 3, 20 (31.25 percent) of them have 3 to 4 children and 14 (21.88 percent) of them have 5 children and above in the family.

Likewise, in cropping activity out of 218 respondents, 110 (50.50 percent) of them have children below 3, 76 (34.90 percent) and 32 (14.70 percent) of them have 3 to 4 and 5 and above children respectively.

Table 4.8: Distribution of the Respondents According to Their Number of Children

Number of Children	Animal husbandry	Cropping	Farm Development
Below 3	30 (46.87)	110 (50.50)	11 (73.30)
3 to 4	20 (31.25)	76 (34.90)	1 (6.70)
5 and above	14 (21.88)	32 (14.70)	3 (20.00)
Total	64 (100)	218 (100)	15 (100)

Source: Field survey.

Note: Figures in brackets are the percent to total.

Further, it has been observed that out of 15 respondents engaged in farm development activities, 11 (73.30 percent) of them have children below 3, 1 (6.70 percent) and 3 (20 percent) of them have 3 to 4 and 5 and above children respectively. Thus, it has been inferred from the overall analysis that above 45 percent of women beneficiaries have children below 3 in the study area.

Type of House: Classification of respondents according to type of house they are residing has been presented in Table 4.9.

It is inferred from the table that out of 67 respondents in animal husbandry, 35 (52.20 percent) of them have Pucca house, 24 (35.80 percent) of them live in Kutcha House and 8 (11.90 percent) of them live in huts. In the case of women engaged in cropping activity, out of 218 respondents, 76 (34.90 percent) of them dwell in Pucca house, 87 (39.90 percent) of them dwell in Kutcha house and 55 (25.20 percent) of them dwell in huts.

Table 4.9: Distribution of the Respondents According to the Type of House

Type of House	Animal husbandry	Cropping	Farm Development
Hut	8 (11.90)	55 (25.20)	-
Kutcha house	24 (35.80)	87 (39.90)	7 (46.70)
Pucca house	35 (52.20)	76 (34.90)	8 (53.30)
Total	67 (100)	218 (100)	15 (100)

Source: Field survey.
Note: Figures in brackets are the percent to total.

In farm development activity out of 15 respondents, 8 (53.30 percent) and 7 (46.70 percent) of them dwell in Pucca and Kutcha house respectively. Thus, it could be concluded that majority of the respondents in the study area dwell in Pucca house except in cropping category where majority of 39.90 percent of them resides in Kutcha house.

Respondents Monthly Income: The distribution of respondents according to their monthly income has been depicted in Table 4.10.

It has been observed from the Table that out of 67 respondents engaged in animal husbandry, 5 (7.50 percent) of them come under above middle income category earning ₹ 5000 above per month, 21 (31.30 percent) of them come under the middle income group of ₹ 2000 to ₹ 5000 and 41 (61.20 percent) of them come under the category below ₹ 2000. They lead a mere subsistent living (hand-to-mouth living). While in cropping activity, out of 218 respondents 98 (45 percent) respondents each come under the income group of ₹ 2000 to ₹ 5000 and above ₹ 5000 respectively and remaining 22 (10.10 percent) of them come under the subsistent income category of below ₹ 2000.

Further, in farm development activity, out of 15 respondents, 10 (66.67 percent) of them come under the monthly income category of ₹ 5000 above followed by 5 (33.33 percent) of them in ₹ 2000 to ₹ 5000 income group.

Thus, it could be concluded from the pooled analysis that majority of the sample respondents in animal husbandry fall under the monthly income category of below ₹ 2000. In cropping majority of them fall in the income group of ₹ 2000 to ₹ 5000 and ₹ 5000 above while in farm development category majority of them fall in the income group of ₹ 5000 above.

Table 4.10: Distribution of the Respondents According to their Income (Per Month)

Income (in ₹)	Animal husbandry	Cropping	Farm Development
Below 2000	41 (61.20)	22 (10.10)	-
2000 to 5000	21 (31.30)	98 (45.00)	5 (33.33)
5000 above	5 (7.50)	98 (45.00)	10 (66.67)
Total	67 (100)	218 (100)	15 (100)

Source: Field survey.

Note: Figures in brackets are the percent to total.

Spouse's Monthly Income: Distribution of the respondents according to their spouse's monthly income is shown in Table 4.11.

It has been deduced from the table that out of 61 respondents engaged in animal husbandry, 52 (85.24 percent) of them have spouses who belong to the category of income below ₹ 5000, 6 (9.84 percent) of the respondents' spouses belong to the income group of ₹ 5000 to ₹ 10000 and 3 (4.92 percent) of their spouses belong to the income group of above ₹ 10000.

In the case of cropping activity, out of 208 respondents, 120 (57.69 percent) of them have spouses who belong to the income category of below ₹ 5000, 88 (42.31 percent) of their spouses belong to the income group of ₹ 5000 to ₹ 10000 and none of their spouses have income above ₹ 10000.

In the case of farm development activities, 5 (35.71 percent) of them have spouses belonging to the income group below ₹ 5000, 6 (42.86 percent) and 3 (21.43 percent) of their spouses belong to the income category of ₹ 5000 to ₹ 10000 and above ₹ 10000 respectively.

Table 4.11: Distribution of the Respondents According to their Spouse Monthly Income

Income (in ₹)	Animal husbandry	Cropping	Farm Development
Below 5000	52 (85.24)	120 (57.69)	5 (35.71)
5000 to 10000	6 (9.84)	88 (42.31)	6 (42.86)
10000 above	3 (4.92)	-	3 (21.43)
Total	61 (100)	208 (100)	14 (100)

Source: Field survey.
Note: Figures in brackets are the percent to total.

Thus, it could be inferred from the overall analysis that, majority of them have spouses who belong to the income group below ₹ 5000 followed by those having spouses belonging to the income category of ₹ 5000 to ₹ 10000 in the case of animal husbandry and cropping activities. While in farm development activity majority of them have spouses belonging to the income category of ₹ 5000 to ₹ 10000 in the study area.

Family Monthly Income of the Respondents: The monthly family income of the respondents has been explicated in Table 4.12.

Table 4.12: Distribution of the Respondents by Their Family Income

Family Income (in ₹)	Animal husbandry	Cropping	Farm Development
Below 10000	63 (94.00)	109 (50.00)	2 (13.30)
10000 to 15000	3 (4.50)	88 (40.40)	7 (46.70)
15000 above	1 (1.50)	21 (9.60)	6 (40.00)
Total	67 (100)	218 (100)	15 (100)

Source: Field survey.
Note: Figures in brackets are the percent to total.

It has been observed from the table that out of 67 respondents in animal husbandry activity, majority of respondents 63 (94 percent) have family income falling in the income group of below ₹ 10000 per month, 3 (4.50 percent) of them have family income in ₹ 10000 to ₹ 15000 group and remaining 1(1.50 percent) of the respondent fall under the family income group of above ₹ 15000.

In the case of cropping activity, out of 218 respondents, 109 (50 percent) of the respondents have family income below ₹ 10000, 88 (40.40 percent) and 21 (9.60 percent) of them have their family monthly income of ₹ 10000 to ₹ 15000 and above ₹ 15000 respectively.

While in the case of women beneficiaries engaged in farm development activity majority of 7 (46.70 percent) of them fall under the monthly family income category of ₹10000 to ₹ 15000, 6 (40 percent) of them fall in the family income group of above ₹ 15000 and only 2 (13.30 percent) of them have their family income of below ₹ 10000 per month. Thus, it could be concluded from the overall analysis that majority of the respondents engaged in animal husbandry and cropping have their family monthly income in the income category of below ₹ 10000. While in farm development activity majority of them have their family monthly income in the category of ₹ 10000 to ₹ 15000.

Variation in Monthly Income among three different groups of Women Beneficiaries

In order to ascertain whether women beneficiaries engaged in three different activities have caused significant variation in their income, one-way ANOVA test has been carried out. The computed results of one-way ANOVA for women beneficiaries has been presented in Table 4.13.

It has been inferred from the result that, since the calculated F value exceeds the tabulated value at 2 and 297 degrees of freedom there was a significant variation in the monthly income of women beneficiaries engaged in animal husbandry, cropping and farm development activities at 5 per cent level. Hence, it may be concluded that the monthly income varied significantly for different groups among women beneficiaries in three different activities.

Table 4.13: One Way Anova Test Results of Monthly Income among Women Beneficiaries in Animal Husbandry, Cropping and Farm Development Activity

Source of Variation	Source of Squares	Degrees of Freedom	Mean Sum of Squares	Calculated F-Value	Tabulated F-Value $F_{0.05}$
Between groups	491960085.804	2	245980042.902	69.053*	2.995
Within groups	1057971282.232	297	3562192.869		
Total	1549931368.037	299			

* Significant at 5 percent level.

Share of Respondent's Income from Activities towards Family Income

Percent share analysis has been used in order to assess the contributional share of respondent's income from activities towards family income (after availing of credit). Table 4.14 explicitly shows the contributional share of respondent's income towards family income.

Table 4.14: Distribution of Respondents According to their Percent Share towards Family Income

Share percent	Animal husbandry	Cropping	Farm development	*Total*
0 to 25	6 (9.00)	--	2 (13.30)	*8 (2.67)*
25 to 50	32 (47.80)	66 (30.3)	11 (73.30)	*109 (36.3)*
50 to 75	24 (35.80)	152 (69.7)	1 (6.70)	*177 (59.0)*
75 above	5 (7.50)	--	1 (6.70)	*6 (2.0)*
Total	*67 (100)*	*218 (100)*	*15 (100)*	*300 (100)*

Source: Field survey.

Note: Figures in brackets are percent to the total.

It is clearly observed from the Table that, out of 67 respondents from animal husbandry activity, 5 (7.50 percent) respondents were found to be contributing more than 75 percent share towards family income after availing of bank credit. 24 (35.80 percent) of them contributed 50 to 75 percent towards their family income, 32 (47.80 percent) of them contributed 25 to 50 percent and only 6 (9 percent) of them contributed below 25 percent towards their family income.

In case of cropping activity, out of 218 women beneficiaries, 152 (69.70 percent) of them contributed 50 to 75 percent in their total family income and 66 (30.30 percent) respondents have been contributing about 25 to 50 percent of share in their total family income.

While, in the case of Farm development activity, majority of 11 (73.30 percent) respondents have been contributing about 25 to 50 percent towards their family income.

On the whole, majority of 177 (59 percent) of respondents have been contributing 50 to 75 percent share income towards family income. It could be inferred from the analysis that in animal husbandry and farm development activities majority of women beneficiaries have been found to be contributing about 25 to 50 percent share towards their family income, while this percent share of contribution has been found up to 75 percent in case of women beneficiaries engaged in cropping activity. Thus, it could be inferred from the analysis that the earnings of women beneficiaries engaged in cropping activity contribute/share more percent in the family income than that of women beneficiaries in animal husbandry and farm development activities concerned.

Conclusion

It could be concluded from the analysis that majority of the beneficiaries belong to the age group of 31 to 40 years. Majority of them were Hindus and belong to most backward class. Most of them were married and formed nuclear family having below 3 children.

The earnings of women beneficiaries engaged in farm development activities have been found higher than that of those engaged in the other two activities. Further, with regard to the contributional share of beneficiaries towards family income it has been observed that women engaged in cropping activity contributed more than that of woman engaged in other two activities. Thus, the socio-economic position of women within and outside the family in Madurai district has been found to be remarkably good.

5

Female Domestic Workers in Punjab

Harvinder Kaur and Monika Rani

Introduction

Mosι of the literature available on economic status of women mainly explores the issues pertaining to women rights and problems of women working in organised sector. To some extent, it also relates to the issues of the women who work in unorganised sector. One major issue that has received very little attention in India and especially in Punjab is related to women domestic workers (both adult women and young girls). In fact, in Punjab, nearly three decades back in 1976-77, Balqis Begum conducted a study which focused exclusively on the socio-economic problems (such as illiteracy and ignorance, low wages, long working hours, insecurity of job, etc.) of female domestic workers in Nabha town of Punjab state Though many years have passed away, yet these women workers are prone to similar types of problems. The state has shown complete indifference towards their woes. Hence, it becomes an important subject to examine the economic condition of female domestic workers in Punjab.

Since the domestic service is considered a tedious job, most of the women workers involved in it come from poor and needy families. There are no minimum wages fixed and the Minimum Wages Act does not cover the domestic workers, the employers are free to pay arbitrarily, irrespective of the quantum and hours of work. The female domestic workers do not have any claim to privileges which the female workers in offices, schools and other establishments have. Further, these women workers do not enjoy any job security, as these matters depend upon the moods and fancies of the employers.

Similarly, any increment in the pay of the female domestic workers again depends upon the mood of the employers. In fact, there are several female domestic workers who have been working for long years under the same employer, without receiving any hike in pay. As there is no written contract between the employer and the domestic worker, there is an immense scope for exploitation of these workers. This scope for exploitation further expands with the fact that the bargaining power of these domestic workers is almost negligible. They do not have any organisation of their own to protect their rights. Of course, they would be lucky if the family/families they work for treat them as human beings.

Hence, it is really an important issue to explore the economic condition of female domestic workers. The present paper is a humble attempt at this. The paper is based on empirical work which examines the economic condition of female domestic workers employed in one or more households. The survey has been conducted in the urban areas of the Sangrur district of Punjab state. In Sangrur district, there are five tehsils, namely Malerkotla, Dhuri, Sangrur, Sunam and Moonak. Out of these five tehsils, Dhuri and Sangrur have been selected randomly. The selected tehsils (i.e. Dhuri and Sangrur) constitute four towns namely Dhuri, Sangrur, Longowal and Bhawanigarh.

The respondents have been selected from various mohallas/wards of these four towns, and the information has been collected through discussion with these workers. The interview schedules were well structured and were filled up for 160 female domestic workers (40 for each town). Besides, the simple statistical techniques such as average and percentage, Chi-Square Test has been used to draw the results.

Definition of a Female Domestic Worker

A lot of definitions have been given for domestic worker from time to time. A few definitions are mentioned here as follows:

1. A bill presented in Rajya Sabha, entitled 'The Housemaids and Domestic Servants (Conditions of Services and Welfare) Bill, 2004', has defined domestic worker as (a) "domestic servant means any person who earns his livelihood by working in household of his employer and doing household chores", and (b) "housemaid means a woman servant who performs household chores for wages" (GOI, 2004).
2. The International Labour Organisation (ILO) broadly defines a domestic worker as "someone who carries out household work in private households in return for wages" (quoted in Kundu, 2007).
3. Unorganised Non-Agricultural Workers' Conditions of Work and Social Security Bill, 2007, has included the domestic servants into the category of wage workers. According to the bill "Wage worker means a person employed for a remuneration as an unorganised non-agricultural worker, directly by an employer or through any agency or contractor, whether exclusively for one employer or more employers, whether simultaneously or otherwise, whether in cash and/or in kind, whether as a temporary or casual worker, or as a migrant worker, or workers employed by households including domestic workers" (GOI, 2007a).

On the basis of above definitions, it can be concluded that a domestic worker is one who carries out the household chores (like cleaning utensils, washing clothes, sweeping and cleaning the floor, cooking or assisting the employer in the kitchen, looking after the small children or accompanying them to school, etc.) on part-time or full-time basis for one or the more employer/employers for nominal wages.

Female Domestic Workers in India

In ancient times, domestic work, in India, was largely performed by "serfs" who generally belonged to lower castes and were denied access to education (Gothoskar, 2005).

However, employing women as domestic servants is a characteristic of a feudal society. Domestic maid servants, better known in the feudal ages as "Dasis", are not new to the country (Mahadevan, 1989). In feudal society, the condition of women domestic workers was quite miserable. Although many centuries have passed away, yet there has been a very little improvement in the economic condition of female domestic workers.

In the recent past, the trend shows that all the big cities of India have become centres to recruit poor women as domestic workers. The non-availability of jobs in rural or tribal areas facilitates continuous supply of women workers to these cities. A major reason for this is a sharp increase in the number of middle class women in employment (Deshkal and FES, 2002). These middle class employed women have shifted their household workload to the poor working women as their maids. In some cases, it has been seen that the middle and upper class in order to keep their upward mobility and status symbol, have withdrawn themselves from household duties (Gothoskar, 2005). Moreover, it does not cost much.

In India, there is an absence of any reliable data about female domestic workers. Although a great deal of literature on women is available, but it does not cover a complete cross-section. Very little information is available on women workers engaged in domestic services, agriculture and construction and also the women workers doing other sundry and piece-meal jobs (Tripathi, 1991).

Despite special provisions in the constitution and various legal and administrative measures to improve the status of women, there has been a little change in the socio-economic attitudinal life of the women domestic workers in India. A few state governments have taken some steps to improve their socio-economic status. For example, Karnataka, Kerala and Tamil Nadu states have introduced minimum wages for domestic workers. Karnataka became the first state to fix a minimum living wage for domestic workers in 2004 so as to establish some kind of fairness in wages. It was fixed at ₹ 1600 per month for an eight-hour day of domestic work (Hamid, 2006). In Maharashtra, the State Labour Board issued guidelines regulating the services of domestic workers in 2000. The service rules included paid leave, travel allowance, fairer wages, etc.

Similarly, in Kerala and Tamil Nadu, domestic workers are recognised as part of unorganised sector and can also form worker unions (Sharma, 2003). These efforts, however, remain half-hearted because the most daunting problem of fair wages still remained as such; followed by provisions for holidays, a pension or some kind of security after work (Hamid, 2006).

Women Employment in Punjab and Sangrur District

As in other parts of India, Punjabi society consists of hierarchies based on caste, class and community. Within these hierarchies, there is yet another hierarchy—of gender—women being at the lower rung (GOP, 2004). Though Punjab witnessed high levels of development since Green and White Revolutions, yet these high levels did not translate into progress of women. Declining sex ratio, strong preference for male child over female child, big gender gaps in literacy and work participation rate are clear indicators of lower socio-economic status of women as compared to men (Kaur, 2005).

But, at the same time, it is also important to note that there has been a dramatic increase in the spaces available to the women, many of which have been a consequence of state initiatives, through the formulation of gender sensitive programmes, initiatives by NGOs and other civil society groups (GOP, 2004). During the last two decades, there has been a considerable improvement in various aspects of both rural and urban women related issues such as literacy rate, overall female work participation rate, percentage share of female workers in total labour force and women employment in organised sector (both in public and private). Further, the female work participation rate among scheduled castes has also improved quite rapidly. Thus, it can be said that though status of women in Punjab is not up to the mark, yet it has been improving rapidly.

The study is related to Sangrur district, which is one of the southern districts of the Punjab state. The district takes its name from its headquarters town, Sangrur. According to Census of India 2001, the total area under the district is 5020 sq. km. with total population 2000173 and population density 399 persons per sq. km. In terms of area and population, the district has been placed at 3rd and 5th ranks respectively (in 2001). Further, the proportion of female population to total population is 46.5 percent (same for rural and urban areas). In the district, sex ratio is 871 females per 1000 males, while the proportion of female scheduled caste population to total female population is 27.7 percent. In the district, female literacy rate (i.e. 53.4 percent) is lower than the state's female literacy rate (i.e. 63.4 percent), while the gender gap in literacy rate for Sangrur (i.e. 12.4) is higher than that of state's (i.e. 11.9). The women work participation rate, on the other hand, is higher in the Sangrur district (i.e. 24.6 percent) vis-à-vis state's average (i.e. 18.7 percent).

Similarly, the proportions of female workers to total workers, female main workers to total main workers and female marginal workers to total marginal workers are also higher for Sangrur district (i.e. 28.1 percent, 22.5 percent and 68.3 percent respectively) than those of state's proportions (i.e. 23.7 percent, 18.0 percent and 58.6 percent respectively). The data clearly reflect that though in case of sex ratio and female literacy rate, Sangrur is far behind the state's average, but in case of women's share in the overall employment, the district has out stepped the state by impressive margin (Table 5.1).

A higher female work participation rate may have enhanced the demand for female domestic workers. Hence, it becomes very important to explore the economic condition of this vulnerable segment of the society in general and of the district in particular.

Table 5.1: Some Socio-economic Indicators of Women Development in Punjab State and Sangrur District* (Census of India, 2001)

Categories	Punjab			Sangrur District		
	Total	Rural	Urban	Total	Rural	Urban
Proportion of female population to total population	46.7	47.1	45.9	46.5	46.5	46.5
Sex ratio	874	887	848	871	871	870
Proportion of scheduled caste female population to total female population	29.1	33.1	21.2	27.7	30.7	20.5
Female Literacy rate	63.4	57.7	74.5	53.4	49.2	63.6
Gender gap in literacy rate	11.9	13.3	8.6	12.4	12.7	11.8
Female work participation rate (FWPR)	18.7	23.2	9.7	24.6	29.9	11.7
Proportion of female workers to total workers	23.7	27.8	14.3	28.1	31.9	16.3
Proportion of female main workers to total main workers	18.0	20.7	12.5	22.5	25.6	13.3
Proportion of female marginal workers to total marginal workers	58.6	61.5	40.9	68.3	70.6	54.2

*Barnala is included here.
Source: Census of India, 2001 (Provisional).

Economic Condition of Female Domestic Workers

The economic condition of female domestic workers has been analysed on the basis of two different aspects, viz. their monthly earnings and per capita monthly earnings of their families.

Economic Condition and Monthly Earnings: Female domestic workers generally belong to the poor strata of the society. Though these women work hard to earn their livelihood, yet the returns for their hard work are shockingly low (Manohar and Shobha, 1983; and Kundu, 2007). In order to examine the economic condition of the respondents, they have been categorised into three categories on the basis of their monthly earnings, i.e. up to ₹ 400, ₹ 401-800 and above ₹ 800. The percentage analysis given in Table 5.2 explains that nearly half of the respondents, i.e. 49.38 percent, are earning between ₹ 401-800 per month, followed by 33.12 percent earning above ₹ 800 per month and 17.50 percent earning up to ₹ 400 per month. The lowest monthly earnings of the respondents are found to be ₹ 200 and the highest monthly earnings of the respondents are found to be ₹ 1500. Further, the average monthly earnings of the respondents are found to be only ₹ 842, which is no where near to the amount of ₹ 2,525 per month which is the minimum wage fixed for unskilled manual labour in Punjab (GOI, 2008).

Table 5.2: Distribution of Respondents According to of their Monthly Earnings

Monthly Earnings (in ₹)	Up to 400	401-800	Above 800	Total	Average Monthly Earnings
Number	28	79	53	160	842
Percentage	17.50	49.38	33.12	100.00	-

Age and Monthly Earnings: Age of the respondents is closely related with their monthly earnings because the different age groups show the different level of efficiency to work. Age-wise differences in the monthly earnings of the respondents have been examined in Table 5.3. The table depicts that 3/4th of the respondents in the age group of up to 14 years (i.e. 75 percent) earn up to ₹ 400 per month. The main reason for this is that the respondents belonging to this age group are children, who work for lesser hours per day than the respondents belonging to other age groups. Similarly, a significant number of the respondents (i.e. 45.95 percent) belonging to the age group of above 44 years also earn up to ₹ 400 per month, because most of the respondents in this category are higher-aged women who prefer to work for lesser hours per day. As far as, the age groups of 15-29 years and 30-44 years are concerned, most of the respondents earn between ₹ 401-800 per month (i.e. 56 percent and 49.28 percent respectively) and above ₹ 800 per month (i.e. 38 percent and 43.48 percent respectively), because these respondents belong to the economically active middle age groups and work for more hours per day than the earlier mentioned respondents. Thus, it can be concluded that the monthly earnings of most of the respondents in the age groups of up to 14 years and above 44 years are relatively lower than that of the respondents in the age groups of 15-29 years and 30-44 years.

Table 5.3: Distribution of Respondents according to their Monthly Earnings and their Present Age

Present Age	Monthly Earnings (₹)			
	Up to 400	401-800	Above 800	Total
Up to 14	3 (75.00)	1 (25.00)	0 (0.00)	4 (100.00)
15-29	3 (6.00)	28 (56.00)	19 (38.00)	50 (100.00)
30-44	5 (7.24)	34 (49.28)	30 (43.48)	69 (100.00)
Above 44	17 (45.95)	16 (43.24)	4 (10.81)	37 (100.00)
Total	28 (17.50)	79 (49.37)	53 (33.13)	160 (100.00)

Note: Figures in parentheses represent row-wise percentage share.

Caste and Monthly Earnings: In our society the work of domestic servants is generally assigned to the lower caste segment of the society. Therefore, the major part of women domestic workers in the present study belong to the lower caste. The earnings of these workers are quite low due to their low bargaining power. Table 5.4 shows the caste-wise distribution of the respondents' monthly earnings. As is clear from the table, a sizeable majority of upper caste and backward caste respondents (i.e. 71.43 percent and 83.34

percent respectively) earns above ₹ 800 per month, i.e. the highest monthly income category. On the other side, among the lower caste respondents only 26.95 percent earn above ₹ 800 per month and 73.05 percent earn below ₹ 800 per month. It is mainly due to the fact that the most of the lower caste respondents are illiterate and their bargaining power is very low. Hence, they agree to work for lesser wages as compared to upper caste and backward caste respondents.

Table 5.4: Distribution of Respondents According to their Monthly Earnings and their Caste

Caste	Monthly Earnings (₹)			
	Up to 400	401-800	Above 800	Total
Upper Caste	0 (0.0)	2 (28.5)	5 (71.4)	7 (100.0)
Lower Caste	27 (19.1)	76 (53.9)	38 (26.9)	141 (100.0)
Backward Caste	1 (8.3)	1 (8.3)	10 (83.3)	12 (100.0)
Total	28 (17.5)	79 (49.3)	53 (33.1)	160 (100.0)

Note: Figures in parentheses represent row-wise percentage share.

Religion and Monthly Earnings: The religion-wise categorisation of respondents' monthly earnings has been presented in Table 5.5. As is clear, monthly earnings of most of Hindu respondents fall in the income categories of ₹ 401-800 per month and above ₹ 800 per month (i.e. 50.86 percent and 41.38 percent respectively). Whereas, monthly earnings of most of Sikh respondents fall in the income categories of up to ₹ 400 per month and ₹ 401-800 per month (i.e. 43.18 percent and 45.46 percent respectively). This makes it clear that most of the Sikh respondents earn less as compared to the Hindu respondents. This may be due to the fact that a lesser number of Sikh women go for such type of menial job and, if they go, they work for lesser hours as compared to Hindu respondents. The value of chi-square, which is greater than the table value, shows that the monthly earnings of Hindu and Sikh respondents differ significantly.

Table 5.5: Distribution of Respondents according to their Monthly Earnings and their Religion

Religion	Monthly Earnings (₹)			
	Up to 400	401-800	Above 800	Total
Hindu	9 (7.76)	59 (50.86)	48 (41.38)	116 (100.0)
Sikh	19 (43.18)	20 (45.46)	5 (11.36)	44 (100.0)
Total	28 (17.50)	79 (49.37)	53 (33.13)	160 (100.0)

Note: Figures in parentheses represent row-wise percentage share.
$\chi^2_{0.5}$ at 2 degree of freedom = 31.76 (greater than the table value 5.91)

Marital Status and Monthly Earnings

Table 5.6 shows the distribution of the respondents according to their monthly earnings and their martial status. Due to heavy economic responsibility, a higher percentage of the widow/separated respondents earn above ₹ 800 per month (i.e. 59.09 percent) as compared to lower percentages of married and unmarried respondents (i.e. 33.05 percent and only 5 percent respectively).

Table 5.6: Distribution of Respondents according to their Monthly Earnings and their Marital Status

Marital Status	Monthly Earnings (₹)			
	Up to 400	401-800	Above 800	Total
Single	6 (30.00)	13 (65.00)	1 (5.00)	20 (100.00)
Married	21 (17.80)	58 (49.15)	39 (33.05)	118 (100.00)
Widow/ Separated	1 (4.55)	8 (36.36)	13 (59.09)	22 (100.00)
Total	28 (17.50)	79 (49.37)	53 (33.13)	160 (100.00)

Note: Figures in parentheses represent row-wise percentage share.

In fact, a higher percentage of married and unmarried respondents earns between ₹ 401-800 per month (i.e. 65 percent and 49.15 percent respectively). Hence, it can be concluded that most of widow/separated respondents' monthly earning are comparatively higher than that of married and unmarried respondents.

Migratory Status and Monthly Earnings: The relationship between the monthly earnings and migratory status of the respondents has been examined in Table 5.7. This table shows that most of the migrant respondents earn above ₹ 800 per month (i.e. 72.22 percent). On the other hand, more than half of the non-migrant respondents earn between ₹ 401-800 per month (i.e. 52.82 percent). It is generally observed that the migrant respondents work for longer hours and in more number of houses as compared to non-migrant respondents. Further, economic condition of the migrant respondents is found to be very poor and, hence, the economic responsibility on the former is comparatively higher than that on the latter.

Table 5.7: Distribution of Respondents according to their Monthly Earnings and their Migratory Status

Migratory Status	Monthly Earnings (₹)			
	Up to 400	401-800	Above 800	Total
Migrants	1 (5.56)	4 (22.22)	13 (72.22)	18 (100.0)
Non-Migrant	27 (19.01)	75 (52.82)	40 (28.17)	142 (100.0)
Total	28 (17.50)	79 (49.37)	53 (33.13)	160 (100.0)

Note: Figures in parentheses represent row-wise percentage share.

Economic Condition and Per Capita Monthly Family Earnings: In order to assess the intensity of poverty among the female domestic workers, the economic condition of the respondents has been further examined on the basis of per capita monthly earnings of their families. Per capita monthly family earnings are computed as total monthly family income divided by total number of family members. Ministry of Labour, Government of India estimated the poverty line as ₹ 466.16 per month for urban areas in Punjab for the year 2004-05 (GOI, 2007b).

Further, in the same year, 8.4 percent of the Punjab's total population was estimated to exist below poverty line. So far as this study is concerned, it has been found that almost 2/5th of the respondents' families (i.e. 39.38 percent) still exist below poverty line. Further, the average per capita monthly family earnings are found to be ₹ 641, which are even below the respondents' own average monthly earnings (Table 5.8).

Table 5.8: Distribution of Respondents according to their Per Capita Monthly Family Earnings

Per Capita Monthly Family Earnings	Below Poverty Line	Above Poverty Line	Total	Average Per Capita Monthly Family Earnings
Number	63	97	160	641
Percentage	39.38	60.62	100.00	

Age and Per Capita Monthly Family Earnings

No parents like their young daughters to get involved in the menial jobs like domestic services. It is the extreme poverty that compels them to do so. The present study shows that 3/4th of the child respondents (i.e. up to 14 years) belong to the families whose per capita monthly family earnings are below poverty line, which is the major cause of their involvement in this menial work. Similarly, per capita monthly family earnings of more than half of the higher aged respondents (i.e. above 44 years) are below poverty line. It can be said that child respondents as well as higher-aged respondents are involved in these jobs mainly due to the extreme poverty of their families.

On the other side, it has been found that per capita monthly family earnings of only 28 percent respondents in the age group of 15-29 years and 36.23 percent respondents in the age group of 30-44 years are below poverty line. Hence, the economic condition of most of the middle aged respondents' families is found to be better than that of child respondents and higher aged respondents' families (Table 5.9).

Table 5.9: Distribution of Respondents according to their Per Capita Monthly Family Earnings and their Present Age

Present Age	Per Capita Monthly Family Earnings		
	Below Poverty Line	Above Poverty Line	Total
Up to 14	3 (75.00)	1 (25.00)	4 (100.00)
15-29	14 (28.00)	36 (72.00)	50 (100.00)
30-44	25 (36.23)	44 (63.77)	69 (100.00)
Above 44	21 (56.76)	16 (43.24)	37 (100.00)
Total	63 (39.38)	97 (60.62)	160 (100.00)

Note: Figures in parentheses represent row-wise percentage share.

Caste and Per Capita Monthly Family Earnings: Caste-wise differences in the per capita monthly earnings of the respondents' families have been presented in Table 5.10. Surprisingly, per capita monthly family earnings of all the upper caste respondents are above poverty line. On the other side, per capita monthly family earnings of 25 percent of backward caste and 42.55 percent of lower caste respondents are found to be below poverty line.

Table 5.10: Distribution of Respondents according to their Per Capita Monthly Family Earnings and their Caste

Caste	Per Capita Monthly Family Earnings		
	Below Poverty Line	Above Poverty Line	Total
Upper Caste	0 (0.00)	7 (100.00)	7 (100.00)
Lower Caste	60 (42.55)	81 (57.45)	141 (100.00)
Backward Caste	3 (25.00)	9 (75.00)	12 (100.00)
Total	63 (39.38)	97 (60.62)	160 (100.00)

Note: Figures in parentheses represent row-wise percentage share.

This may be due to the fact that most of the upper caste respondents have small family size and higher family income than that of lower caste and backward caste respondents.

Marital Status and Per Capita Monthly Family Earnings: The economic responsibility on the widow/ separated women is generally found to be higher because most of them have to play the role of bread winner for their families. Even then, their per capita family earnings remain quite low. The similar situation has been found in the case of female domestic workers. Table 5.11 shows that per capita monthly family earnings of an overwhelming majority of the widow/separated respondents (i.e. 86.36 percent) is below poverty line, followed by single/unmarried respondents (i.e. 60 percent) and married respondents (i.e. 27.12 percent). Hence, it can be concluded that the economic condition of most of the widow/separated respondents is worse than that of the other respondents.

Table 5.11: Distribution of Respondents according to their Per Capita Monthly Family Earnings and their Marital Status

Marital Status	Per Capita Monthly Family Earnings		
	Below Poverty Line	Above Poverty Line	Total
Single	12 (60.00)	8 (40.00)	20 (100.00)
Married	32 (27.12)	86 (72.88)	118 (100.00)
Widow/ Separated	19 (86.36)	3 (13.64)	22 (100.00)
Total	63 (39.38)	97 (60.62)	160 (100.00)

Note: Figures in parentheses represent row-wise percentage share.

Status of House and Per Capita Monthly Family Earnings: Table 5.12 shows the distribution of the respondents according to per capita monthly family earnings and their housing conditions. The percentage analysis shows that 48.19 percent of the respondents' families with Katcha house are living below poverty line, followed by 44.74 percent of the respondents' families with Semi-Pacca house and 15.38 percent of the respondents' families with Pacca house. This leads to the conclusion that the living conditions (or housing conditions) of these workers greatly depends upon their per capita monthly family earnings. Similarly, the value of chi-square, which is found to be greater than the table value, also shows that living conditions of the respondents is significantly associated with their per capita monthly family earnings.

Table 5.12: Distribution of Respondents according to their Per Capita Monthly Family Earnings and Status of their House

Status of House	Per Capita Monthly Family Earnings		
	Below Poverty Line	Above Poverty Line	Total
Katcha	40 (48.19)	43 (51.81)	83 (100.00)
Pacca	6 (15.38)	33 (84.62)	39 (100.00)
Semi-Pacca	17 (44.74)	21 (55.26)	38 (100.00)
Total	63 (39.38)	97 (60.62)	160 (100.00)

Note: Figures in parentheses represent row-wise percentage share.
$\chi^2_{0.5}$ at 2 degree of freedom = 12.57 (greater than the table value 5.99)

Anti-Social Habits of Husband/Father and Per Capita Monthly Family Earnings: Drug addiction is a serious problem all over India and especially in Punjab. Many families are victims of drug addiction of their male members. This is also the case with female domestic workers. Table 5.13 shows that nearly 3/5th of those respondents whose husbands/father are drug addicts (i.e. 60.87 percent) are living below poverty line. On the other side, a lesser percentage of those respondents whose husbands/fathers are not drug addicts (20.29 percent) are living below poverty line. Further, the value of chi-square is also found to be greater than the table value which shows that the per capita monthly family earnings of the respondents vary significantly with the drug addiction habit of their husbands/fathers.

Occupational Status of Husband/Father and Per Capita Monthly Family Earnings: In the present study, it has been found that the economic condition of those respondents whose husbands/fathers are self-employed is comparatively better than that of those whose husbands/fathers are either wage workers or non-workers.

Table 5.13: Distribution of Respondents according to their Per Capita Monthly Family Earnings and their Response towards Question 'A'

Attitude 'A'	Per Capita Monthly Family Earnings		
	Below Poverty Line	Above Poverty Line	Total
Yes	42 (60.87)	27 (39.13)	69 (100.00)
No	14 (20.29)	55 (79.71)	69 (100.00)
Total	56 (40.58)	82 (59.42)	138 (100.00)

Note: Figures in parentheses represent row-wise percentage share.
(Question 'A' - Is your husband/father a drug addict?)
$\chi^2_{0.5}$ at 1 degree of freedom = 23.56 (greater than the table value 3.84)

As is clear from the Table 5.14, more than 3/5th of those respondents whose husbands/fathers are non-workers (66.67 percent) and nearly 2/5th of those respondents whose husbands/fathers are wage workers (i.e. 39.18 percent) are living below poverty line.

Table 5.14: Distribution of Respondents according to their Per Capita Monthly Family Earnings and the Occupational Status of their Husbands/Fathers

Occupational Status of Husbands/Fathers	Per Capita Monthly Family Earnings		
	Below Poverty Line	Above Poverty Line	Total
Wage Workers	38 (39.18)	59 (60.82)	97 (100.0)
Self-Employed	4 (20.00)	16 (80.00)	20 (100.0)
Non-Workers	14 (66.67)	7 (33.33)	21 (100.0)
Total	56 (40.58)	82 (59.42)	138 (100.0)

Note: Figures in parentheses represent row-wise percentage share.

On the other side, only 1/4th of those respondents whose husbands/fathers are self-employed (i.e. 25 percent) are living below poverty line.

Hence, it can be concluded that the economic condition of those respondents whose husbands/fathers are self-employed is better than that of others.

Summary and Conclusion

To sum up, it can be concluded that economic condition of the female domestic workers is quite vulnerable. The analysis of economic condition of the respondents on the basis of their monthly earnings shows that monthly earnings of the majority of the respondents in the age groups of up to 14 years and above 44 years is worse than that of the respondents in the age groups of 15-29 years and 30-44 years. Monthly earnings of the lower caste respondents and Sikh respondents are also found to be lower than that of others. The monthly earnings of the migrant respondents are found to be relatively higher than non-migrant respondents because the former prefer to work for longer hours. Due to the heavy economic responsibility, widow/separated respondents and those who have rented houses have to work for more hours and in more number of houses and, thus, they earn more.

Similarly, the per capita monthly family earnings of the respondents show that the economic condition of these women workers is very weak. The per capita monthly family earnings of most of the respondents in the age groups of up to 14 years and above 44 years are found to be below poverty line. Similarly, the per capita monthly family earnings of most of the scheduled caste and widow/separated respondents are found to be below poverty line. Nearly half of those respondents who have either Katcha house or Semi-Pacca house are living below poverty line. Further, the per capita monthly family earnings of majority of those respondents whose husbands/fathers are drug addicts and those whose husbands/fathers are non-workers are below poverty line. Hence, though all the respondents belong to the poor section of the society but the above mentioned respondents are found to be the poorest of the poor section of the society.

To improve the overall economic condition of these female domestic workers, the following suggestions are put forward:

- Keeping in mind the workload in a house for a day or so, the wage rate should be fixed and there must be a provision for time to time increments in their wages. Further, these workers must be covered by the Minimum Wages Act of the respective State governments.
- To improve the economic condition of the families of the respondents, the Self-Employment Scheme must cover the poor families of domestic workers. Further, the government should also introduce some additional employment schemes in the area, so that their husbands and children can get some profitable work.
- In the present study, the economic condition of widows/separated respondents are found to be very poor. To improve this, they must be provided some financial help. These respondents and their children must also be specially considered in the provision of social security benefits.
- The female domestic workers must be registered under the Trade Union Act. This effort will enable them to enjoy their strength, unity and also satisfy their grievances towards their employers through different kinds of pressure building and bargaining strategies.
- The study has found that exactly half of the respondents' families are negatively affected by anti-social habits of their husbands/fathers (like drug addiction). There is a need to start some Drug Counselling Centres in order to help these families overcome their problems.

To conclude, it can be said that the economic condition of female domestic workers (especially child domestic workers, widow/separated domestic workers, lower caste domestic workers and those whose husbands/fathers are drug addicts) in Punjab is a matter of concern. The state government is indifferent towards their woes. In order, to improve the economic condition of these women workers, the above suggestions must be considered and applied promptly.

References

Begum, B. (1976-77), *The Problems of Female Domestic Servants at Nabha*, project report submitted to the Department of Political Science and Public Administration, Punjabi University, Patiala.

Deshkal and FES (2002), *Working Conditions, Coping Strategy and Legal Status of Female Domestic Workers*, a one day seminar presented in Delhi on 12th October, 2002.

GOI (2004), *The Housemaids and Domestic Servants (Conditions of Services and Welfare) Bill 2004*, Bill No. 35, presented in Rajya Sabha, Government of India, available at www.rajyasabha.nic.in.

GOI (2007a), *Unorganised Non-Agricultural Workers' Conditions of Work and Social Security Bill 2007*, Press Information Bureau, Government of India, available at www.nceuis.nic.in.

GOI (2007b), *Poverty Estimates for 2004-05*, Press Information Bureau, Government of India, available at www.planning commission.nic.in /news/prmar07.pdf.

GOI (2008), *Punjab: Minimum Wages*, Ministry of Labour, Government of India, available at www.paycheck.in/main/officialminimumwages/punjab.

GOP (2004), *Human Development Report 2004: Punjab*, Government of Punjab, India.

Gothoskar, S. (2005), *New Initiatives in Organizing Strategy in the Informal Economy-A Case Study of Domestic Workers*, Committee for Asian Women, July.

Hamid, A. (2006), Domestic Workers: Harsh Everyday Realities, *Economic and Political Weekly*, Vol. 61, No. 13, April 1, pp. 1235-1237.

Kaur, H. (2005), Socio-Economic Status of Women (With Special Reference to Indian Punjab), in B. Singh (ed.), *Punjab Economy: Challenges and Strategies*, Twenty First Century Publications, Patiala, Punjab (India), pp. 146-163.

Kundu, A. (2007), Conditions of Work and Rights of Female Domestic Workers of Kolkata, *The Indian Journal of Labour Economics*, Vol. 50, No. 4, pp. 853-866.

Mahadevan, U. (1989), Plight of Women Domestic Workers, in R.K.

Sapru (ed.), *Women and Development*, Ashish Publishing House, New Delhi, pp. 127-134.
Manohar, K.M. and V. Shobha (1983), Selected Case Studies: Maid Servants, in K.M. Manohar (ed.), *Socio-economic Status of Indian Women*, Seema Publications, New Delhi, pp. 31-45.
Sharma, K. (2003), In the Name of Servitude, *The Hindu*, Sunday, August 24.
Tripathi, S.N. (1991), *Informal Women Labourers in India*, Discovery Publishing House, New Delhi.

6

Women Workers in Handloom Weaving

Minaxi Pathak and Nandita Bhattacharyya

Introduction

Assam has a rich and fairly ancient tradition of handloom weaving. Handloom weaving is not a mere occupation; it has become a way of life. Essentially a female craft, it is customary for the girls of Assam to learn the art of weaving. Over the ages weaving has come to be associated closely with their emotional life. When a girl etches a floral design on the '*Bihuan*', a gift to be given to her beloved one on the occasion of the *Bihu* Festival, she naturally, puts her heart into it. The design on the *bihuan*, etched with the coy love of a maiden heart, eventually becomes a spiritual creation. On a conservative estimate there are about nearly 1.4 million weavers in the entire North Eastern region. The total production of handlooms in the region is valued around Rs.1145 million on an annual basis. The commercial production of cotton handloom is oriented heavily towards meeting the requirement of the local market. In Assam, items like *Gamucha, Chaddhar, Mekhala, Lungi* and *dhoti* etc. that are basically the local dresses, dominate the product mix. Besides traditional items Assam also produces articles like *bedsheets*, furnishings fabrics, pillow covers, *laishingphee* and the like.

Handloom weaving industry is one of the most important cottage industry in the State of Assam and it has a long tradition in the socio-economic life of the people for supplementing the family income to a great extent and self-employment opportunities to lakh of people of poor and down trodden section of the society. At present Assam has the highest number of handlooms in the whole country. With nearly 6.48 lakh looms and a sizeable number of weaver population, Assam accounts for well over 60 percent of the total production of handloom goods in the NE region.

Handloom Industry in Assam

Handloom industry in Assam is the largest segment in the unorganized sector and plays a very important role in the economy of the state. This age-old traditional industry, known for it's excellence in workmanship and value addition the world over, produced 133.44 millions sq. mt. handloom fabrics (Handloom Census, 1987-88). In the state, handloom sector alone produced more than 40 percent cloth against total requirements of textiles. The pattern of consumption of handloom fabrics has also undergone a significant change due to consumer preference.

One important feature of handloom industry is that it offers employment opportunity to all the categories of people (right from highly skilled to totally unskilled labour). The participation of women workers in handloom industry is very high. Women constitute a major portion of workers in handloom industry. In 1982, 10 million persons were dependent on a single traditional industry i.e. handloom. It ranked only next to agriculture as far as employment was concerned (India, 1982). According to Das (1982), the handloom industry of Assam engages about 12 lakh persons as full time and part time weavers. Ninety percent of these weavers are women. Most of the weavers entering the occupation at an early age show the utter necessity of assuming family responsibilities.

According to the Handloom Census, 1987-88 conducted by the Government of India, there are 12.23 lakh weaver households in Assam. Almost 84 percent of the weavers are working independently, 6 percent under co-operatives, 3 percent under private owners and 5 percent under master weavers and the rest under Handloom Development Centre and Khadi and Village Industries Board. In Assam, 20 percent looms are considered as commercial looms which produce garments for sale. The rest are mainly utilized for supplying family needs.

Most of the handloom industries fall under the category of unorganized sector. Being unorganized sector women suffer discrimination in terms of employment opportunities and wages, irregularities and uncertainties in the employment. The weavers in the weaving are paid on the basis of designs and number of articles produced.

Problems of Workers Engaged in Handloom Industry

Handloom industry is highly labour intensive. Although both male and female are involved, a large portion of labourers is women. They are involved in performance of varieties of activities starting from preparation of yarn to weaving. Apart from problems in production, marketing, raw materials, credit facilities, the weavers are forced to work in poor workplace with unscientific technologies leading to occupational stress. While at work the weavers sometimes have to assume postures without giving consideration to their individual capability and limitations, which results in stress and trauma the workers experience. Most of the weavers spend time on their loom and sometimes squatting on the floor. Poor working postures have a great impact, which might likely to cause many health problems in the musculoskeletal system, in the long run. These may lead to body deformities and incapacitate them, thereby reducing their ability to perform work, which might have an indirect effect on their earnings and livelihood.

The health status of the work force in every country has an immediate and direct impact on national and world economy. Total economic losses due to occupational illness and injuries are enormous. Such losses are a serious burden on economic development. The international labour organization (ILO) has estimated that in 1997, the overall economic losses resulting from work related diseases and injuries were approximately 4 percent of the world's gross national product. It is therefore essential to improve the working condition of these industries to reduce their work related problems.

Prospect of Handloom Industry in Rural Assam

Though the rural women in Assam have enough entrepreneurial potentialities i.e. traditional skills and capacity for initiation of viable small enterprises, they are not able to convert their entrepreneurial dreams into reality. It is generally observed that the traditional rural industry, which is mostly based on skills acquired outside the formal school system, suffers from technological obsolescence, low productivity, inconsistent quality, etc. Moreover, the rural women are unaware of the opportunities and facilities available for setting up of rural business ventures in spite of having necessary elements for entrepreneurship development.

One of such ideas for women entrepreneurship development is weaving sector where women are solely involved. Unlike other parts of India, weaving is practiced universally by all sections of the indigenous population of Assam. But women are not able to get significant benefit from weaving as a source of subsidiary income. The present study was conducted to collect data on extent of involvement of women in handloom weaving and the problems faced by the women workers in handloom industry of Assam.

Methodology

The present study was carried out in two phases. In the phase-I a survey among the households was conducted to gather information on extent of involvement of women in handloom weaving at household level, types of handloom products produced, their problems. Attempt was also made to work out the economic estimation of time spent in handloom weaving at household level. For the phase-I to select representative samples, a multistage sampling method was adopted. A total of 120 households were selected purposively from five villages of Lakhimpur District of Assam. Data were gathered with an interview schedule, prepared keeping the objectives of the study in mind. In the phase-II, an attempt was made to study the occupational stress of the women workers engaged in handloom industry. For the purpose 120 women workers were selected purposively from seven handloom industries of Jorhat and Nagaon District of Assam. Occupational stress of the workers were studied in terms of Rating of Perceived exertion (RPE) by following modified rating of Perceived Exertion scale (Varghese *et al.*, 1989), postural stress, and musculoskeletal problems faced by the workers. The collected data were coded, tabulated and statistically analyzed. A market survey was conducted to find out the value of the time spent on handloom weaving. For the purpose value added method was used.

Results and Discussion

Phase I: Extent of Involvement of Women Workers in Handloom Industry: Weaving is the unique leisure time activity of the homemakers of Assam and it was carried out by all the women folk during their lean agricultural season. The present study revealed that cent percent respondents were found to be highly involved in handloom weaving.

Types of Handloom Products Produced: Handloom weaving, organized in cottage level not only meet the family requirement but also supplement family income. Handloom products usually produced by the women are analyzed and presented in Table 6.1. It was observed from the table that interest of women in producing women's clothing was higher than that of men' clothing. *Mekhela chadar* both for daily and occasional wear was woven by almost all the women, followed by shawls (71.67 percent). *Riha* (a part of Assamese costume) was rarely woven by the respondents. It may be because of the fact that use of *Riha* is day by day decreasing both in urban and rural areas of Assam. Out of Men's clothing *Chelang Kapoor* and *Endi Chadar* were woven by majority of the women as reported by 81.67 percent and 70.83 percent of the respondents respectively. *Dhoti* was woven by a few number of respondents because mill made *dhoti* was preferred to the hand-woven one.

Table 6.1: Distribution of Respondents by Different Textile Items Produced by them in General

Different Handloom Items	N=120	
	Frequency	Percentage
I. Women's Clothing		
1.Mekhela		
i. For daily use	120	100
ii. For occasional use	117	97.5
2. Chadar		
i. For daily use	120	100
ii. For occasional use	116	96.6
3. Riha	2	1.6
4. Ornamental Border		
i. For chadar	12	10
ii. Both chadar and Mekhela	16	13.33
5. Shawls	86	71.67
6. Saree	5	4.17
II. Men's Clothing		
1. Borkapoor	2	1.67
2. Khania Kapoor	34	28.33
3. Cheleng Kapoor	98	81.67
5. Endi chadar	85	70.83
6. Dhoti	4	3.33
III. Linens		
1. Gamossa	120	100
2. Mosquito net	77	64.17
3. Fata-Kani Kapoor	61	50.83
4. Bed sheets	29	24.17
IV. Furnishing Materials		
1. Curtain	15	12.5
2. Table cloth	9	7.5
3. Table mat	9	7.5

It was also observed that a wide variety of linens were produced by the women, out of which production of *Gamosa* both for daily and occasional use was significantly high which was followed by *mosquito net* (64.17 percent), *fatakani Kapoor* (50.83 percent) and *bed sheets* (24.17 percent). As regards to weaving of furnishing materials, a very few percent of respondents were found to be involved. Weaving of furnishing materials may be encouraged as it can be a good venture for the weavers to capture a good market.

Economic Estimation of Time Spent in Handloom Weaving

The study revealed that the activity of handloom weaving was considered as leisure time activity by majority of the respondents in lean agricultural season. Except a very few fraction, most of the respondents (93.33 percent) took handloom as non-commercial pursuits. Quantum of time spent during the year in handloom weaving indicated that majority of the respondents spent 100 hrs to 200 hrs. The average time spent was found to be 392 hours per women during the year. The value of one hour spent on handloom weaving was computed to be ₹ 5.77 only (revised rate).

Problems Faced by Handloom Weavers

It was observed that the weaving industry, which is mostly based on skills acquired outside the formal school system, suffers from different problems. In the present study attempt had been made to study the general problems as well as the work related problems of handloom weavers. Data summarized in Table 6.2 shows the general problems faced by the respondents. Lack of time was as one of the reason given by 80 percent of the respondents. This is because they are overloaded with both farm and household activities. Lack of capital was another problem faced by 60 percent of the respondents. The increasing price of the raw materials was the major bottleneck in the growth and development of handloom industry. Ignorant about the demand of various textiles items in the market (41.67 percent), lack of commercial value of their handloom products (27 percent), lack of technological knowledge in terms of colour combination, size and design of different linens (27.5 percent) were the problems faced by the respondents, so they were not able to take handloom weaving as an income generating activity. The study also revealed that as the economic contribution through the handloom weaving was not visible, the respondents were not able to get encouragement from their male counterpart.

Table 6.2: General Problems Faced by the Respondents Regarding Handloom Weaving

Problems	N=120	
	Frequency	Percentage
1. Lack of time	97	80.83
2. Lack of capital	72	60
3. Lack of recognition of commercial value of their handloom products	31	25.83
4. Lack of idea about marketability and demand for various products	50	41.67
5. Lack of initiative to find the sources of financial assistance for handloom weaving	8	6.67
6. Lack of technological knowledge in terms of colour combination, size and design of different linens	33	27.5
7. Absence of encouragement from the male counterpart.	15	12.5

Phase II

Hours of Work: It was found that in all the handloom industries surveyed, both govt. and non-government, the hours of work were more or less the same i.e. 8 hours per day.

Rest Period: The rest period on working days in all the selected industries were found to be almost the same which was one hour during lunch time.

Extent of Involvement of Women Workers in Handloom Industry: The handloom industry of Assam engages about 12 lakh persons as full time and part time weavers. Ninety percent of these weavers are women. The handloom industry is practically monopolized by women not only from the idea of economic necessity but also from the sense of social customs (Das, 1982). The women workers are highly involved in these industries starting from spinning to weaving. In the present study the involvement was studied in terms of extent of involvement, which can be defined as women's participation in various activities to the extent of daily, sometimes and rarely and were scored 3, 2 and 1 respectively. After calculation of the weighted score and mean score, ranking of extent of involvement in different activities in handloom industry was done.

It was found that women workers were highly involved in weaving activity as compared to the other activities. Majority (95.83 percent) of the respondents performed the activity daily followed by spinning, which was performed by 38.33 percent of the respondents daily, 56.66 percent sometimes and only 5 percent rarely. Most rarely performed activities were threading the reeds (82.5 percent). This may be due to the fact that these two activities were needed to be performed after one warp was completed.

Weaving was found to be the most highly involved activity (Rank I). This was followed by spinning (Rank II), winding and twisting (rank III), setting the warp on the loom (rank IV), wrapping (rank V), preparing the loom for weaving (rank VI), threading of healds (rank VII). Threading the reed was assigned as rank VIII.

Postures Assumed by the Respondents in Performance of Various Activities in Handloom Industry

Posture is a relative arrangement of bodily parts, specifically the orientation of the limbs, trunk and head during the work. The working posture is largely dictated by the needs created by movements of bodily segments and there in turn depend on the demands deriving from the task, work station design and machine layout. Women engaged in different occupations perform various activities with high postural load due to constraints of work methods and working condition. While performing various activities in handloom industry, the workers assume a variety of postures which were studied by observation and the still photography technique, wherefrom postures were analysed.

Different Types of Postures Assumed by the Respondents: The study revealed that sitting with slight forward bending at the neck and at the back with both the hands and legs moving were assumed by majority of the respondents while they performed the weaving operation. Similar postures with the legs in static position and hand stretched forward was also found to be assumed by the respondents while performing other activities like threading the healds and threading the reed for a long period of time without changing the postures. Sitting on ground/pidi was assumed while performing spinning and preparing the loom for weaving. Standing posture with arms stretched forward was assumed while performing winding, twisting and setting the warp on the loom and warping operations.

Feeling of Comfort and Discomfort While Assuming Different Postures: Further analysis of data pertaining to comfort and discomfort while assuming different postures revealed that the majority of the respondents found the postures uncomfortable while performing the weaving operation (94.78 percent), setting the warp on the loom (96.33 percent), preparing the loom for weaving (86.48 percent). This may be the fact due to that the respondents were perform forced to the activities in awkward postures which involved more of static muscular efforts. The comfortable postures as reported by majority of the respondents, i.e., 81.66 percent, 80 percent and 78.18 percent were sitting on pidi while performing spinning, sitting on the stool with the hands out stretched while performing threading the healds and threading the reed respectively. Most comfortable posture was found only by 14.55 percent of the respondents while performing the threading the reed operation followed by the threading the healds operation only by 10.9 percent of the respondents.

Exertion Perceived by the Respondents: Despite rapid strides of mechanization and automation, manual work is still pre-dominant in many occupations. It puts considerable loads on the workers and show deviations from the resting level depending on the intensity and duration of work which results in some sort of exertion perceived by the respondents in performance of various activities.

In the present study an attempts was made to find out the work stress of workers in terms of exertion perceived by women workers in performance of various activities in handloom industry. Perceived exertion may be termed as the subjective rating of feeling of tiredness in performance of activities. Exertion perceived by the respondents were recorded as light to heavy according to the modified Borg's rating of perceived exertion scale (Varghese, 1989).

It was found that weaving was found to be perceived as very heavy activity by 51.43 percent of the respondents, 16.52 percent as moderately heavy and 32.17 percent as heavy. Among the activities which were perceived as light were spinning, threading the healds, threading the reed by 95 percent, 72.12 percent and 75.72 percent of the respondents respectively.

From the calculated mean scores of rating of perceived exertion (RPE), categorization of activities performed by women workers in handloom industry was done (Table 6.3).

It was found that the activities graded as heavy were warping, setting the warp on the loom, preparing the loom for weaving. The moderately heavy activities were spinning, winding, twisting, threading the healds, and threading the reed. The only activity that was found as very heavy was weaving. It is noticeable that not a single activity was found light or very light.

Table 6.3: Categorization of Workload Based on Rating of Perceived Exertion Scale

Categories	Score	Activities
Very light	Below 1	-
Light	1-2	-
Moderately heavy	2-3	Spinning, winding, twisting, threading the healds, threading the reed
Heavy	3-4	Warping, setting the warp in the loom, preparing the loom for weaving
Very heavy	4-5	Weaving

Musculoskeletal Problems Faced in Performance of Different Activities in Handloom Industry

From the study it was revealed that work related problems of the respondents were very high. Many of the respondents demonstrated a high degree of physical effort due to bad working postures and static muscular efforts which might have lead to feeling of fatigue as well as musculoskeletal disorders. While performing various activities the respondents were forced to assume different unnatural postures because of task demand and the work environment. Findings of the present study (Table 6.4) revealed that majority of the respondents were found to perform the weaving activity in a prolonged sitting postures which demanded the worker to assume certain bad working postures and resulted in the occurrence of low back pain which was quite high (85 percent). The incidence of pain in the elbow joints and knee pain were also quite alarming i.e. 55 percent and 60 percent of the respondents Due to long hours of sitting postures with the neck and the back bent forward with extended arms while performing most of the activities like threading the healds, threading the reeds, warping, twisting, winding etc. the respondents reported to suffered from pain in neck (67.5 percent), shoulder joint pain (65 percent), hand pain (60.83 percent), shoulder pain (56.66), back pain (52.5 percent), leg pain (46.66 percent) and finger pain (23.33 percent).

Table 6.4: Distribution of Respondents According to Musculoskeletal Problems Faced in Performance of Different Activities in Handloom Industry

Musculoskeletal Problem	*N=120*	
	Frequency	*Percentage*
Backache	63	*52.5*
Shoulder pain	68	*56.66*
Shoulder joint pain	78	*65*
Neck pain	81	*67.5*
Leg pain	56	*46.66*
Elbow joint pain	66	*55*
Hand pain	74	*60.83*
Finger pain	28	*23.33*
Knee pain	73	*60*
Low Back pain	*102*	*85*

Conclusion

On the basis of the findings of the present study, the following conclusions are drawn and few suggestions are put forward for uplifting the economic status of rural women for rural development. Handloom weaving as commercial or non-commercial preposition plays an important role in the socio-cultural and economic life of Assam.

The analysis of extent of involvement of women in handloom weaving was observed to be low as their main problem is lack of time. They do the weaving operations as leisure time activity during lean agricultural period. With the adoption of improved technologies while performing different activities both in agricultural as well as in home activities much time and energy could be saved and availability of leisure time will be more for the respondents. There is a great scope for development of handloom weaving. with modern technique, design and management together with marketing facilities which will encourage the weavers to take handloom weaving as commercial pursuit.

Analysis of various problems faced by weavers showed

that due to lack of capital, handloom weaving could not be considered as commercial basis. This indicates that commercial channel have not yet been able to make the desired impact on rural life of people. Rural women must be educated the financial assistance offered by the Directorate of handloom and Textile through their District and Sub-Divisional offices. Handloom Textiles particularly the linens have gradually replaced the mill made furnishings in the effluent society. The rural women with proper training on colour combination, design, texture, etc will be able to meet the growing demands to some extent.

The key to improve the economic status of women is positive motivation. Rural women should be motivated in a positive direction. Since they are less educated they neither expected to take part in developmental activities at their own initiative, nor do they have skill and abilities to draw program for uplifting the economic status. In this respect, technical experts and administrators should provide a blue-print, which will enable the rural women to raise their existing economic status. To have more productivity as well as to avoid work related problems of he workers, the workplace should be ergonomically designed. It is advisable that correct postures should be adopted to counteract some of the problems of stressful environment and long working hours.

References

Census of Handloom in India, 1987-88.

Gayan, M. (2000). Ergonomic study on postures adopted by women engaged in handloom industry. Unpublished thesis in the Department of FRM, C.H.Sc., AAU, Jorhat.

Varghese, M.A.; Atreya, N. and Saha, P.N. (1994). A rapid appraisal of occupational workload from a modified scale of perceived exertion. Ergonomics 37, 485-491.

7

Stress and Coping among Women Managers in Indian Organizations

H.L. Kaila

Introduction

This is a qualitative study of 140 female managers interviewed in 81 organizations in order to review trend of problems faced by women managers, the ways in which the problems affect them, and the coping strategies used by them to overcome their problems. In-depth personal interviews were conducted with the help of a structured questionnaire using open-ended questions. The narratives of managers have provided a broad base in understanding managerial life and profession of women. The implications are underlined for better organizational health and performance. This paper is an extract from a larger study.

Though women workforce has risen to a greater extent, the old attitudes of men still exist in organizations. For example: a woman was not introduced while sharing a stage with men when everyone else was. Another woman was asked repeatedly by his boss whether she can work in shifts even though she happened to be a qualified engineer holding senior manager position. A senior man in the organization denied concession in work timings to a pregnant lady who requested so. Do these instances indicate that men lack sensitivity on women specific issues?

Women in offices quite often have to travel along with men as part of their duties or stay together during conferences. Men would readily agree to travel with a woman whereas a woman would face several questions from various fronts. She herself is in dilemma sometimes, whether should she accept this? How the family would react to it? How would organization address such gender issues? Whether this is an issue for young women working in MNCs?

In a study on stress coping styles among German managers (Kirkcaldy and Furnham, 1999), the abbreviated German version of Occupational Stress Indicator's Coping Scale was completed anonymously by over 160 managers. No difference in coping profiles of men and women was found, but different levels of management and educational status did influence preference for coping styles. More specifically, it was seen that at the most senior levels of management, delegation and maintaining stable relationships are considered the most useful forms of coping with stress.

A comparative study on managerial stress in Hong Kong and Taiwan by Oi-ling, Luo, and Cary (1999) investigated occupational stress in managers in Hong Kong and Taiwan using the Occupational Stress Indicator-2 (OSI-2). The results showed that there were gender differences in managerial stress in Hong Kong: female managers scored higher in sources of stress and quitting intention; but had lower job satisfaction, worse mental and physical well-being than male managers. These differences could not be found in Taiwanese managers, yet Taiwanese female managers did report more stress related to "managerial role" than their male counterparts.

Kaila (2002) studied 120 managers in metropolitan Mumbai and found that 80 percent of them experienced the most common workplace stresses and challenges such as: meeting deadlines, working in a competitive industry, managing finances, exhausting working hours, and rotation work in addition to handling regular tasks (such as sales, marketing, training, research and development, and accounts of core clients).

A Malaysian survey on occupational stress among managers (Taap, Fontaine, and Chong, 2003) examined sources of stress among Malaysian managers working in multinational companies. A total of 440 managers participated in this survey. Data was collected through a questionnaire distributed to the managers in 34 multinational companies operating in Malaysia. It was found that workloads, working conditions and relationship at work were main concerns of the managers that lead to stress at the workplace. The results also indicated that certain demographic variables do influence the level of stress among managers.

Kasper, Meyer, and Schmidt (2005) conducted an explorative analysis on managers dealing with work-family conflict. The sample was drawn largely according to the principles of theoretical sampling; family-work constellations provided the basis of selection. Thirty problem-focused interviews were content analyzed. Results showed three distinct prototypes of dealing with work-family-tension: career as subject of social fascination, family as a factual task, the tradition of two worlds, double burden and the pressure of tasks. One outstanding result was that if both partners were professionally active, the family was increasingly dominated by merely functional requirements.

Armstron-Stassen (2005) compared the reactions of executive-level and middle managers prior to a large-scale downsizing, during initial and final phases, and following the downsizing. Compared with executives, middle managers perceived greater job insecurity, were more likely to use escape coping, and reported lower job performance and higher levels of health symptoms. Over time, both executives and middle managers reported a decline in perceived threat of job loss but an increase in sense of powerlessness, a decrease in the use of control-oriented coping strategies, and reduced job performance in the initial phase of downsizing. Although less so, executive-level managers were also adversely affected by the downsizing, suggesting that this group should be included in stress management interventions.

The studies on managerial psychology recently as well as in the past depict that cross-culturally there are similarities and differences on managerial behaviours. Secondly, female managers report more stresses regardless of cultural background. Thirdly the sources of managerial stress across cultures are similar. Moreover the managerial researches so far have been based on quantitative methodologies. Hence, it is postulated that the use of qualitative and narrative methods on the study of managerial issues would broaden our understanding and provide us more depth in the field.

Methodology

A structured questionnaire using the following three open-ended questions was presented to individual managers in their respective organizations.

- What do you think was the greatest problem you faced in the past 12 months? Please describe below.
- Please explain in which ways did it affect you personally or professionally?
- Could you give a title or heading to this problem above and how did you overcome this problem? Please explain.

The managers were asked to narrate their experiences. The women managers took time out of their really busy and hectic schedule to share their problems and issues in organizations. Though managerial problems and coping have been researched using quantitative research techniques, the depth of understanding on managerial issues is lacking. Hence a narrative approach was attempted in this study in order to enrich the managerial research.

The sample consisted of 140 female managers between 26 to 55 years of age in 81 organizations (including private and public sector, and MNCs) from different parts of India such as Mumbai, Bangalore, and Hyderabad, ranging from banks to IT, pharmaceutical companies to call centres. Data were collected from varied work backgrounds, different age groups and different levels of management: upper, middle and lower working in various departments through in-depth personal interviews and e-mails in a few cases with the help of a structured questionnaire using open-ended questions.

Results and Discussion

The survey results have been presented under the following section:

Problems faced by women managers, the ways in which the problems affect the women managers, and the coping strategies used by women managers to overcome their problems

The first question asked to managers was: What do you think was the greatest problem you faced in the past twelve months? Please describe. The second question asked was: Please explain in which ways did problems faced by you affect you personally or professionally? The third question asked to managers was: Could you give a title or a heading to the problem faced by you and how did you overcome the problem? Please describe. In this way, the manager herself titled the problem.

The Women Managers Responded:

Time Crisis: The greatest problem I have faced during the last 12 months is Time Constraints to meet deadlines. At a managerial level, I am assigned with a lot of responsibilities and the expectation of the superiors from me is also high. Since I have a family to look after it is even more difficult to attend to my work responsibilities. Many a time it leads to an injustice on my part towards either the home responsibilities or work responsibilities.

My problem has affected me positively and negatively. In a negative manner it brought about a lot of work pressure as I was falling short of time and I could not spend appropriate time on the assignments given to me by my superiors. Secondly, I found it difficult to maintain a balance between my home and work responsibilities also. But in a positive manner because of my constant efforts as well as correct planning I have become "immune to stress".

I overcame the problem by planning and prioritizing the tasks based on urgency, discussion with my colleagues and collectively resolving issues leading to lesser burden of work.

Since, I cannot take long holidays I take short breaks of 20 minutes from my work and listen to soothing music. I also watch plays in the theatre with my family to keep me in good spirits.

Relocation Trauma: During the recent times I faced the problem of relocation and shifting of archives because of the merger. Since we relocated from our old office to the current one, we had to physically shift more than 100 cartons of important documents and arrange it in the new location. Since there was very little time and less help I had to manually fill the boxes and arrange them in the new location.

Manually shifting archives affected me personally and professionally. Personally, it caused physical discomfort and muscle pull due to manual shifting of archives. Professionally it affected because being a qualified professional I did not find it a pleasing task to do the work of shifting files and cartons by myself.

I overcame the first problem of shifting by doing what was required i.e. shifted all the cartons manually with colleagues help and took proper medications for the muscle pull.

Time Constraints to Meet Deadlines: The greatest problem I have faced is the time constraint to cope up with multiple activities. Since I am a family woman I have to manage both the home as well as office. My responsibilities in office are also tremendous and I have to do multitasking but the time is so little that I sometime have difficulty in completing my assignments on time.

The problem of coping with multiple activities in a limited time has affected me personally because I have to complete many assignments together I have to stay late in office which amounts to a lot of physical strain as well as neglect in my home responsibilities. I also tend to miss important events in my personal life. It affected me professionally as I find it difficult to finish projects on the given deadline because of the limited time available to me thus causing stress. It also leads to crashed expectation from my superiors as they expect a lot out of me. Therefore I am constantly under pressure to prove myself in front of them.

I have managed to overcome my problem by prioritizing my work based on urgency of the tasks. I plan and organize my time so that multiple activities can lead to their goals. Sometimes I take a day or two off after hectic work schedules and go to resorts. When I return from there I feel recharged and like a new person altogether.

Glass Ceiling/Competition: The greatest problem was related to my up-gradation. Despite performing well year after year, I was not promoted to the higher cadre. I neglected a lot of areas of my life in the bid to get promoted but unfortunately I was never noticed when it came to promotion. Despite achieving all the goals on time, I saw that a higher number of males had risen to good posts and were the preferred candidates for promotion, resulting in humiliation.

The problem affected me very badly personally. I started neglecting my personal life in the bargain to do well so that at least in the next appraisal I could get promoted. Similarly, I endured a lot of mental trauma and physical strain as I used to work till long hours in office and remain tensed about my promotion. Communication with my family decreased. My self-esteem took a huge blow as I started doubting myself. Professionally I did not let if affect my work; in fact I started working more so that I could do my best.

I have not completely got over the problem as I am still struggling to understand why there was a bias towards the males and why hardworking deserving women like me were left out. But off late I have stopped thinking about it anymore, as it does not lead me anywhere. I constantly take support or spend time with my friends by going out for movies or dinner. I am doing my best but do not harbour the hopes of promotion any more. Volunteering or buying things for my nieces and nephews also helps me divert my attention from core problems..

Job Insecurity/Uncertainty: During the recent times I

have faced the problem of insecurity and uncertainty in my job. This is due to the recent merger that took place between the two pharmaceutical companies. The merger changed the whole structure of our organization. Many posts were declared unnecessary leading to ouster of many employees from the organization. I was constantly living under the fear of being asked to leave from the organization. With many new colleagues joining in there was uncertainty in what I was supposed to do and whether I was required by the organization or not.

Personally I felt lost. I felt stressed as I was constantly thinking about my work. For a short while I began to avoid pleasurable events. Professionally, I was very unclear as to where my job was leading me. For a while I was also contemplating to leave my current job and look for a new one. I was confused, as my role in the organization was not defined.

I have tried to overcome my problem with the support of my colleagues at work and seniors. Secondly, I started spending more time with my child and being with her itself was extremely de-stressing as for some time I would forget about my own problems. It's been nine months since the merger so I am now getting acquainted with the new structure and begun to understand my job responsibilities better. There have been constant talks with the Management and I been assured that my job is secure hence I have stopped worrying about that aspect also.

Clash with Superiors: The problem I suffered recently is altercation with my boss. He wasn't particularly happy with the way one of our core team members was performing. But instead of reprimanding him, my boss started to blame all the core team members. Since I am the project leader of the team I had a few altercations with my boss. I was aware of the performance deficiency of my team-mate and the remaining team was compensating for that person. Instead of appreciating the good contacts and trust we were building with the customers/clients, he was getting upset about it. So in order to overcome this he started to mentally harass a few of us. He started to bad mouth about the team members against each other.

This affected my social as well as professional life. Since my manager could not find any faults with my work he started criticizing me for my behaviour. This made me lose interest in my work and as a result I was not able to give my 100 percent to my job. It also increased my stress level and I was not able to concentrate on my social life.

This problem can be solved if my boss handles this situation in a more mature and intelligent manner. Instead of harassing us to gain an upper hand he can make use of the good connections and trust that we have built up to get more business. Secondly, he can speak to our team member about his performance deficiency and guide him to perform better. In this way not only will our organization benefit but also all the team members will feel secured by having a good boss around us. I haven't been able to overcome the problem but whenever I feel stressed out I go with my friends for a movie or have a good meal somewhere and then I feel better for sometime.

Honesty is the Best Policy in the Case of Fraud: Due to bogus stamp papers distributed in the workplace and stolen National Savings Certificate issued through authorized vendors, my employees and I faced serious problems. We were accused of creating a fraud in the organization. The customers of my bank could not repay the amount within the stipulated period of time.

Though there was no mistake on our part we as employees underwent serious problems. We were taken to court where enquiries were made. Professionally, it affected me because as a Manager I was under pressure to save the reputation of my organization. Secondly, it was my duty to support my subordinates and participate honestly in the enquiries made by legal authorities. Personally, I was under tremendous pressure and stress. I suffered from a mild heart attack because of the pressure I underwent. My family also underwent massive worries.

If people were honest and did not commit such a crime then we would not have undergone such stress. Being an honest person, I participated in all the enquiries made on the organization and me, as I had nothing to fear. I fully supported my subordinates and stood by them. I was constantly in discussion with the top management regarding this scam. We won the court case and the culprits were arrested. Thus, we all stuck together like one family at the time of crisis. During stressful times I would either read books so that I could divert my attention from problematic issues or involve myself in making painting and handicrafts to get away from the problems.

Non-cooperative Subordinates: The greatest problem I faced in the past 12 months was un-cooperative attitude of my workers due to the interference by the internal union. Some of my workers were a part of the internal union. For silly reasons they used to be instigated by their core members to suspend work at the drop of a hat.

The above problem affected me personally and professionally. Personally because I used to be under constant stress because I was unable to understand why the workers were behaving so erratically and why they were not working. Professionally, it affected me because our daily production was affected because they were suspending work. Secondly, my superiors were under the impression that I was unable to handle the workers under my department.

I called the workers under my department in groups of 5 and advised them about the losses incurred because of suspending the work for some silly reason. I asked them the reason for suspending work and 50 percent said that they didn't know the reason and they were doing it because their fellow workers were doing it, 40 percent said that they were doing it because their union head had asked them to do so. Whereas the remaining 10 percent were among the ones who were lazy and liked to drop work at the slightest reason. I looked into the matter with the help of our top management and as far as my workers were concerned I brought in an Industrial/Occupational Counsellor who gave them appropriate counselling regarding the disadvantages of being instigated by others to suspend work and generally made them aware of their contribution towards their organization so that they could work sincerely in the future. As far as my personal coping was concerned spending time with my baby was itself quite a stress buster and secondly since I am religious by nature, I would say my prayers and keep full faith in God.

Loss of Communication: The greatest problem I faced was loss of communication with colleagues in my prior organization. The merger brought about a whole lot of changes. One of them being the shifting of the heads of all departments to the Head Office. This relocation led to loss of communication with my colleagues because a lot many of them were not at higher posts so they remained in the old office.

Loss of communication affected me personally by the way of setting in monotony and boredom. I was not in touch with many of my colleagues due to the merger so I was not aware of what was happening with them. In a way my social support system has broken down because with my job I rarely got the time to give them a call or keep in touch with them. In a professional way, less communication means I was not clearly aware of what was happening in different business areas because of the merger. Since I was new in the current organization and not well acquainted with my new colleague there was ambiguity on the professional front.

I haven't been able to overcome the second problem because I have completely lost touch with my old colleagues due to my hectic routine. I feel as if I have lost a backbone, as now I have no one to share my problems with. In the current organization there is still loss of communication as I am new here and not well acquainted with my new colleagues. So there is still ambiguity with respect to my job role also. In order to get away with tension I spend some time on my own "me time" so that I feel much better and relaxed.

Shift Work Problem: The greatest problem I face is working Night Shifts. Since I am in a call centre, night shifts are inevitable.

Working night shifts affected me personally and professionally. Personally, it becomes very difficult to manage my home and work together because at home I have to attend to my 2 yrs old baby and responsibilities in office are equally pressurizing. I felt guilty since I do not get time to spend with my family. Night shifts disrupt the whole schedule due to which I encountered a lot of health problems such as fatigue, headaches and a lot of stress. There is often a spill over of tensions from home to work and work to home. Professionally, my health problems decreased my productivity at work. Though I was unable to handle my team, my appraisal rating from my superiors took a blow.

I have been able to overcome the problem with the support of my family. When I am not around my husband takes care of our baby. Secondly, I spend some of my times with my friends who are not from call centres, which takes some load off. I am a member of an N.G.O named Aakansha and there is no other bigger pleasure than buying gifts for the needy children and seeing a smile on their face. I plan and organize my schedule during night shifts so that I can spend adequate time with my child too.

The above responses revealed that majority of the women managers faced the problem of meeting deadlines due to time constraints. Many women managers combine their full time paid work with parenthood or household responsibilities. They tend to remain the primary caretakers on the home turf in spite of being assigned with a job which requires long hours of physically and mentally demanding work. Other main problems included getting work done from subordinates, relocation problems as well as feelings of job insecurity and uncertainty. It was also found that women managers find internal politics between their colleagues/subordinates as well as altercations, lack of communication with colleagues/friends and clashes with their superiors extremely stressful. The "Glass ceiling effect" was also reported by one woman manager who said, "She felt that there was a bias against women who wanted to move up the ladder." Lastly, night shifts too posed a major hindrance for a woman manager who reported "Nights shifts are inevitable in call centres, but I feel guilty for not spending time with my family". According to a woman manager "The glass-ceiling effect and not being able to handle ones subordinate are problems that are very gender specific. In many organizations, in spite of working so hard, many women still face discrimination".

Women Managers Reported that their Problems affected them personally as well as professionally.

Women managers who faced the problems of meeting deadlines due to time constraints, working night shifts and insecurity and uncertainty regarding ones job reported that personally overwork was causing a strain on their families and relationships as it robbed them of time, energy and attention needed to maintain healthy relationships with partners and children. They also reported missing out on important social events such as weddings or outings with families. According to one female manager "I have to complete many assignments together so I have to stay late in office which amounts neglect in my home responsibilities". Feelings of insecurity and uncertainty regarding ones job created a lot of anxiousness and stress in women managers because they were constantly bombarded with thoughts about their future in the organization. They also remained tensed, as they were unclear regarding their job function in the organization. Many of these women also reported a spill over of tensions about ones work to home and from home to work. This spill-over resulted in conflicts between them and their spouses. Their problems are further compounded because they also tended to suffer from health problems due to long working hours or disruptions in shift hours.

They complained of headaches, back pain, fatigue, weakness and other physical ailments. Their problems also brought along professional hazards for them in the form of dissatisfaction of superiors regarding their quality of work and low productivity in their performance in the organization.

Women managers who were concerned of interpersonal conflicts at work felt de-motivated and stressed out seeing the conflicts between their colleagues. According to a woman manager “it’s a challenge to remain neutral and listen to both sides of the story”. As far clashes with bosses were concerned managers felt de-motivated to work especially when the clash was a result of misunderstandings or feelings of insecurity harboured by the superiors. A woman manager reported “Constant clash with my boss made me lose interest in my work and as a result I was not able to give my 100 percent to my job”. Uncooperative subordinates posed a problem for women managers because the attitude of the subordinates gave an impression to their superiors that the manager was unable to handle the subordinates. This problem also affected the productivity of the organization as the subordinates used to suspend work. Women managers reported a lot of confusion as they were unable to understand the real reason behind their subordinates erratic behaviours. They also reported being under constant work pressure as they felt a need to prove themselves in front of their superiors.

Women managers who faced the problem of discrimination in the workplace reported “feeling humiliated” and left out because of unfair appraisals. Decrease in their self esteem was another apparent effect due to the discrimination in the workplace. They also reported of neglecting their family life in a bid to do well resulting in less communication with their family. Stress, feelings of anxiousness and work pressure were their chief problems.

Complaints of monotony, boredom and lack of social support were stated by women managers who reported the problem of communication. They also complained of feelings of ambiguity as they were unaware of the ongoings in different business areas due to restrictive communication. Health problems such as muscle pulls were the chief complaints of women managers who suffered from the problem of relocating from one office to another.

So far we saw the negative effects of problems faced by the women manager. But the results of this survey also revealed a welcome change. According to a few women managers, the stress, tension and anxiety caused to them because of work pressure and deadlines had made them "immune to stress" as a result of which they reported handling work pressure much better than before. This effect is called as eustress as it connotes a positive change in the behaviours with respect to handling of stressful situations.

Thus, it can be seen that the problems faced by women managers affected them personally and professionally and the effects of the problems they faced were positive as well as negative.

As far as coping with problems among women managers is concerned, it was seen that only a few managers were not able to overcome their problems. But overall, the responses towards coping with problems were positive.

Different individuals have different styles of coping with their problems. It was seen that many women managers worked actively towards eliminating their problems by meditating, going on holidays, taking short breaks and having appropriate medications. Other common coping strategies reported by women managers included, discussing problems with colleagues and seeking advise from superiors, spending time with friends by going for movies and holidays, planning and organizing ones schedule.

Many women managers were spiritually inclined as a result of which they participated in different kinds of religious activities to relax their minds such as singing bhajans, visiting temples or saying prayers. According to a woman manager "whenever I face a problem I send a small prayer up there so that things go well with me". Other interesting ways of coping with problems included pampering oneself by going for shopping or having a good meal. Many women managers joined NGOs where they generously donated gifts. One such manager exclaimed "There is no other pleasure than seeing a smile on children's face. It's very destressing". Many of them indulged in giving gifts to relatives and friends in order to feel better. But the unanimous votes went in the favour of spending time with ones family especially ones children. According to one manager "It's extremely destressing to spend time with my child because for sometime I forget that I have a problem. Other indulged in activities like painting or watching plays in a theatre to keep their minds off work pressure.

Conclusion

When we observe International Women's Day on 8th March every year, we need to ponder over the gender issues in organizations. Male attitude is an issue to be addressed, attitudinal barriers from men trouble women. Though male dominance in organizations is changing a bit, still an issue remains to be addressed. Some suggestions can be considered to deal with these problems:

- Successful women or women at higher positions should act as mentors to other women and make women friendly organizations.
- Women' leadership training need to be emphasized so that they can tackle their issues more effectively.
- The perspectives of international women's day need to go beyond gender and look at relationship building.
- Include men in women's seminars and other programmes.
- Gender sensitivity programmes at schools and organizations must be conducted on regular basis as a part of Human Resource Development.
- Organizations need to develop women development cell for soft skills training and personality development

programmes.

- It is sexual harassment for some women and romance at work for others especially young people. These different sets of responses of women to the opposite gender need to be understood and addressed accordingly.
- Essentially organizations have to take up work-family balance mechanisms such as pick-up facility, ATM machines, flextime, compressed week etc.
- Women must come united, raise their voices on issues that haunt them, don't leave any single case of harassment un-attended.
- Introduce Employee Assistance Programme and counselling in organizations.
- Psychosomatic ill-health of women working on computers is an issue to tackle. Yoga and health check-ups are necessary.
- International women's day should be called as International Gender Day.

Though men and women are socialized differently, women are more rigorously trained for family and social roles; whereas men remain weak in these roles or opposite gender related responsibilities. Do men need to be re-socialized at the organizations for becoming gender-friendly or gender-just people? MNCs today are becoming inclusive organizations and open to people's issues (both male and female employees as equal partners).

A few common solutions are suggested to make a woman's life easier in organizations such as compressed working week, crèches at the workplace, employee counselling at workplaces, flexitime, compulsory periodical medical examinations, providing the facility of working from home, yoga for improved physical and mental health (Kaila, 2004; 2004a; 2005).

References

Armstrong-Stassen M. (2005). Coping with downsizing: A

comparison of executive-level and middle managers. *International Journal of Stress Management, 12,* 117-141.

Kaila, H. L. (2002). Stress is a way of life for Mumbai workers. *Psychology International*, 13, *Fall 2002.*

Kaila, H.L. (2004). Indian women managers: Their stresses, health and coping behaviour - A Survey in Mumbai. *Journal of Health Management, 6*, 147-161.

Kaila, H. L. (2004a). *Women of Mumbai towards new millennium.* Mumbai: Himalaya Publishing House.

Kaila, H. L. (2005). *Women, work and family*. New Delhi: Rawat Publications.

Kasper, K; Meyer, M. and Schmidt, A. (2005). Managers dealing with work-family-conflict: an explorative analysis. *Journal of Managerial Psychology. 20,* 440-461.

Kirkcaldy, B. D. and Furnham, A. F. (1999). Stress coping styles among German managers. *Journal of Workplace Learning. 11,* 22-26.

Oi-ling, S.; Luo, L. and Cary, C. (1999). Managerial stress in Taiwan: A comparative study. *Journal of Managerial Psychology. 14,* 6-25.

Taap, A. M.; Fontaine, R. and Chong S. C. (2003). Occupational Stress among managers: A Malaysian survey. *Journal of Managerial Psychology. 18,* 622-628.

8

Wage Discrimination against Women Agricultural Labourers

A. Sangamithra and S.C. Karpagavalle

Introduction

Indian women in Vedic times enjoyed an exceptionally high status. The Vedic 'dampati' used to denote jointly husband and wife; etymologically it means ancestors created a Plethora of the concept 'Ardhanareeshwarar' where god is depicted as half man and half woman. Presently, the picture seems to be very different and paradoxical. In a male-dominated society, women suffer from variety of gender-bias and repressive laws in all field of life. Exploitation of the so-called weaker sex became the target of the society. In the economic sphere women have less opportunity than men; they earn half of men's income. Another problem is the limited mobility of women doesn't allow them to access to improved opportunities in skill development or economic betterment. According to the first Women Director- General of the World Health Organization (WHO), Gro Brundtland, 70 percent of the 3.1 billion people living in poverty are women; of this majority are illiterate and women are paid 30 to 40 percent less than men for comparable work. Unfortunately, these statistics portray the vicious cycle of inequality, poverty of large number of women.

Status of Women in Agricultural Sector

Agriculture is the mainstay of the Indian economy, a way of life for million of farm families with pre-domination of small and marginal farmers and landless labourers. As per the 2001 Census, work participation rate is 39 percent with 41.8

and 32.2 percent in rural and urban areas, respectively (Singh, 2006). The participation of both men and women in agriculture takes place in mutually dependent as well as independent roles, in the sector.

In a rural society where more than 62 percent of the labourers are working in the agricultural sector, the wage rate is an important indicator of their level of living. It is strongly affected by the performance of agricultural sector among men and women workers. As agricultural labourers are from informal sector in India, they could not have collective bargaining power in determining high wage rate. Though many rural development programmes have been implemented from time to time, it could not solve the agricultural labour issues. Further, the wage differentials between male and female labour becomes a serious issue at present. So to analyse the above mentioned problem, an attempt has been made to study the wage differentials among men and women in agricultural sector in Athani village of Gobichettipalayam taluk, Erode District, Tamil Nadu.

Objective of the Study

- To analyse the socio-economic conditions of the farmers in the study area.
- To analyse the consumption pattern of agricultural labourers.
- To analyze income inequality among men and women.
- To examine the wage differentials among men and women on account of different field operations in agricultural sector.

Profile of the Study Area/Data Collection

Erode district is agriculturally progressive area in Tamil Nadu. In this district most of the farmers cultivate crops like Paddy, Sugarcane, Turmeric and Banana. Athani village is agriculturally progressive village in Gobichetti Palayam Taluk. And the main occupation for most of the farmers is agriculture in this village.

Primary data was collected in the agricultural field of Athani village. We went to the field and collected the particulars directly through direct interview method from 120 respondents of both male and female. However, it was very difficult to contact the labourers in the farms as they were engaged in different operations in the field at the time of survey. But still we have managed to obtain the information.

Athani block is situated at the North West corner of Gobichettipalayam Taluk. It is one of the fertile areas in the district. Its geographical area is 184.47 sq. km. The total geographical area is 184.47 hectares. The forest constitutes 3605 hectares of the geographical area. Out of this 12,088 hectares are in agricultural use and 2,754 hectares are put to non-agricultural uses. The main occupation of this block is agriculture. The principal crops grown in this block are paddy, sugar cane, turmeric, onions and banana. Out of this sugar cane and turmeric are the major crops placed in the agricultural sector of this area. This block has a special feature of sandy soil type. The soil of the block is divided into (a) alluvial soil (b) dry soil (c) red coamy soil and (d) black with sandy soil. These soils are found in Bhavani river and lower bhavani project area of the block. The block gets rain during north-east and south-west monsoon season. The average rainfall of the block during the north east monsoon season was recorded to be 619.2mm. The average rainfall during south- west monsoon was only 264.3mm. The major crops grown here are paddy, sugar cane, turmeric, onions, and fruits under the canal system. Tube well irrigation is utilized mostly in this area.

Gender Discrimination

Gender discrimination is discrimination against a person or group on the grounds of sex or gender identity. Socially, sexual differences have been used to justify societies in which one sex or the other has been restricted to significantly inferior and secondary roles. There are number of studies mainly focus on gender disparity in the agricultural sector. Economic inequality between men and women is an important problem deserving wage discrimination of in depth study because of the large number of people it affects. Not only do current gender wage gaps affect women, they also likely affect their future generations. A number of relevant studies have found evidence that women tend to receive low wage income compare to men in their earnings in agricultural sector.

Gender inequality is an acute and persistent problem, especially in developing countries. Gender discrimination in wages and differentials in earnings are widespread in India and particularly in the informal sector where equal pay legislation is not applied. Moreover, a large proportion of women and men working in the informal sector are doing so as unpaid family labour. In agriculture, wage rates vary widely across regions and by season; but rates for women, are particularly low compared to men. Female wages as a proportion of male wages range from around half to over three quarters depending on the state. There is no consistent trend in and little recent data on gender differentials in agricultural wages. In most industrial categories, women earnings in the informal sector were around half those of men. Even in the formal sector, however, inequalities in earnings are marked because women are concentrated at lower occupational levels. In regular waged employment, women earnings are only on an average 83 percent of men.

General wage inequality in the agricultural sector that has received a great deal of attention in the economic literature. Differences in wages between men and women, particularly in the agricultural sector and variation in the size of the gender gap, has been studied as thoroughly. The difference in wage income between men and women is of great importance because it affects a very large number of people.

More than two-thirds of the population of India is dependent on agriculture. Though Green Revolution technologies enhanced agricultural productivity, they also widened economic disparities and deepened gender discrimination in community life. The introduction of labour intensive technologies in the agricultural sector has had differential impact on men and women and women have been adversely affected due to lack of access to technology now days.

There is a distinct gender division of labour within the agricultural sector in the study area and gender discriminatory practices are evident not only in allocation of types of work and rates of wages but in timings of work as well. Irrespective of the differentials in socio-cultural dimensions and consumption pattern across communities and classes, of men and women, only women shoulder the responsibility of domestic labour. Among the agricultural worker households too the case is not different; women perform an overwhelming proportion of the various items of unremunerated domestic work in addition they attend to work in the farms.

Nearly 70 percent of the women in the agriculture sector reported they do not get any help from their men in the discharge of domestic responsibilities such as cooking, fetching water, washing clothes, cleaning floors or caring of children. There is no difference in this regard even in the better off families among them. The few women who get support get it either in fetching water or in the care of children. The gendered relations have created an environment at home which does not allow women to put their feet up even after long hours of tedious, backbreaking work such as transplanting, weeding or harvesting. After collecting wages, these women rush to the nearby shops for buying food articles and then to their kitchen for preparing dinner.

Usually, women do food articles and other household items, in addition to the work in the kitchen. Obviously, most of these works are invisible and not reckoned as work at all. They are considered women's responsibility. It will not, however, be entirely correct to believe that all women internalize such gender roles uncritically. It is largely the social pressures that impose such burdens on them. So this may be the main reason for getting low wage compared to men in the agricultural sector.

Usually, gender wage discrimination is identified as the difference in earnings between male and female workers who are otherwise identical in their attributes and thus in their expected productivity. Gender discrimination in the employment sector is enduring, an overwhelming majority of women working within the boundaries of informal sectors. Tamil Nadu is agro-based and a major proportion of both men and women are in the labour force work in agriculture. Men were able to opt out from agriculture and seek new employment avenues elsewhere when they encountered low prospects in agriculture. But women have remained, however, in the agricultural sector, accepting the traditional practice of paying wages to women at half of the rates compared to men. Employment opportunities in the agricultural sector are diminishing quite rapidly due to changes in land use and cropping patterns associated with commercialization of agriculture.

Women are paid lower wages in many rural areas on the assumption that women are less productive. Mencher and Sardamoni (2002) pointed out that this is not based on any fact. "No one has ever measured the amount of paddy harvested by a woman and that harvested by a man in the sector. Only because of assumption made by the owners the wage rate are providing high for men compared to women". Now let us see the objectives and the relevant findings in this section.

Findings

Socio-economic Conditions of the Sample Respondents: The first objective deals with socio-economic conditions of the sample respondents. From the analysis, it is found that the respondents age comes under the category of 30-40. 60 respondents are male workers and 60 respondents are females.

And majority of the respondents belongs to the category of scheduled caste and scheduled tribes. They are working mainly in the agricultural field in that sector of the selected field. Workers education status is very poor in this sector. The reason is 25 members of the total respondents they did not even enter in to school. But a total of 63 respondents entered in to primary education at least.

Consumption Pattern of the Sample Respondents: The second objective deals with consumption pattern of the sample respondents for their daily necessities namely food, clothing, and medical and recreation facilities. According to the level of consumption of the respondents it mainly deals with their earning level of income. So according to the wages received by the agricultural workers they have spent mainly for consumption. We have done a survey for the pattern of consumption for whole month and it is concluded that people working in the agricultural sector are consuming less amount ranges from ₹ 2001-2500 for the whole family per month. Again we observed that most of them are spending their income only to consume food and next is for Schooling. And most of them spent a very little amount of money on clothing and recreation facilities.

Income Inequality among the Sample Respondents: Agricultural wages are an important indicator of the standard of living of the large mass of agricultural labourers in the country. Historically, the agricultural labour force was constituted by the lowest sections of the social order who lived in great penury and deprivation. Income is considered as one of the important resources. Every individual will have different level of wage rate. So according to wage the workers will receive the income. And the income is mainly based on Age of the respondents, type of agricultural operations, time taken to finish the particular task are all based on their income. So from the work performance income level may increase or decrease to the wage earners.

The third objective explains the income inequality of the

respondents working in the agricultural field with different field operations. To prove whether there is the income inequality among the respondents we have used Lorenz curve. And it is estimated from the Lorenz curve that 0.35012347 of value has made a change among the respondents for those who are getting wage in agricultural field and it shows that there is income inequality among the workers better male and female.

The Lorenz Curve is a tool used to represent income distributions among men and women and it tells us which proportion of total income is in the hands of a given percentage of population. The Lorenz curve has been selected for the study to show how income distribution worsened during the period of collection of the data. If illustrated, the value X represents the sample respondents and value Y represents the amount of inequality among one and others. These curves graphically present the state of income distribution and how income distribution shifted among high wage earners to lower wage earners. And it shows the underlying movements in male and female real earnings that gave rise to the reduction in the gender gap.

Wage Differences in Different Field Operations in Agricultural Sector: Gender discrimination in the employment sector is enduring, and over whelming majority of women and men working within the boundaries of informal sectors. So the size of the aggregate (or national-level) gender pay gap can be influenced by a wide variety of developments in the economy or society that influence employment rates, the composition of the workforce, wage levels, and the structure of wages.

Equal proportion of both men and women are taken for analysis in this sector Men were able to opt out from agriculture and seek new employment avenues elsewhere when they encountered low prospects in agriculture. But Women have remained, however, in the agricultural sector, accepting the traditional practice of paying wages to women at half the rates for men. So this may cause main reasons for wage discrimination.

From the paired T-test it is proved that there is a significant difference between men and women. It is empirically proved that there is wage difference between men and women and also in different fields of operations. All the fields were statistically significant at 5 percent level which gives strong support for our analysis.

Overall Wage Difference between Men and Women

Hypothesis Test: To compare the Gender discrimination in the agricultural fields Null Hypothesis (Ho)=There is a significant difference between men and women earnings in the agricultural sector among the field.

Alternative Hypothesis (H1)=There is no significant difference between men and women earnings in the agricultural sector among the field. ANOVA test has been applied to find out if there is any significant difference between gender while receiving the agricultural wage rate in all the three field operations.

Gender inequality in wages is created and maintained by many different fields of operation namely paddy, turmeric and sugarcane. Agriculture used to be the major source of employment for both men and women in the village. Gender inequality is reflected in the unequal sharing of benefits of wage rate between man and woman. And the employment of the majority of the women in our sample in the low-paid work in the informal sector is seen to be the outcome from the estimated results. So from the over all wage rate it is found that wage rate may differ according to time spent, completion of hours of particular task, and main reason is made according to gender.

The lower wages paid to female workers in comparison with males can easily be checked empirically from the analysis. While analyzing wage discrimination from a point of view, considering gender in the field of Paddy, Turmeric and sugar cane, we come out with the following conclusion.

To test the wage difference between men and women, we used Analysis of Variance (ANOVA). From Table 8.1, we understand that there is a significant difference between male and female wage rates. We used all the field operations like Paddy, Turmeric, and Sugarcane wage rates of both men and women for our analysis. It is statistically significant at 5 percent level, which means that there exists mean difference between male and female wage rates. So we accept (Ho) null hypothesis that there is wage difference between men and women.

Table 8.1: Analysis of Variance (ANOVA)

	Sum of Squares	df	Mean Square	F	Sig.
Between Groups	22344.318	1	22344.318	52.716	.000
Within Groups	64426.623	152	423.859		
Total	86770.942	153			

Source: Primary Data.

We have analysed and concluded for the agricultural operation for the field of paddy and it is found the mean value of men has got the Total value of 91.7000 and in the same field women has got the mean value of 71.4167 for the same time period and for the same type of work (Table 8.2). From these findings it is concluded that there is lot of difference made in their mean value of both men and women in their operation. And from the analysis of variance it is proved significant for the gender discrimination. From the analysis of turmeric we found that the mean value of men has got the total value is 103.5833 and for the same field and same type of operation for women workers has got the total mean value of 80.4167. And from the findings it is proved that there is significant difference between the wages of men and women in the field of turmeric operation among the workers.

Table 8.2: Mean Difference between Men and Women Wages

Fields	Men (₹)	Women (₹)
Paddy	91.7000	71.4167
Turmeric	103.5833	80.4167
Sugarcane	169.8333	111.1667

Source: Primary Data.

From the finding in the field is sugar cane we found that the mean value of men wage earners has got the total of 169.8333 and for the mean value women wage earners has got the total of 111.1667. From the analysis of variance it is proved that there is significant difference between the wages of men and women among the sample respondents. And finally from the comparison of all the three field operation which has been chosen for the study period we found a significant difference of all the three operations. And it is found highest mean value for the sugar cane for both the male and female wage earners when compared to other agricultural operations.

Conclusions

Hence according to the earnings of wage among men and women and among individual difference we have proved that there are gender differentials among the sample respondents. Other than underemployment, illiteracy and inadequate facilities for life, women's access to livelihood is rendered increasingly difficult by men's lack of economic and emotional support and violence against women. Further, it seems that despite shouldering the double burden of work–within home and outside home–and stretching themselves beyond their physical capabilities to procure adequate economic security for their families, nearly four-fifths of the households are not able to have two square meals a day round the year. Indeed, women bear the brunt of the deprivation due to the gender inequities. In short, the poverty of the women agricultural workers encompasses a wide rage of unmet needs and gender-specific inequities including lack of adequate access to education, employment, resources as well a range of violence, relative powerlessness, feelings of hurt, low self-esteem and denial of identity.

Women are the key to sustainable development and quality of life. "Women are the heart of development." So investing in women's "capabilities" and empowering them to achieve their "choices" and "opportunities" is the surest way to contribute to economic growth and development. Women have a decisive role to play in the alleviation of household poverty. Empowering women with property rights and saving and investment facilities would contribute much more to the household income. Moreover women work participation in the income earning activities would raise the gender per capita income. The economic empowerment of women is sine-qua-non for eradiation of poverty in general and rural poverty in particular. Goals of poverty eradication and empowerment of women can be effectively achieved if poor women could organize into groups. The group-based activities not only enables them to participate in income generating programmes but also paves the way for skill development, leadership, decision-making and participation in various programme as effective partners and articulation of their hopes and desires.

Policy Suggestions

Agriculture is considered as the biggest unorganised sector among all other sector where large number of rural men and women takes part actively. About 75 percent of the Indian male and female population are from rural families, who belonged to the small and marginal farmers and landless agricultural labourers. Though women's primary responsibility is indulging in domestic work greater emphasis is laid on women's earning in the form of money by working outside the four walls. In India, a significant proportion of the women are earning below the minimum wage level in this field and it is a fact that women labour force participation will increase with poverty and low standard of living in their economy. The mind set of the people must change and the government must also take effective steps to eliminate such discrimination practices in the agricultural sector.

Gender discrimination against women in the market place reduces the available talent in an economy, which has negative economic consequences. Gender discrimination takes many forms. Many social practices seen as normal from a religious or cultural point of view (which may have deep historical roots) leave women out of the economic main stream. These social practices may have profound economic consequences because they do not allow society to take advantage of the talent inherent in women. Although gender discrimination may have a myriad of other important consequences, including psychological, sociological, and religious, these are not discussed in this paper. But this type of study will certainly pave the way for further research in future.

References

Abiodun O. Falawewo (2006) "Determinants of informal sector labour demand: Does methodology matter?" The Indian Journal of Labour Economics. Vol. 49.

Akinumi, Adesina. A and Kouakou. K. Djato (1997) "Relative Efficiency of Women as Farmer Managers", Agricultural Economics, Vol. 16, No. 1.

Amit Kundu (2006) "Wage-Employment relationship in the agricultural labour market of West Bengal" The Indian Journal Labour Economics Vol. No. 49.

Arulampalan, W. Booth, A. L. and Bryan, M. L. (2006) 'Is there a glass ceiling over Europe? Exploring the gender pay gap across the wages distribution', Industrial and Labour Relations Review, 60 (2).

Aysot Tansel (2000) "Wage Earners, Self-employment and Gender in the Informal Sector in Turkey" Department of Economics, Middle East Technical University, Ankara, Turkey.

Aysot Tansel (2000) Wage Earners, Self-employment and Gender in the Informal Sector in Turkey.

Banaerjee G. D. (1988) "Changes over years in employment wages and earning of agricultural labourers of the rural community"-

Economic Affairs, Vol. 30, No. 9, 1988.

Berta Esteve-Volart (2004) "Gender Discrimination and Growth– Theory and Evidence from India" London School of Economics and Political Science, London, January.

Blau, Francine and Lawrence Kahn (1997) 'Swimming upstream: trends in the gender wage differential in the 1980s.' Journal of Labour Economics, 15(1) pt.1:1- 42

Boserup, Ester (1970) Women's Role in Economic Development. New York: St. Martin's Press.

Clementina Santos, Pilar González (2003) Gender Wage Differentials in the Portuguese Labour Market, Research Centre on Industrial, Labour and Managerial Economics, Portugal.

Coral del Río, Carlos Gradín, Olga Cantó (2006) The measurement of gender wage discrimination: The distributional approach revisited, The International Association for Research in Income and Wealth, Joensuu, Finland.

Himanshu (2005) "Wages in rural India: Sources, Trends, and comparability". Indian Journal of Labour Economics, Volume 48, Number 2.

Indu Grover and Nishi Sethi (2007) "Mapping out gender dynamics of farming systems of Haryana" Journal of social science, Vol. 14(3)

Jeemol Unni (1994) "Labour participation decisions of married women in rural India"- Indian Economic Review Vol. XXIX No. 2.

Jenkins, S. (1994) Earnings discrimination measurement: a distributional approach. Journal of Econometrics, 61(1):81–102.

Kanchana N. Ruwan Pura (2005) Impact of new farm technology on farm labour use in Punjab 1966-67 to 1969-70.

Klaus Deininger1, Songqing Jin1, and Hari K. Nagarajan (2006) Gender discrimination and returns to self-employment Evidence from rural India National Council for Applied Economic Research, New Delhi, India.

Leela Gulati (1975) "Sex discrimination in Wages" Social Scientist, Vol. 4.

Lopamudra Banerjee (2005) "Effects of flood on agricultural wage formation in Bangladesh-An empirical analysis" Department of Economics, University of California, Riverside October.

Luca Flabbi (2004) Gender Discrimination Estimation in a Search Model with Matching and Bargaining, Georgetown University and IZA Bonn, Germany. Discussion Paper No. 1764.

Manajari Bhattacharyay and Manabendu Chattopadhyay (2006) "Efficiency of family versus hired labour in Indian agriculture - Findings from west Bengal"-Indian journal of Labour economics, Vol. 49, No. 2.

Michael Schultz (1995) Background report on gender issues in India: key findings and recommendations BRIDGE (development - gender) Institute of Development Studies University of Sussex Brighton BN1 9RE, UK

Pallavi Chavan, Raj Shree Bedamatta (2006) "Trends in agricultural wages in India 1964-65 to 1999-2000" Economic and political weekly, November 3 Vol. XL1 No. 38.

Parthasarathy. G (1996) "Recent trends in wage and employment of agricultural labour"–Indian Journal of Agricultural Economics. Vol. 51.

Patel. J.B and Sundangai. B.N. (1995) "Work and time analysis of farm women in farming systems operations" Manpower Journal Vol. XXX.1 No. 2.

Rajesh Bhatia (2002) "Measuring gender disparity using time use statistics" Economic and Political Weekly, Vol. XXXVII, No.33

Sasank Sarmah (1995)–"Agricultural wages in India"-The Indian Journal of Labour Economics.

9

Gender Implications of New Work Order

Kaistha Sunita and Amar Nath Singh

Introduction

Gender as a structural principle operates at several levels. Societal gender structures find expression in norms and how women and men "are" or "ought to be", as manifested for instance through public discourse, politics and media. But gender structures are also at work in the organization of the labour markets and workplaces, as well in the way we behave in private relationships within families and with friends. Gender has a powerful impact on the development of a person's identity.

The understanding of the complex processes that lead to the consequences for the individual both in work life as well as life outside work is a difficult task. Although research in a gender perspective has made many important contributions to working life research in recent decades, most research within the sphere of working life has a gender-neutral perspective, in which gender as a social category has no significance. Thus explanatory models continue to be produced which continue to not satisfactorily address the problem.

Gender Processes in Development

Gender segregation, and the structure on which women's relatively subordinate position in the work force is based, keeps women working at lower level jobs, concentrating power in the hands of men. This subordination is most clearly seen at the overall level in two dimensions lateral subordination, where female–dominated sectors and occupations have a lower status than male dominated sectors and occupations, and subordination in the vertical dimension, where women as a group are to be found at a lower level in the hierarchies than men. Researchers have shown that women's chances of development are better in network organizations than in hierarchical organizations (Gunnarsson and Ressner 1983; Ressner 1985). In one study, Kvande and Rasmussen, 1990 compared the hierarchical organization with the network organization. They summarised their findings as given below:

Hierarchy Organisations:

- Specialisation and strict division of labour.
- Vertical communication.
- Centralised decision-making systems.
- Influence according to hierarchical position.

Network Organisations:

- Flexible and team-based work organization.
- Transverse communication.
- Decentralised decision-making systems.
- Influence on basis of knowledge and experience.

A comparison between hierarchy and network organizations shows that a hierarchical organization limits people's exposure to new challenges. On the other hand a network organisation offers considerable, in principle limitless, challenges. *Hierarchical or*ganizations are likely to make women invisible as bearers of knowledge, and isolate them, often at the bottom of the hierarchy. A hierarchical organisation promotes a gender order where men are given pride of place over women. *Network* organizations become more female-friendly, largely by virtue of their flexibility. Network organizations are more amenable to change, make women visible as working individuals and allow all employees to take on greater challenges. Network organizations are also more female-friendly because they better reflect women's attitude to work, women's values and their general way of being (Gunnarsson 1991; Kvande and Rasmussen 1990).

The structures in a work organization are often seen as

gender neutral, as independent of whether the organization's members are women or men. However, one has to question how gender affects the processes and structures of the organizations. Organisational structures must be understood and analysed as gendered systems. Different forms of organization have different gender-political effects. The so-called gender power systems, i.e. underlying conceptions, standards and practices in modern companies, are constituent elements in the logic of organizations and in fact more or less make women's conditions "invisible" (Acker 1987; Baude et al. 1987; Gunnarsson et al. 1991; Kvande and Rasmussen 1990).

However, gender based power structures are not static since society, norms and values change over a period of time. Structures arise out of social relations and are therefore the result of actions by individuals and groups. Gender is thus viewed not as something that is being constructed, by ourselves and by others in constant interaction, within the framework of the structures that surround us.

Gender segregation is the process in which women and men end up in different types of occupation, so that two different types of labour market may be said to exist, female and male. Gender marking and gender segregation interact, and are determined by the social structure of gender.

So gender marking takes place by a process in which the qualifications and characteristics of an occupation become associated with gender. This gives us an idea of which gender a person should have for a particular job. Gender marking becomes apparent when occupations become female or male. In theory, gender segregation may be seen as a result of gender marking of qualifications, characteristics, occupations and work functions. However, there is interplay between the gender-segregated society in which we live and the gender-marking process, one result of which is that the conditions that lead to gender marking change over time.

In many situations, the thought process is that if only the

number of women within an occupation, organization, company, board of directors or in the government etc. becomes more equal, then gender segregation will decline and society will become more equal. But research shows that the values and processes that result in occupations becoming gender-marked and gender-segregated do not change especially when more women enter what was previously a clearly male-dominated area (Westberg, 2008). As Westberg suggests, gender segregation is not synonymous with gender marking–a process that renders an occupation typically female or male. If a society can deal with gender marking, gender segregation will fade away. *Notions and ideas about what is feminine and masculine legitimize the placement of women and men in different occupational categories or the same occupational categories, but with the content differently defined.* This leads to notions that "female" qualifications and qualities differ from "male". The gender structure of the workplace is underpinned by the kind of generally shared perceptions of which requirements are posed by various jobs and by notions of which skills are possessed by women and men. Such qualities do not necessarily come from the individual; they may also be associated with what a particular job attributes to the individual, such as power, status and pay.

Women's Working World

The lack of freedom of choice, power and material resources, traditional gender roles and norms, stand in the way of development, as is evident in most parts of the world. Significantly, a large proportion of women in the world live in poverty and in fact efforts to reduce poverty are inseparable from the aspirations for greater equality. Research indicates that gender equality in the long run has lead to reduction of poverty. *In fact unequal power structures for women and men constitute an impediment to economic growth and democratic development.* Equal opportunities for women and men to own land and assets, to earn money and to participate in working life, are essential for sustainable and democratic development in the long run.

For a number of reasons it is important to impose a perspective of gender on women's and men's working life. One fundamental reason is that it is assumed that the conditions in working life are the same for women and men.

A number of studies, show that women are more often overqualified for their job than men. Other studies show that women have less influence over their work organisation and content than men. Women also generally have a greater degree of monotonous, repetitive motion in their work. Further, studies show that occupations where women predominate have a lower status than male dominated occupations, even if the occupations require equivalent education and training. In workplaces with as many women as men, in apparently the same occupation, the women often perform different tasks, which most of the time are classified differently in status and pay. The work women almost always perform is valued lower.

A consistently large proportion of female workers in both the public and private sectors are employed part-time. The number of temporary and short-term contractual jobs is steadily increasing. This weakens common pay policies, starting a trend towards more local and individual pay agreements. Because employees in managerial position very rarely work part-time, the dualistic model causes immense problems for highly educated women as far as work is concerned. Budget cutbacks in the public sector, which already has undervalued jobs (as compared to the private sector) in care occupations, worsen conditions for the majority of working women. The current emphasis on giving preference to market solutions has also aggravated these cutbacks.

When building families, men are usually learning their trade or occupation, and establishing their position in the labour market. Women still have responsibility for care, both at home and in the public sector. She therefore plans a larger part of her life around the combination of gainful employment and her responsibilities in the home and for the family. She does this by using different strategies for both caring for the family and maintaining her employment. Only by fitting together different working hours, part-time work, and temporary jobs, and relying extensively on public services, can she meet these varying demands.

Consequences of the New Labour Market

As a consequence of the new conditions in the labour market, there is a strong tendency to demand a work force which is available only when needed. These changes to the labour market affect the unemployed, those with temporary employment, and even permanent employees. The recent changes in the work and jobs environment places higher demands especially on women for greater flexibility and adaptability (the economic meltdown of the latter half of 2008, 24x7 jobs). This means that women will have greater difficulty in planning and combining work and family life. However, women feel greater anxiety than men about the changes to the labour market that will affect them. A look at the type of employment for women indicates they have a more insecure situation on the labour market. Women have temporary jobs to a greater degree than men. And to a much greater extent, they feel they must adapt their working life to their family.

What is Work?

For the framing of development policies, national level statistics is the principal data input, but this is largely impaired by the undercounting of women, both as workers and those available for work. The first barrier is off course the definition of work vis-à-vis women's work. We continue to relate work only to remunerative aspects of work as work. The ideology that all women are primarily 'housewives' and whatever work they do is marginal and secondary to that of men pervades the data system from the formulation of the schedule design to actual data collection and reporting, Conceptually, the multiple roles played by women at different levels of economic life are not perceived because of the definition of work as 'for pay or profit'.

The total share of employment by women world-wide is around 40 percent (2006); this makes them indispensable contributors to the national economies. But still the women's proportion of the world's poor and working poor continues to increase. Estimates suggest that more than 60 percent of the world's working poor comprise women, and given the inequalities in the labour market women will find it more difficult to escape poverty.

As mentioned earlier women and men commonly perform divergent tasks, work in different sectors and in different positions. The majority of women work in the informal economy in domestic work and street vending and from their homes.

Globally, women suffer more from job insecurity, limited possibilities for training and promotion, and low or no social benefits (e.g. insurance, sick leave).

Women all over the world have generally retained the main responsibility of unpaid work associated with household, childcare & other unpaid duties, such as taking care of sick & elderly relatives. This may continue to be a greater total workload and reduce women's opportunities for rest and restitution outside work. We today are looking at the total workload (paid and unpaid work) of women and men who have chosen to combine an occupational career with family responsibilities

Indian women are engaged in two kinds of work; one that produces an income and other that does not. The former in turn has home-based work and work outside the home. Even within the latter, there are many components that are not 'pure' domestic work like cooking, cleaning, child care but encompass post-harvest processing, livestock maintenance, gathering of fuel, fodder, water and forest produce, unpaid family labour in the family farm or family enterprise and so on.

Even where women are doing work which is market-oriented, the special characteristics of women's work make such work 'invisible', as for example, home-based piece rate workers. The Census concept of 'work' overemphasize production for exchange and although it does include some non-market production for own consumption such as cultivation where men are also involved, it excludes by a strange logic other types of production for own consumption such as livestock maintenance (done mostly by women) and hence these figures do not correspond with the non-market output in the national accounts. According to the 1981 Census only a little over 13 percent women are shown as workers, whereas the Report of the National Commission on Self-employed Women, Shram Shakti (1988), states that 89 percent of women workers are in the 'unorganized sector'.

In India, the organized sector accounts for a very small proportion of total employment in the country. At present, the organized sector employs about 8 percent of workers as almost 92 percent employment is provided by the unorganized sector. The unorganized or informal sector consists of production or business units that employ less than 10 persons. This sector is the main source of employment. About 92 percent of country's population is employed in the unorganized sector within this sector; agriculture contributes the largest share of employment. It accounts for nearly 55 percent of total employment in the country. Trade, transport, tourism, roadside restaurants etc; that are run on a small-scale are also sources of informal employment.

Feminization of Work

The phrase feminization of work in the sense it is being used now was probably first employed systematically by Guy Standing of the ILO (Standing, 1989). The article included data from various countries at different stages of development; it showed that, since about the mid-sixties, there has been a widespread trend towards a higher share of women workers in the labour force of both developed and developing countries.

Without getting into the question regarding Standings viewpoint the question is: if feminization of the workforce were to take place, would it necessarily be empowering for women? Of the two current views on this issue, that of Standing and his friends is that feminization does little to reduce women's subordination and may even enhance it. The other point of view has been put forward, among others by Sen (1990), and claims that wage work increases the bargaining power of women in the household and the economy and is therefore empowering. This though is more complex and more research needs to continue.

As Banerjee (2008) suggests the problem is, in most cases that the initial position of the woman at the entry to the labour market is such that her expected income from the work is poor and uncertain; it is by no means sufficient for her to live singly. Added to that are the problems associated with the society's reaction to women who seek divorce or try to find a living on their own. Therefore, at least in South Asian countries, women are rarely able or willing to walk out of the marital home. In that case, wage work outside the house increases her sharing her housework. Perhaps the jobs in the export factories, however exploitative they might be, at least give women an opportunity to find a way of living with other women and to draw strength from them in her deals with the family. So, unlike what Sen has claimed, Banerjee does not think that work by itself would always give women the necessary bargaining strength; but factory work, especially when it brings women into close contact with others in a similar situation, may well do so.

How Women and Men Conceptualize Health?

It is a well known fact that women report more health problems than men, almost regardless of the type of complaint; at the same time there is no consensus on the reason for this phenomenon. But what is interesting in the context of gender differences in health complaints is how women and men conceptualize health. Blaxter (1990) found that women showed a stronger tendency to express multi-dimensional concepts of health and were much more likely than men to identify psychological factors, family structure and social relationships as being important influence on health.

In addition Walters (1993) found in study that stress became central theme among women they asked to identify three main health problems. This is true both for developed and developing countries and raises the question of whether women experience more unhealthy or stressful psycho- social conditions than men. A condition that might contribute to this possibility is if women in paid jobs assume the main responsibility for home and family to a much higher degree than men.

The point at which work related problems will be accepted by the legislators and other concerned persons/organizations depends on the current social climate and is related to historical and cultural factors in a society including attitudes toward men and women. Societal values and preconceptions are being constantly altered, by new knowledge, which contains both apparent and obscure messages that affect society sub-consciously. This is important for understanding working conditions for men and women and their relationship to health in different countries, different classes and social group a look at the official statistics for the distribution of the labour force by area of work in any country always shows a more or less skewed distribution.

New technology is being developed and used in both new and old industries. Demand for outdated skills therefore shrinks, while workers with training in the newer techniques are in high demand. "Flexible specialization" production has been developed, resulting in quick changes to the products made. New forms of training are developed within the company rather than in colleges and universities.

At the same time, new forms of production and working are being used. These include systems such as flexible tasking, distance work, "just-in-time" employment, short-term employment, and "consultant" hiring. The public debate is focused largely on the conflict between the goals of a profit oriented economy and the goals of public well-being aimed at meeting certain societal needs. The new conditions also affect employee attitudes towards employers. The worsened conditions at the workplace and in working life may result in decreased confidence in employers. Ill-health caused when patterns of reliance between employees and employers break down as a result of the insecure labour market. Loss of confidence in employers can be seen as the cause of a type of ill-health. Because women have a more insecure position in this market, they are more likely to experience symptoms related to this ill-health syndrome than men.

Occupational Safety and Health of Men and Women

Michael Quinlin in the Australian Journal: Labour History (No. 37, 1997), suggested that occupational safety and health has been neglected by historians in most countries, despite an increasing interest in social history and labour history since 1960's. Problems concerning working conditions and work safety have not been acknowledged as an independent field of research. The issues of occupational safety and health remain largely ignored because of the nature of women's work itself which continues to be largely invisible, unpaid and home-based. The individual's outlook on the future employment situation, considering both the possibilities and risks, can be related to such problems as fatigue, listlessness, indigestion, insomnia, and more among both women and men there are problems which are work related but have not yet been acknowledged as such.

Women's visible presence in paid employment, formal as well as informal, has initiated research on one hand on how their health should be protected, and on the other on how gender affects their health related to work Differences in ill-health are referred to two main categories; the biological that stress the body and the socio-cultural that stress health related behaviour and life-conditions. It is important to note that both modes of explanations simultaneously are necessary to understand the concept. Hence, the concept of health should be understood in this wider perspective. Access and regulations in work life regarding health resources, economic and social factors and power-structures in work-life have a crucial importance in relation to where the line is drawn between health and ill-health.

The integration of a gender perspective in occupational health should be made to ensure that work is safe and healthy for both men and women, taking into account their social specificities. When consideration of women 's family roles is integrated, it may also be necessary to make a different definition of a risky paid work schedule, in order to include those that make it particularly difficult to combine work and family.

When considering women in health and safety work questions, relevant questions to men will be considered at the same time. For example in the case of weight and size differences among persons of one sex are much greater than those between men and women. Therefore, if you make work and work-tools better adapted to women it means that you also make them more accessible to all.

Adjusting statistically for gender instead of analyzing data separately for women and men limits information on the entire population...In fact less information loss will be the result if you analyse data separately for men and women that means to use data in a gender-sensitive way (Westberg,)

As mentioned before women and men are often found in different occupations but also when they are supposed to have the same occupation their job-tasks often differ. One result of the separated labour-market is that in many occupations there are significant differences between the tasks women and men perform and this naturally leads to their experiencing different problems related to the work environment.

As gender inequality both in and outside the workplace can have an impact on women's occupational safety and health, it should be included or 'mainstreamed' into equality agendas. The risk of ignoring gender or taking a gender 'neutral' approach has in fact led to:

- gender differences being obscured or overlooked,
- less attention being paid to some research areas more related to women, and
- the extent of risks to women being underestimated.

But on the other hand when gender has been taken into account the focus has been on women as child bearers, which has led to other reproductive hazards faced, such as menstruation, menopause. Relationships within the family have also changed over time, not least with the introduction of dual-earner model.

Negotiations and practical compromises in daily life mean that women and men spend a lot of time, commitment and energy piecing together the 'jigsaw' of daily life. However, women still assume a relatively large share of the responsibility for ensuring that the balance between work and family life functions they interrupt their careers when the children are born and then in order to cope with everyday family business, often work part while the children are small.

Usually, it is the women who make adjustments in their lives to help aged parents or other close relatives in need of care. Responsibility for the family's social connections with friends and relatives as well as the task of keeping track of school outings, doctors appointments or parent meetings, are further areas of responsibility that often fall to women's lot. A gender based division of labour is thus noticeable, despite progress towards greater equality.

The strategy in present day development policy and planning should be to (a) follow a policy of gender mainstreaming and (b) Focus areas. Gender mainstreaming means that a gender equality perspective is to be incorporated at all levels and in all stages in the decision-making processes. Focus areas are representation, that is, equal access to positions of power and influence and equal work for equal pay.

Women Work and Health Congresses

A very successful initiative to improve the situation for women's occupational safety and health took place in Spain 1993. This initiative has had a great importance for the interchange and stimulation of research, knowledge and actions in the field of women, work and health. The Centre for Analysis and Sanitary Programs (CAPS) in Barcelona organized an International Workshop Women, Health and Work, in 1993. At this workshop the participants decided to launch the International Congress on Women, Health and Work with the intention to gather research and knowledge about the differences between disease in women and men.

The First "Women, Work and Health" Congress took place in Barcelona, Spain in 1996. The Congress decided to continue working as a network so as to preserve the information gathered from the research done by the different groups. Another important outcome from the Congress was the intention to make special efforts to introduce gender issues and point out differences in disease for women and men at universities and at all teaching levels in Health Sciences.

The second Congress was held in Rio de Janeiro, Brazil in 1999 and the outcome was a wide variety of approaches, experiences and proposals. From the scientific point of view important subjects were looked into and new issues added about the relationship between gender, work and health.

The third Congress was held in Stockholm, Sweden in 2002 with the intention of having an international and inter-disciplinary Congress to bring together scholars, activists, representatives of civil society organizations and trade unions, of government agencies and persons involved in practical work from all parts of the world for critical discussions on questions related to women's working conditions, their living conditions and gender-specific issues related to health/ill health. The intention was to continue the intense debate that started in Barcelona and Rio de Janeiro and to leave a legacy in practice. Therefore, sessions were organized to discuss how best to disseminate information related to women, work and health and how to develop change in practice.

One of the main outcomes of the congress was the creation of different working networks (the most important was an African network) on women's health and work.

The fourth Congress was held in New Delhi, India 2005 and was cantered on the three main themes gender, paid and unpaid work, the changing world of work and scientific health practiced in development. The reason why the organizers of the Congress chose these themes was a result from preparatory country-wide regional workshops where researchers, non-governmental organizations, unions and persons involved in practical work gathered and discussed gender, work and health issues.

In India, as in other developing countries, women have always worked in informal sectors, and their work is not acknowledged as such. The work of women is still ignored in the agendas of developing countries, as well as their security and health, including their reproductive health. An initiative called "Woman, Work and Health Initiative Asia" was created for the advancement of the research findings linked to the reality experienced by women, so as to have a positive impact in their lives and work conditions.

The mission of this initiative is to recognize women's work in its entirety in the organized, unorganized sectors and the domestic sphere.

Create awareness on women's issues e.g. gender discrimination, decent work, violence at work and home, knowledge dissemination, life style related health issues, adult literacy and sustainable development.

The Fifth Congress was held in Zacatecas in Mexico 2008

with the general objective to give continuity to the four previous events, in respect to the discussion and creation of an agenda focused on women's work and health issues, as well as organizational issues. The following specific objectives were the focus:

- To continue the discussions on the main subjects related to women's work and health issues at the local, national, Latin American and international levels.
- To make progress in the organization of women for the improvement of paid and unpaid work conditions at the local and global levels.
- To network/promote the coordination of efforts amongst all actors, whose mission is a commitment towards women, focused on work and health issues?

The Congress laid emphasis on the themes of Situation of the work market, non-remunerated work, work organization; work conditions and work environment, public and private policies, rights and justice, methodologies (training, action, human resources education and research).

The series of Women Work and Health Congresses have played an important role as they have opened up for an interchange of knowledge between developed and developing countries and between researchers, different organizations, unions, persons involved in practical work with the focus on issues that are central above all for women and their conditions of work and health.

References

Bannerjee Nirmala. How real is the bogey of Feminization? In Women's Studies in India Edited by John E. Mary (2008).

Bildt Carina. A theoretical Model of Various Causes of Musculskeltal Disorders. In selected readings IV International Congress Women, Work and Health. Edited by Sahaya Amita, 2008.

Blaxter, M. Health and Lifestyle, London, Routledge, 1990.

Copsey Sarah. Gender Issues in safety and health at work-A Review, European agency for Safety and Health at work: 2003.

Gender Equality, Work and Health: A review of the evidence. World Health Organization 2006.

Ghosh J. Macro-economic dynamics and female employment: India in the Asian context. Paper presented at the seminar on Gender and Employment in India, organized by the Indian Society of Labour Economics and the Institute of Economic Growth, New Delhi.1996.

Krishmaraj Maithreyi, Women's Work in Indian Census: Beginnings of Change in Women's Studies in India Edited by John E. Mary (2008).

Lundberg Ulf, Krantz Gunilla. Gender, Work and Health. In Selected Readings IV International Congress Women, Work and Health. Edited by Sahaya Amita, 2008

Messing Karen, Ph.D. CINBIOSE, Université du Québec, Montréal, Canada and Östlin Piroska, Ph.D. Karolinska Institute, Stockholm, Sweden in Women's Health at Work. Kilbom Åsa, Messing Karen and Bildt Torbjörnsson Carina (eds.) 1998.

Omvedt, Gail. Effects of agricultural development on the status of women. Paper prepared for ILO Tripartite Asian regional Seminar on Rural development and Women, Mahabaleshwar, India, April 6-11, 1981.

Sen, A. K. Gender and cooperative conflicts. In *persistent inequalities,* ed. I. Tinker. Oxford University Press, Oxford, New York. 1990.

Shah, N. et al. Structural adjustment, feminization of labour and organizational strategies. *Economic and Political Weekly,* Vol. 24, No. 18. 30 April, 1994.

Standing. G, (1989), Global feminization through flexible labour. World Development, Vol. 17, No. 7.

Visaria, P. Levels and pattern of women's employment in India, 1911-1994 Paper presented at the seminar on Gender and Employment in India, organized by the Indian Society of Labour Economics and the Institute of Economic Growth, New Delhi.1996.

Westberg H. Flexible Labour Markets and Welfare Systems in Sweden. (Working Paper) National Institute for Working Life, Stockholm.1996.

Westberg Hanna. Development in Gender Processes. Paper presented at V Women, Work and Health Congress, Zacatecas, Mexico, and 27-31 October, 2008.

Westberg Hanna. Different Worlds. In Women's Health at Work. Kilbom Åsa, Messing Karen and Bildt Torbjörnsson Carina (eds.) 1998

10

Gender Differences in Financial Decision-making

Bindu Arora, Patiraj Kumari and Yasmeen Ansari

Introduction

When dealing with financial decision making, one is often confronted with a gender stereotype, i.e. with the opinion that women are more risk averse than men. An increasing number of financial studies conclude that women invest their asset portfolios more conservatively than their male counterparts. Although there is a large body of literature on gender differences in investments, examination of differences in investment behaviour is a relatively new avenue for research. The existence of gender differences raises important questions, particularly in light of the recent trend toward investment patterns of men and women. However, assuming that this is a cause for concern, appropriate policy interventions can be more effectively designed with better understanding of the fundamental causes for differences. This issue is important not only to investors, but also to sponsors and professionals who provide investment information to clients. Hence, this paper focuses on the gender differences in investment behaviour, their demographic characteristics and development of gender-specific guidelines to develop investment habits among the investors.

Background Review

Recent economic trends have shown that individuals and households are becoming increasingly responsible for their own financial security. Financial security greatly depends on the ability to save and invest one's earnings. It can help individuals and households better cope with unexpected life events. Perhaps most importantly, it can be a significant source of retirement income for individuals and families who are less able to rely on Social Security alone. One source of concern, especially in today's economic climate, is the persistent gap in investment behaviour between men and women. Women's investment has historically been lower than men's for several reasons, including social and various demographic concerns. However, the difference continues to be significant even after controlling for individual characteristics (Schmidt and Sevak, 2006).

Women's investment choices are different from men's. Sunden and Surette (1998) found that demographics, financial characteristics, and attitudes were important controls, but that these did not fully explain gender differences. While there is not a known psychological reason why gender should matter, it may be that gender is a parody for other factors that influence financial decisions like risk aversion and financial literacy. There is evidence that women are more risk averse than men in general and this translates to investing in less risky assets in their investment plans (Agnew, Balduzzi and Sunden, 2003). Differences in financial literacy between men and women may also explain differences in their investment decision. In most studies measuring financial literacy, women score lower than men, and it is possible that literacy is driving the investment decisions among men and women. In fact, Dwyer, Gilkeson and List (2002) find that the gender differences observed in mutual fund investment decisions can be largely explained by differences in knowledge.

Risk tolerance is the acceptable amount of risk an individual investor is willing to undertake. While risk tolerance is only an individual preference, large deviations of risk preference between social groups of people (e.g., race, education) can lead to different portfolio returns and wealth inequalities. High-risk investors are more likely to invest in annuities, corporate bonds, and stocks than cash deposits, money market accounts, and cash (e.g., savings accounts and money market funds). It is a widespread belief that women are more risk averse than men in making financial decisions. This belief can have critical implications for the financial well-being of women (Schubert, Brown, Gysler, and Brachinger, 1999). In a survey of mutual fund investors, Dwyer et al. (2002) found that women took less risk than men in their mutual fund investment decisions. However, the impact of gender on risk-taking was reduced significantly when they controlled for the investor's financial knowledge.

Methodology

On the basis of preceding discussions, this study is based on the responses of an incidentally selected national sample of 500 respondents. The study is mainly confined to north India while few more states have also been included in this study. The population of U.P., Bihar, Uttarakhand and Delhi are mainly covered while few cases from Mumbai, Bangalore and Chennai have also been included. The two variables of this study are investment patterns and demographic variables (age, profession, education and income) of the investors in relation to gender. In order to measure the demographic characteristics and investment patterns of the investors, a self-designed questionnaire was constructed and administered on the selected sample. The questionnaire is based on various aspects of respondents' investment behaviours, attitudes and beliefs. The investors' were contacted through share brokers, banks, financial institutions, relatives, family and friends.

Findings

Demographic Characteristics in Relation to Gender: In this section, different demographic characteristics of the respondents with emphasis on gender were analyzed. These characteristics include age, education, profession, and income.

About three-fourth (84.4 percent) of the respondents were males and one-fourth (15.6 percent) of the respondents were females. It is evident from the information presented in Table 10.1 that the percentage of males and females was 15.8 percent and 7 percent below the age group of 25 years. In the age group of 25 to 40 years the percentage of males was 38.8 percent and females were 6.8 percent respectively. 23.6 percent and 1 percent respectively were between 40-60 years in comparison to small percentage of above 60 years of age (6.2 percent and 0.8 percent) (Table 10.1).

Table 10.1: Age, Education, Profession and Income of Respondents

Variables	Total		Men		women	
	N	percent	N	percent	N	percent
	500	100	422	84.4	78	15.6
Age						
Below 25 years	114	22.8	79	15.8	35	7
25-40 years	228	45.6	194	38.8	34	6.8
40-60 years	123	24.6	31	23.6	5	1
Above 60 years	35	7	31	6.2	4	0.8
Profession						
Professional	124	24.8	108	21.6	16	3.2
Academicians	127	25.4	85	17	42	8.4
Managers	83	16.6	76	15.2	7	1.4
Businessman	106	21.2	101	20.2	5	1
Any other	60	12	52	10.4	8	1.6
Education						
Intermediate	21	4.2	18	3.6	3	0.6
Graduates	149	29.8	130	26	19	3.8
Post-graduates	283	56.6	235	47	48	9.6
Any other	47	9.4	39	10.4	8	1.6
Income (in ₹)						
1 lakh-1.5 lakh	108	21.6	78	15.6	30	6
1.5 lakh-3 lakh	261	52.2	225	45	36	7.2
3 lakh-5 lakh	107	21.4	96	19.2	11	2.2
Above 5 lakh	24	4.8	23	4.6	1	0.2

Respondents were asked to provide information about their

current profession. As can be seen from the Table 10.1, there were notable differences between the profession of males and females in the study. The percentage of males employed in the professional category was 21.6 percent in comparison to females (3.2 percent). They were engineers, physicians and architects. On the other hand, more males (17 percent) than females (8.4 percent) were academicians. Much more males (15.2 percent) than females (1.4 percent) held managerial positions such as financial analysts, executives and managers. Much more males than females were self-employed in business and management. 10.4 percent of males in comparison to females (1.6 percent) employed in any other areas such as administrators, technicians and programmers etc.

Participants were also asked to indicate about their education status. More males (47 percent) in comparison to females (9.6 percent) were holding postgraduate degrees while 26 percent and 3.8 percent males and females. Respondents' Demographic Characteristics were holding graduate degree respectively.

Very negligible percentage (3.6 percent and 0.6 percent) of respondents held intermediate certificates while 10.4 percent and 1.6 percent respectively were holding any other degree such as M.Phil, Ph.D, and LL.B etc. Respondents were also asked to report about their income status. It has been found that the largest income group earned by the respondents was between ₹ 1.5 lakh to ₹ 3 lakh. Compared to their male counterparts, women had lower income group and faced greater financial obligations.

Investment Patterns

Investment patterns mean putting one's money to work for them or it's a different way to think about how to make money. This includes putting money into stocks, bonds, mutual funds, real estate and gold etc. Participants were asked to indicate their objective for money investing/spending. Response categories include *car purchase, children's education, payment for a home/down payment, savings for retirement, vacation, business and any other*. Responses showed that 9.2 percent of males invest for car purchase in comparison to females (1.8 percent). 26.2 percent and 5.4 percent correspondingly invest for their children's education.

As per findings the males take the most responsibility for making the payment of home/down payment as compared with females. The percentage is being 9.6 percent and 1 percent respectively. 10.2 percent of males and 1.6 percent of females invest for their retirement while 3.4 percent of males and 1.6 percent of females invest for their vacation. 16.8 percent of males and 3 percent females invest for business and a very small proportion of males (6 percent) and females (1.2 percent) invest in any other activities such as children's marriage, higher education etc.

Participants were asked to respond whether they contribute regularly for their saving plan for future needs or not. A larger percentage of males (75.6 percent) than females (10.8 percent) reported 'yes' for regularly contributing for their savings for future needs. On the other hand, a very small proportion of males (8.8 percent) and females (4.8 percent) reported 'no' for contributing for their future needs.

Participants were asked to account for their investment reasons for investing. Possible responses include *risk coverage, tax benefits, returns, safety and protection from inflation*. 33.4 percent of males in comparison to females 6.2 percent reported that they preferred for safety than returns (18.2 percent and 2.8 percent). More males (16 percent) than females (4 percent) reported for risk coverage, tax benefits (11.6 percent and 1.6 percent) and negligible percentage of the sample investigated would like to protect them from inflation. The percentage being 5.2 percent and 1 percent respectively.

Source of Financial Information

It explored the various sources of financial information that respondents used for financial decisions. We asked how frequently they have obtained investment information from *TV, radio, books, magazines, newspapers, internet, investment newsletter, family/friends, professional advisors* and *any other*. More males (15.8 percent) in comparison to females (1.6 percent) read newspapers for investment guidance, 13.8 percent males and 2 percent females reported that they access internet or investment related websites, 12.4 percent and 3.2 percent correspondingly take advice from their family/friends, whereas 10.8 percent and 2.4 percent seek advice from professional advisors in order to make right investment decisions. A small percentage (9.2 percent and 1.8 percent) watches TV programs while very small percentage of respondents (2.4 percent and 0.2 percent) listen radio for getting information related to investment and financial institutions. A much smaller percentage refers books (5.8 percent and 2.2 percent), magazines (8.2 percent and 1.6) and investment newsletters (5.8 percent and 0.4 percent) for this purpose. The negligible but the same percentage (0.2 percent) in both the cases of the investigated sample shows interest in any other areas such as participating in investment clubs, conferences, seminars or workshops.

Time Spent on Investment Activities

Participants were asked to think about the time duration they devote for their investment activities. Responses include *2-5 hrs./week, 2-5 hrs./month, 2-5 hrs./year, most of my spare time* and *as little time as possible*. More males (23.4 percent) than females (5 percent) devote their 2-5 hrs./month in investment related activities. More males than females spend as little time as possible (18.6 percent and 2.8 percent) whereas 17.2 percent and 2 percent spend 2-5 hrs/year in investment actions. More males (16.8 percent) than females (3.6 percent) spend 2-5 hrs./week whereas small percentage (8.4 percent and 2.2 percent) spent most of their spare time in investment activities.

For information gathered in response to the question, "how

much you rate your investment knowledge", the possible responses were *minimal, modest, moderate, good* and *very good.* It can be found from the information provided by the respondents that much more males (30 percent) in comparison to females (4 percent) reported for moderate knowledge. Similarly, more males (21.8 percent) than females (3.8 percent) reported for good knowledge. A small percentage of the sample investigated (12 percent and 2 percent) reported for modest knowledge and 11.6 percent and 4.6 percent respond for minimal knowledge and similarly 9 percent and 1.2 percent have a very good knowledge about investment related activities.

Participants were asked to respond the reasons for which they tend to sell their liquidate investments. Various responses included here are *my advisors recommends I sell, of market fluctuations, need money for buying a home/car, the news lines suggest the market is going down* and *any other.* The information reveals that a majority of males (25 percent) than females (3.4 percent) sell because their advisor recommends them to sell whereas more males (19 percent) than females (4.4 percent) sell because the news lines suggest the market is going down. 18 percent and 5 percent respectively sell because of market fluctuations. A small percentage of respondents (16.6 percent and 2.6 percent) sell because they need money to buy a home/car whereas a very small percentage (5.8 percent and 0.2 percent) sell for any other reason such as for higher education, invest in some other assets or for expanding their business.

It explored the actions investors take when they would sell their investments. They were asked to respond to the following responses: *buy another investment, put money in a money market fund, partly invested and partly use to buy something, ask for investment advice* and *don't know what they would do.* As per the findings the males (30 percent) partly invested and partly use to buy something as compared to females (7.2 percent). More males (19.8 percent) than females (1.8 percent) put the money in a money market fund. Similarly, 17.4 percent and 3.8 percent respectively, buy other investments. A small percentage of respondents (13.2 percent and 1.8 percent) asked for investment advice and a negligible percentage (3.6 percent and 1 percent) of respondents don't know what to do with the sold investments.

Opinions of Investors towards Financial Advisor

Participants' were presented the various qualities such as *trust, education, helps in dealing with financial stress, confidentiality, investment knowledge, fee structure* and *an ongoing relationship*. The findings indicate that the most of the males (19.9 percent) look for investment knowledge in their financial advisor than females (3.4 percent). A large percentage of males (18.8 percent) in contrast to females (2 percent) favoured educated financial advisor. More males (17.6 percent) desire confidentiality in comparison to females (2.4 percent) similarly, (14.6 percent and 4.4 percent) likes advisors who help them in dealing with their financial stress. Small percentages (7.6 percent and 2.4 percent) of respondents have faith in their financial advisor. More males (3.4 percent) than females (0.6 percent) have a liking for fee structure and an ongoing relationship (3.4 percent and 0.4 percent) with their financial advisor.

How long they have been the investors? This question inquired about for how long they have been the investors. This measure captures respondents' confidence in investment activities. Respondents were asked to respond in the categories of, *0-2 years, 2-5 years, 5-10 year*, and *more than 10 years*. Overall more males (26.2 percent) than females (5.2 percent) have been in investment activities for 2-5 years; more males (21.2 percent) in contrast to females (6 percent) have been into investment from 0-2 years. 18.6 percent and 2.8 percent respectively have been into the investment for the last 5-10 years whereas 18.4 percent and 1.6 percent are continuing their investment for more than 10 years investment.

Short-term vs. Long-term Investments

To gather rather extensive information about participants' confidence about the time period they consider that they would like to remain in their investment activities, they were asked to respond for: *less than 3 months*, *3-6 months*, *1-2 years*, *2-3 years* and *more than 3 years*. As per findings, most of the males (23.2 percent) than females (3.6 percent) would like to remain invested for more than 3 years. Findings suggest that 20.2 percent males than 6.8 percent females would like to invest for 1-2 years and 17.6 percent and 2 percent respectively would like to be invested for 2-3 years and the percentages for the 3-6 months are 16.4 and 1.6. Negligible percentage of the sample investigated (7 percent and 1 percent) reported for less than three months investment period.

Types of Investment

Participants were asked to respond for the investment avenues they hold from the available choices: *stocks, mutual funds, real estate, government securities such as NSS, NSC, PPF and KVP, gold, art and paintings and any other*. The information indicated more males (28.4 percent) than females (3.8 percent) have invested in government securities such as NSC, NSS, PPF and KVP. 25.4 percent of males in comparison to females 3.8 percent would like to invest in mutual funds while 14.2 percent and 4 percent respectively invest in real estate. A small percentage (9.4 percent and 2.4 percent) likes to invest in gold and a much smaller percentage (4 percent and 0.8 percent) would like to invest in stocks. It is also supported by the findings of Bernasek and Shwiff (2001) who found that women invested a significantly lower percentage of their money in stocks. Participants (2.2 percent and 0.6 percent only) report that they invest in any other areas such as diamonds, gems, or bank deposits and similarly negligible percentage of respondents (0.8 percent and 0.2 percent) reported their investment in art and paintings.

Participants were asked to respond by saying '*yes*' or '*no*' about their awareness of financial planning. Responses collected show that majority of males (70 percent) in comparison to females (11 percent) respond for 'yes' whereas a small percentage (14.2 percent and 4.6 percent) respond for 'no' for their awareness about financial planning.

Strategy of Investors in Case the Stocks Slide

Participants were asked to identify about their decisions they will take if their stocks went down 50 percent. They were asked to select any one out of the following choices: *sell it, buy more, hold on at least until it reached at price I originally purchased, consult a professional, contact the company*, and *ignore the loss*. The findings suggest that 25.6 percent of males in comparison to females (4.6 percent) will hold on at least until it reached at price at which they originally purchased, 21.2 percent and 4.6 percent respectively would like to consult a professional and 17.4 percent and 1.8 percent correspondingly would like to sell it. 11.4 percent and 2.4 percent respectively buy more and a negligible percentage of respondents (5 percent and 1.2 percent) want to contact the company and ignore the loss (3.8 percent and 1 percent).

Apprehensions about Investment

This question explored respondents' actions when they have fear about investing. The possible responses include *loosing o money, making a mistake, others finding out I failed, lack of knowledge*, and *lack of experience*. The information reveals that most of the respondents (33.8 percent and 6.2 percent) fear about loosing money, while 20.8 percent and 5 percent point out of making a mistake. Respondents also indicate lack of experience (11.8 percent and 1.8 percent) and knowledge (10.8 percent and 2.4 percent) in investment activities. And a small percentage (7.2 percent and 0.2 percent) shows that they fear from others finding out that they failed.

Gender-specific Guidelines to Develop Investment Habits

On the basis of obtained results we have proposed

following guidelines for developing investment habits among men and women:

- Financial professionals and educators should interpret measures of risk tolerance, especially when working with women. Women may tend to understate their risk tolerance and their observed preference for more conservative investments may result from a lack of financial knowledge. Thus, before recommending overly conservative portfolios to women, there may be a need to better educate women about the risk-return trade-off and help them make more informed choices.
- In addition, there is a need for more specific and targeted financial education to help men and women with their investment decisions. Men may need to be cautioned about the pitfalls of trading excessively, which leads to a fall in investment returns. Women may need additional guidance on how to make investment choices that carry a certain amount of risk so that there is sufficient growth in their savings, particularly for retirement. This information could significantly enhance their retirement security.
- Financial professionals and educators can also use the results from the household bargaining literature to better inform married couples about their financial options and the importance of not leaving the financial decisions entirely to one's spouse. Indeed, husbands and wives could achieve more efficient outcomes by cooperating in the financial planning process rather than by making independent choices.
- Keeping in view of the legislative proposals, it is important that financial professionals and educators communicate to policymakers how the decision-making process within households can affect financial investments. The literature has shown decision-making power and respondents' characteristics can significantly affect their retirement savings decisions. Some investors are likely to be at greater risk than others for being

inadequately prepared for retirement.

Conclusion

In the present investigation we have made efforts to determine whether the variables such as demographic characteristics (age, profession, education and income) and investment patterns could be used individually or in combination to both, differentiate among levels of men and women investment decisions and risk tolerance and develop some guidelines to suggest investors in their investment related activities. This research endeavour has been successful in addressing the dual purpose of the study. First, the demographic characteristics have been found to be effective in differentiating among men and women and secondly studying the investment patterns of both the gender individually and in combination indicates the difference in their investment patterns. These findings may help the investment managers and differentiate them in their investment patterns.

References

Agnew, J. Pierluigi, B. and Sunden. A 2003. "Portfolio choice and trading in a large 401(k) Plan." *The American Economic Review,* 93 (1):193-215.

Bernasek, A., and Shwiff, S. (2001) Gender, risk, and retirement. *Journal of Economic Issues*, 35(2), 345-356.

Dwyer, P. D., Gilkenson, J. H., and List, J. A. (2002). Gender differences in revealed risk taking: Evidence from mutual fund investors. *Economic Letters*, 76(2), 151-58.

Schmidt, Lucie and Sevak, P. (2006). Gender, marriage, and asset accumulation in the United States. *Feminist Economics*, 12(1-2), 139–166.

Schubert, R., Brown, M., Gysler, M., and Brachinger, H. W. (1999). Financial decision-making: Are women really more risk averse? *The American Economic Review Papers and Proceedings*, 89(2), 381-385.

Sundén, A. E., and Surette, B. J. (1998). Gender differences in the allocation of assets in retirement savings plans. *American Economic Review*, 88(2), 207-211.

11

Male-Female Productivity Differentials in the Unorganised Services Sector

Atanu Sengupta, Soumyendra Kishore Datta and Susanta Mondal

Wage-productivity differential between men and women have been studied extensively from a long period of time from the angle of human capital and discrimination. Very few studies cover the unorganised service sector. In this paper, we have studied the productivity differential between male and female in the unorganised service sector in West Bengal and Bihar using the NSSO unit level data. Our study reveals considerable differences in the male-female productivity differential between the male and female labour force in the unorganized service sector. In general, women are less productive in the family farms while they are more productive in the commercial sectors. Increased commercialization has enhanced productivity of female labour force to a considerable extent.

Introduction and Motivation

The interrelationship between productivity differences and wage differential between men and women have been studied extensively from a long period of time from the angle of human capital and discrimination. Most of these studies centres around the field of agriculture and industry. Though a lot of studies have been done on agriculture and industry, there are a very few studies for the informal sector. However, this sector represents an important arena of the nation's overall economic activity. [1] The service sector is often personalized and non-standardized. Here the qualities of the product as well as the delivery are important. Any wage-productivity differential among male and female in this sector remains an interesting subject of study. In the present paper we deal with male female productivity differential in the unorganised service sector in West Bengal and Bihar.

Theoretically a number of issues emanate here. Classicists believed that wage differential exists due to difference in level of skill. According to human capital theorists male-female productivity differential might exist when women accumulate less human capital through work experience due to their relatively short stay in labour market compared to male counterparts. It is also argued that male female productivity differential may be due to a combination of varying degree of work effort as well as mental and physical capabilities. [2] It is argued that male is more suitable for works that requires considerable amount of physical effort than their female counterparts. On the other hand, woman has to bear the burden of household chores (such as baby rearing, cooking, cleansing etc.). [3] This tends to depress their work effort. With increasing commercialization and expansion of market such difficulties should be reduced. In this context it may be said that increased market opportunities could improve female productivity. In the backdrop of the aforesaid analysis it seems imperative to study whether there exists productivity differential between male and female in the informal service sector. Our data set allows us to study such a scenario.

Data and Descriptive Analysis

For our analysis we have used the unit level data of the 57th round of NSSO (National Sample Survey Organisation) published by the Ministry of statistics and programme Implementation of Government of India. This round covered a wide range of economic activities that focused primarily on unorganised service sector [4] (excluding trade and finance) both in *rural* and *urban* areas.

Enterprises are classified into two broad categories-Own account enterprises (OAE) and Establishment. According to the NSSO report "an OAE is an undertaking run by household labour, usually without any hired worker employed on a 'fairly regular basis'. By 'fairly regular basis' it was meant that the employment was for a major part of the period of operation(s) of the enterprise during the last 365 days." On the other hand, "an establishment is an enterprise that employed at least one hired worker on a 'fairly regular basis'." Paid or unpaid apprentices paid household members/servant/resident workers in an enterprise were considered to be hired workers. In short, we can treat OAE as household enterprises while establishment as fully commercial enterprises. Their comparison would shed light on the impact of commercialization in the informal service sector.

Among the 35 states and union territories of India we have selected only two states—West Bengal and Bihar for our study. Because of neighbouring these two states have many common features. Again there are wide socio-economic differences between these two states. It is interesting to study how these socio-economic differences have been reflected in the service sector activities.

First we consider the region wise (rural/urban) and type wise (OAE/Establishment) breakdown of the enterprises as provided in Table 11.1 below. It has been observed that nearly 74 percent of all enterprises in WB and Bihar were OAEs that operated without engaging any hired worker on a regular basis and the remaining 24 percent enterprises operates with hired labour. The picture clearly depicts the features of an underdeveloped economy where labour market has not been fully commercialized.

We now consider the ownership pattern of these enterprises. From Table 11.2, we see that male dominates in the proprietorship of enterprises in both states. However the percentage is higher in Bihar than WB. Female proprietorship in WB is doubled than Bihar. This directly hints at a lower social status of females than males in Bihar compared to WB.

Table 11.1: No. of Enterprises

Type	West Bengal			Bihar		
	Rural	Urban	Total	Rural	Urban	Total
OAE	12156	13085	25241 (73.93)	7026	10457	17483 (74.26)
Establishment	2680	6219	8899 (26.07)	1752	4308	6060 (25.74)
Total	14836	19304	34140	8778	14765	23543

* Figures in the bracket represent the percentage of total.

Table 11.2: Ownership of Enterprises

	West Bengal	Bihar
Proprietary (Male)	87.37	94.06
Proprietary (Female)	7.78	3.87
Partnership with members of the same household	1.75	0.76
Partnership between members not all from the same household	1.41	0.93
Co-operative society	0.08	0.05
Limited company (Outside public sector)	0.44	0.07
Others	1.17	0.27

* All the figures are in percentage form.

An important socio-economic characteristic is the social group of ownership of the enterprises (Table 11.3). In WB, ST-SC-OBC group accounts only 26 percent whereas in Bihar it figures 67 percent. Thus, social ownership of enterprises is biased towards upper class in WB, while the opposite happens in Bihar.

However, a majority of the enterprises in both the states are not registered under companies act (Table 11.4). The percentage is slightly higher in Bihar than WB. That is why from Table 11.5 we see that most of the enterprises do not maintain any account of their activities. This depicts the feature of unorganised sector of an underdeveloped economy where the administrative control over the unorganised sector is not so strong.

Table 11.3: Social Group of Owner

	West Bengal	Bihar
S.T.	1.07	0.31
S.C.	18.35	11.88
OBC	7.68	56.11
Others	71.41	31.30
Code not mentioned	1.49	0.39

*all the figures are in percentage form.

Table 11.4: Whether Registered under Companies Act?

	West Bengal	Bihar
Yes	2.79	3.33
No	97.21	96.04

* All the figures are in percentage form.

Table 11.5: Whether Accounts Maintained

	West Bengal	Bihar
Yes	3.46	1.38
Otherwise	96.50	98.18
Not mentioned	0.04	0.01

* All the figures are in percentage form.

We now consider the composition of labour force in the unorganized service sector of both the states (Table 11.6). In both the states most male and female work in the unorganised sector on full time basis. The figures are slightly higher in Bihar than WB. However the dominance of full time job in this sector is considerably diluted for the females as compared to the males.

However if we consider the distribution of labour according to hired-family category, a different picture emerges. In both the states, a huge proportion of female labour employed is hired labour.

Table 11.6: Full Time and Part Time Workers

Nature of workers	West Bengal	Bihar
Full time male	90.72	94.96
Part time male	9.28	5.04
Full time female	79.62	81.97
Part time female	20.38	18.03

* All the figures are in percentage form.

In fact this is larger than the proportion of male labours that are employed and hired (Table 11.7). This shows that females are more preferred to males as hired workers. This tend to support the general view that many service activities are disproportionately represented by female workers as there are relatively few barriers such as skill and education to enter this sector. Higher percentage of (both family and hired) female workers in WB shows that women in WB have been able to take advantage of increased commercialization of service activities. This increased participation may be guided by the urge to generate more income for the family to increase the standard of living.

Table 11.7: Own, Hired and Other workers

Nature of workers	West Bengal	*Bihar*
Family Labour-Male	49.56	55.14
Hired Male	44.19	33.37
Others Male	6.45	11.49
Family Labour-Female	31.35	29.82
Hired Female	59.06	41.50
Others Female	6.24	28.69

* All the figures are in percentage form.

Framework of Analysis

In order to assess male female productivity differentials

across different types of enterprises, we consider a simple production function of the type:

$$y = g(K, L(L_f, L_m)) \tag{1}$$

Where K is the capital stock and L the labour input that is a function of female labour input (L_f) and male labour input (L_m). The exact form of the labour input function will depend on the assumption of separability.

A group of economists (Jacoby 1992, 1993; S Koufias 1994, Abdulai and Regmi 2000) assumed that:

$$L(L_f, L_m) = \varphi(L_f)\delta(L_m) \tag{2}$$

The production function can be written simply as:

$$y = f(K, L_f, L_m) \tag{3}$$

In this case, the *shadow wages* (or marginal products) are (Jacoby 1992, 1993; Skoufias 1994, Abdulai and Regmi 2000):

$$w_f^* = \frac{\partial y}{\partial L_f} \tag{4a}$$

$$w_m^* = \frac{\partial y}{\partial L_m} \tag{4b}$$

these shadow wages reflect male-female productivity differential in the *perfect separability* case. The basic assumption in this model is a utility maximizing productive unit [5] that consumes leisure, home goods and market produced goods (Jacoby 1992, 1993; Skoufias 1994, Abdulai and Regmi 2000).

$$U = U(C, T_f^e, T_m^e, Z) \tag{5}$$

where T_f^e and T_m^e are the leisure enjoyed by female and male members, C is the total consumption that is the sum of home produced goods (Q) and market purchased goods (G) while Z captures certain family characteristics. The budget constraint is given by the amount of market good that is purchased from the market. This in turn depends on family's income. Jacoby (1993) assumes that the income has three components: (i) net profit from family business (Π) (ii) labour income from hiring out family member (*FML*) and (iii) household's non-farm non-labour income net of fixed costs (*V*). Symbolically the budget constraint is:

$$G = \Pi + FML + V \tag{6}$$

Now it is clear that these components of (6) depend on a set of parameters. Net profit from family business (Π) is determined among other things the volume of marketed goods (*y*). Similarly, the labour income (*FML*) depends on the running market wage (*w*). Lastly, household's net non-labour income (*V*) can be assessed from the volume of home goods (*Q*). In effect thus, the productive unit faces two types of production functions. The production function for the good that the unit sells in the market is given as:

$$y = f(K, L_f, L_m, E) \tag{7}$$

The equation is basically the same as (3) with *E* representing some fixed inputs that are relevant for producing *y*. Similarly one can describe home goods' production function as:

$$Q = Q(S_m, S_f, A) \tag{8}$$

where S_i is the amount of labour of the type *i* *(i=f, m)* that is used in home production and A is vector of fixed inputs necessary for home production.

A productive unit is assumed to maximize the utility function (5) given the budget constraint (6) that incorporates both the production functions (Equation 7 and 8). It is assumed that the commodity *y* (that is either produced by the firm or purchased from the market) is perfectly substitutable with home produced goods *Q*. [6] The first order conditions for this problem state that labourers equate their marginal rate of substitution between consumption and leisure or *shadow wage* either to their market wage or to their marginal product in either farm work or housework. The decision of a labourer to participate in the labour market depends on the shadow wages [7] and the income net of such shadow costs. In the home production literature is defined as *full income*.

For empirical estimation of the model we did not have any data regarding home production. Hence, we concentrated only on the firm production side of these sectors. In this case, the production function will be:

$$y = AK^{\alpha} L_f^{\beta_1} L_m^{\beta_2} \tag{9}$$

Following Jacob (1993), the shadow wage rates (or marginal products) of male and female labourers are calculated from the estimates of Cobb-Douglas production function [8] using the formula:

$$\hat{w}_i = \frac{\hat{\beta}_i \hat{y}_i}{L_i} \qquad i=M, F \tag{10}$$

However even then there exists considerable difference between *actual income* and *full income.* [9]. We may now turn to our empirical results.

Estimation and Results

Next we have considered a few factors which play a significant role on labour productivity. These are given in Table 11.8A and 11.8B. Our results indicate that capital intensity played a significant positive role on labour productivity in both types of enterprises in both the states. The most interesting finding is that the coefficient of the proportion of female to total worker is significantly negative in both the OAE in both the states. This might indirectly hint at a lower productivity of female labour in the OAE. As for Establishment, the coefficient is significantly negative for WB while positive for Bihar. Thus though in Bihar female are more productive than males in the commercial sector, this is not so in the case of West Bengal. The findings seem to support the extended Becker's hypothesis regarding male female dichotomy in work effort that incorporates the effect of increased commercialization is applicable for Bihar though not for WB. However since this an overall estimate for the states as a whole, much conclusion may not derive from it.

Table 11.8A: Sources of productivity variation (WB) (Dependent variable =labour productivity =y/L)

	OAE		Establishment	
Independent Variable	Linear	Log-Linear	Linear	Log-Linear
Constant	18474 (83.74)	72.695 (-0.780)	23677 (19.63)	-1500.1 (-5.556)
K/L	0.025512 (47.80)	0.0097689 (5.068)	0.015027 (14.49)	0.19162 (4.822)
L_f/L	-13088 (-23.47)	-0.00011274 (-0.12630)	-11974 (-3.972)	-0.0045459 (-1.932)
D_1	8773.5 (28.62)	-214.87 (-3.723)	12794 (8.870)	515.37 (2.482)
R^2	0.1284	0.0016	0.0333	0.0033

Notes: 1. Figures in the parentheses represent t-values.
2. K/L = capital Intensity, L_f/L =female labour/total labour.
3. D_1 is the locational dummy (rural/urban).

Table 11.8B: Sources of productivity variation (BIHAR) (Dependent variable =labour productivity =y/L)

	OAE		Establishment	
Independent Variable	Linear	Log-Linear	Linear	Log-Linear
Constant	183.44 (79.68)	-49.423 (-0.5441)	252.61 (33.32	-814.15 (-2.804)
K/L	0.086683 (46.14)	0.024893 (7.051)	0.83310 (27.68)	0.87266 (41.09)
L_f/L	-14435 (-22.02)	-0.00022788 (-0.2532)	1.1693 (10.13)	-0.0059289 (-2.349)
D_1	6086.4 (21.14)	-146.78 (-2.521)	-177.88 (-0.2057)	-83.718 (-0.4796)
R^2	0.1735	0.0030	0.1286	0.2182

Notes: 1. Figures in the parentheses represent t-values.
2. K/L = capital Intensity, L_f/L =female labour/total labour.
3. D_1 is the locational dummy (rural/urban).

In order to solve into this matter at a more micro level, we consider the district break-up in both the states. We have considered averages of six variables–(a) net value of output produced in the unorganized service sector (y), (b) amount of capital used (K), (c) male labour force (L_m) (c) female labour force (L_f), total labour force (L) and proportion of female labour force (L_f/L).

Consider the case of West Bengal. So far as the OAE are considered there is very little variation in L_f/L among the districts-highest being Darjeeling (0.17) and lowest is Murshidabad (0.02). However, highest output produced as well as capital used is in Kolkata. Similarly for Establishment, the highest L_f/L being Maldah (0.14) and lowest is Coochbehar (0.02). However for output and capital the dominating district is Kolkata. The dominance of Kolkata in output produced and capital used for both the categories is quite natural.

Now consider Bihar. For OAE, the highest female proportion is in Siwan (0.14) while the lowest is Araria (0.01). As for output produced the dominating district is Khagaria while that for capital used it is Khagaria. Considering Establishment the highest female proportion is in Nalanda (0.09) while six districts have no female workers. Thus the commercialization of female labour is still very low in Bihar. As for output produced the dominating district is Bagusarai while that for capital used it is Patna.

Next we consider the estimation of shadow wages using the econometric model discussed above. From Tables 11.9A and 11.9B we see that on average male female shadow wage ratio is greater than 1 in OAE in both the states and less than 1 in establishment implying that males are more productive than females in OAE and females are more productive than males in establishment. However, at the district level the picture shows a mixed pattern. In WB out of 18 districts in 13 districts (72 percent) males are more productive whereas in Bihar out of 37 districts in 23 districts (62 percent) males are more productive in OAE. In WB, Burdwan (1.72) and Uttar Dinajpur (1.49) are the top districts in terms of male productivity in OAE. In Bihar Gaya (1.37) and Champaran (E) (1.35) are the toppers in OAE so far as the male productivity are concerned.

Table 11.9A: Male, Female Shadow Wage Ratio: West Bengal

	OAE	Establishment
District	SHL_m/SHL_f	SHL_m/SHL_f
Coochbehar	0.91468051	0.42464268
Jalpaiguri	1.15879267	0.499672542
Darjeeling	0.878281194	0.374184108
Dakshin Dinajpur	0.982429874	0.585171743
Maldah	1.216104522	0.609862385
Murshidabad	1.023216621	0.56512661
Nadia	1.179393664	0.328977062
North 24 Pargana	0.858747037	0.37819939
South 24 Pargana	1.378486876	0.40528866
Kolkata	1.257927827	0.370142546
Howrah	1.179292513	0.318935989
Hoogly	1.192314247	0.423997786
Midnapur	1.218773965	0.489847755
BanKura	0.716357269	0.683302058
Purulia	1.176384922	0.328785277
Burdwan	1.722312206	0.572974612
Birbhum	1.360153304	0.157735477
Uttar Dinajpur	1.497155174	0.378924825
All	1.122577689	0.185961289

However, the situation is totally different in case of establishment enterprises. Here on average females are more productive than males in both the states. However in WB all the 18 states show greater productivity of females as compared to males. Birbhum (0.15) and Howrah (0.31) are at the top of the list. But in Bihar out of 31 districts for which female labour data is available, in 28 districts females are more productive than males. Champaron (E) (0.163) and Sitamarhi (0.169) are the top districts in terms of female productivity.

Table 11.9B: Male, Female Shadow Wage Ratio: Bihar

	OAE	Establishment
District	SHL_m/SHL_f	SHL_m/SHL_f
Champaran (w)	1.071334807	0.522231436
Champaran (E)	1.355989128	0.163839846
Sheohar	0.929079519	0.264395441
Sitamarhi	0.97050719	0.169913503
Madhubani	1.04022226	0.405316015
Supaul	0.811295448	**
Araria	0.615427369	1.090330914
Kishanganj	1.110051143	0.906170885
Purnia	0.951914322	0.392692049
Katihar	1.240893401	0.342762487
Madhepura	1.381758392	**
Sharsa	1.216471423	0.317987124
Darbhanga	1.174774473	0.290528469
Muzafarpur	1.145110642	0.517225027
Gopalganj	1.258252468	0.708894855
Vaishali	0.912172726	0.215976506
Siwan	1.272093803	0.697650647
Vaishali	1.089763554	0.326772593
Samastipur	0.818569983	0.193428637
Bagusarai	0.798691822	0.463303014
Khagaria	0.80421226	0.295942171
Bhagalpur	0.918795374	0.312332305
Banka	0.746788089	**
Munger	0.775070811	1.34646311
Lakhisarai	0.889377704	1.278071757
Sheikhpura	1.152709485	**
Nalanda	1.085338534	0.460939921
Patna	1.049729027	0.378458988
Bhojpur	1.044118104	0.355555723
Buxer	1.180400204	**
Kaimur	1.14143609	0.406636206
Rohtas	1.11906782	0.279409581
Jahanabad	1.094270865	0.321639879

Contd...

Aurangabad	1.049712766	0.178847371
Gaya	1.379490159	0.53946742
Nawada	1.216082159	0.45304563
Jamui	0.742828992	**
ALL	1.090294898	0.376290627

SHL_m- Male shadow wage, SHL_f- Female shadow wage.
** represents non-availability of female data.

Thus in general, males are more productive in OAE and females are more productive in establishment enterprises. This is a potentially significant finding and throws considerable light on the male-female status in the unorganized service sector in India. In the household enterprises (OAE) a women has to conduct several household chores (such as cooking, washing child rearing etc.) besides being a contributor to the family labour force. Male generally do not share equally with women in this context. Naturally women's productivity is adversely affected. Thus, following Becker (1985) a proper evaluation of women's contribution in the household sector must include not only her direct contribution in the production sphere but also her contribution in the reproduction sphere, simply because the latter is essential for successful production activity. [10] The beneficial impact of commercialization on female productivity is manifested in establishments.

Conclusion

In this paper we wished to study male female Productivity differential in the context of unorganized service sector in two states—West Bengal and Bihar. For this we used the NSSO unit level data. It is generally conjectured that female workers have comparative advantage in this sector over males. In a family firm, females are generally weighed down by household chores that prevent them from being productive. However under commercial enterprise where this shackle is not present, they are found to be more productive than the male workers. However, several studies indicated the hapless condition of female labour in these two Eastern states. Increased commercialization may have increased the female productivity but their deprivation goes unabated.

Notes

1. According to an ILO estimate in 2002, about 41 percent of GDP share in the Sub-Saharan Africa may be attributed to the informal sector while the corresponding figure is 31 percent for Asia.
2. Pioneering work has been done by Gunderson (1975, 1989). Oaxaca (1973) was first to decompose of the male female premium into two parts: one that is explained by economic characteristics and a residual. This residual is alleged to be an indicator of gender discrimination (Blau, Ferber and Winkler 1998,). On the other hand a group of writers attribute these differences to the *inherent* differences among men and women (Wise 1975, Duncan 1976, Becker 1985, Long 1995, Hakim 2000, Paarsch and Shearer 2004). These differences may be manifested in mental and physical attributes (such as motivation, aggressiveness, ability to conduct strenuous physical jobs, family attachment etc) as well as preference to certain types of jobs.
3. In fact Becker (1985) has suggested that women have a comparative advantage in high effort domestic tasks which may cause them to supply less effort in the labour market than men.
4. Service activities covered in this survey includes hotels and restaurant; transport, storage and communication; real estate, renting and business activities; education; health and social work; other community, social and personal services.
5. The model is useful in comparing the OAE and Establishment units under informal service sector. OAEs are mostly family enterprises making the analysis appropriate. Arguing that family labour is used even in the Establishment units, the model can capture sufficient amount of reality.
6. This is the standard assumption made by all the authors (Jacoby 1992, 1993; S. Koufias 1994, Abdulai and Regmi 2000). The unit is assumed to have no preference for *home produced goods.*
7. They are already defined in equation (4a) and (4b).
8. Since the inputs themselves are likely to be endogenously determined (Abdulai and Regmi 2000), we have used

instrumental variable method rather than simple OLS to estimate the production function. OLS method may give biased estimates.

9. For example Sen (1964) argued that if we value the family labour according to their market wage, most of the firms would become unremunerative. He suggested the use of shadow price that could appropriately capture such situation.
10. However, Abdulai and Regmi (2000) have found no significant differences in male-female productivity by incorporating time allocated for household purposes in their estimation of labour supply functions. This may however reflect an inherent heterogeneity between time allocated for household chores and that allocated for productivity effort. For females, the former may include a greater intensity of effort per unit of time allocated.

References

Abdulai, A, Regmi, P.P.: "Estimating labour supply of farm households under non-separability: Empirical evidence from Nepal." *Agricultural Economics* 22 (2000) 309-320.

Becker, G. (1981): *A treatise on the family*. Cambridge, Harvard University Press.

Becker, G. (1985): "Human capital, effort and sexual division of labour." *Journal of Labour Economics*. 3(1).

Blau, F., M. Ferber, and A. Winkler, (1998): *The economics of women, men and work*. Prentice Hall, Toronto.

Chattapadhyay, M & Sharma, C.S. (2001): "Is labour a homogeneous quantity in Indian agriculture?" Indian Statistical Institute.

Deoiaiikar, A.B. and Vijberberg, W.P.M.: "A test of heterogeneity of family and hired labour in Asian agriculture." *Oxford Bulletin of Economics and Statistics*. Vol. 49. No 3. (August 1987).

Duncan, G. (1976): "Earnings functions and non-pecuniary benefits." *Journal of Human Resources*. 11(4): 462-483.

Ghosh, B. Neogi, C.: "Liberalisation in India: Quality differentials between public and private employees." *The developing Economics*. XXXIV-1 (March 1996).

Gunderson, M., (1989): "Male-Female wage differentials and policy responses." *Journal of Economic Literature* 27(1): 46-72.

Gunderson, M., 1975: "Male-Female wage differentials and the impact of equal pay legislation." *Review of economics and statistics*. 57(1): 462-469.

Hakim, C., (2000): *Preference theory: Work lifestyle choices in the 21st century*. Oxford University Press, Oxford.

Jacoby, H.G. (1993): "Shadow wages and peasant family labour supply; An econometric application to the Peruvian Sierra." *Review of Economic Studies*. 60, 903-921.

Long, J. (1995): "The effects of taste and motivation on individual income." *Industrial and labour Relations Review*. 48(2): 338-351.

Oaxaca, R. (1973): "Male-Female wage differentials in urban labour markets." *International Economic Review*. 14(October): 693-709.

Paarsch, H. and B. Shearer. (2004): "Piece rates, fixed wages and incentive effects: Statistical evidence from payroll records." *International Economic Review*. 41(1): 59-92.

Sen, A.K. (1962): "An aspect of Indian agriculture." *Economic and Political Weekly*. 16, Annual number, February.

Sen, A.K.(1964) : "Size of holdings and productivity." *Economic and Political Weekly*, 16, Annual number, February.

Skoufias, E. (1994): "Using shadow wages to estimate labour supply of agricultural households." *American Journal of Agricultural Economics*. 76. 215-227.

Wise, D. (1975): "Academic achievement and job performance." *American Economic Review*. 65(3): 350-366.

12

Life Stress and Mental Health among Women Workers

Tejpreet Kang, Vandana Kumari and Rekha Kumari

Women constitute about 50 percent of country's population. But they are the largest excluded category in almost all aspects. They have been denied their rights and liberties by the male dominated Indian society for which their social, economic and political status has remained relatively low. For centuries they have discriminated in all walks of life and treated as "Second class citizens". However the 73rd Constitutional Amendment, 1993 opened a new chapter in the history of democratic decentralization in India by developing power to the people and gives opportunities to women folk to express their voice in the decision making process.

As we look back at ancient times, we find that in India there were eminent women philosophers like Gargi and Maitreyi who were given as much respect as men and participated in discourses and discussions at part with men. In our national freedom movement, the contribution of women has been no less than that of men. Women responded to the call of Mahatma Gandhi to join the freedom struggle, at a time when only two percent were educated. This should give an idea as to how difficult it would have been for women to come out of their homes but yet they did. After Independence, women as members of the Constituent Assembly participated in the task of drafting of a constitution for free India. It is a matter of pride that as per the proposal of Dr. Baba Saheb Ambedkar, the constitution from its very inception has given the right to vote to women, making India one of the very few countries to have done so.

In present time women workforce constitutes an important part of total workforce in India. The work participation rate for women has increased significantly. In 1981, work participation rate for women was only 19.67 percent which increased up to 22.73 percent in 1991 and 26.68 percent in 2001(Census of India). In the women workforce, women from rural areas are more in number as compared to the urban women. Amongst rural women workers, majority is employed in agriculture and some are employed in cottage industries. In the urban areas, women workers are primarily employed in the unorganized sector. A total number of 50.16 lakh women employees were engaged in the organized sector, out of which 29.21 lakh (58 percent) in the public sector and 20.95 lakh (42 percent) in the Private Sector (Census of India, 2001).

An increasing number of women today are becoming career conscious professional in their outlook. Earlier women preferred jobs like nursing, medicine, clerical but now the number of women executives is on the increase. The reasons for such a change are: increase in women's education, changing socio-cultural values, increasing awareness and consciousness in women and the rise in economic independence. Women are in a dilemma facing queries regarding self and their rights. Balancing work and family frequently means irregular work hours for women professionals leading to stress and various problems related to it (Snell, 2004). The working women, regardless of job status, marital status faces higher stress levels. This is not only at work place but at home also. She may feel guilty for leaving and neglecting her children while she works. This increases her stress level.

Weiten (1994) defined stress as "a particular pattern of disturbing psychological and physiological reactions that occur when an environment threaten important motives and taxes one's ability to cope". According to Ojha and Rani (2003) stress refers to the responses elicited by the physical or psychological events that an individual perceives to be harmful or emotionally threatening.

A 'stress' condition seems 'relative' in nature. Moderate stress can compel us to action and stimulate the brain emotionally and bio-chemically to sharpen its performance. It can result in a new awareness and an exciting new perspective. But extreme stress conditions, psychologists say, are detrimental to human health. It can become destructive and can turn into distress. Too much stress on mind and body can make us feel miserable, worried, sad and ill.

Dohrenwend and Dohrenwend (1978) defined life stress in terms of characteristics of stressful events and the individual's reaction to them. It is mainly concerned with an individual's recent traumatic events and the meaning she may attach to such events. Stress can cause psychological, physiological and behavioural problems. Psychological symptoms include job dissatisfaction, tension, anxiety, irritability, boredom and procrastination. The physiological symptoms include high blood pressure, ulcers, loss of appetite, coronary heart diseases, backache, stomach and intestinal disorders. Behaviourally related stress symptoms include changes in productivity, absenteeism, accident proneness and high turnover. There can be also changes in eating habits, increased smoking, consumption of alcohol, drug abuse, rapid speech, sleep disorders and fidgeting.

Stress not only affects the physical health but it also affects their mental health of an individual. The concept of mental health is as old as human beings. Mental health commutates those behaviours, perceptions and feelings that determine a person's overall level of personal effectiveness, success, happiness and excellence of functioning as a person. Bhatia (1982) describes mental health as the ability to balance desires, feelings, ambitions and ideals in one's daily living. It may also be understood as the behavioural characteristics of a person. A mentally healthy person shows a homogenous organization of desirable attributes, healthy values and righteous self-concept and scientific perception of world as a whole. Mental health presents a humanistic approach towards the understanding and assessment of self, positive feeling, attitudes towards self and others. It is an important factor that influences individual's various activities, behaviour, happiness and performance.

Jagdish and Srivastava (1983) defined mental health as a person's ability to make positive self-evaluation, to perceive the reality, to integrate the personality, autonomy, group oriented attitudes and environmental mastery. It is a combined outcome of five types of health-physical, emotional, moral, spiritual and social (Gill and Kaur, 2005). Mental health depends upon the existing conditions that relate to changes taking place in the life of an individual and his/her environment.

In the changing scenario of world lot of changes have been taking place in the role of women. Now days, women may be classified as Working and Non-working. Non-working woman works inside her home as housewife and is fully involved in the management of her home affairs. Whereas, working woman is one who is in gainful employment in some office or institution. The resultant outcome is that modern women live in a system that requires them to perform both familial as well as professional roles, which in turn, leads to number of stresses and strains among them. Nelson and Quick (1985) pointed out that the interface between work and family life that has the potential to be more stressful for women who work outside than for men.

The number of women who are employed outside home increased significantly in recent years in urban India. It is true that employment generates resources for women on one hand but simultaneously it also creates stress in their lives on the other hand. Gender discrimination, sexual harassment, combining work and family life are major contributors of stress in the lives of working women. Working women still retain primary responsibility for dependent care (care of children and elders) and household chores. Hence their overall work-family load is high. As a consequence of greater role strain they are likely to display more stress as compared to the non-working women (Spalter *et al.* 1997). But on the other hand employment has many benefits for women, including increased financial resources, a sense of achievement and reduced social isolation, all of which can benefit their mental health (Swanson *et al.* 1997).

Hence, the present investigation aimed to compare life stress and mental health among working and non-working women. It was hypothesized that the two groups differ on the level of life stress experienced and mental health status.

Methodology

Sample: The present study was conducted in Ludhiana city. Two hundred women belonging to working category (N=100) and non-working category (N=100) were selected for the study. Sample of working women was official staffs working in different departments of Punjab Agricultural University, Ludhiana, having at least 3 years of job experience. While the non-working sample comprised of housewives residing in and surrounding areas of Punjab Agricultural University Campus i.e. Maharaj Nagar, Krishna Nagar and Type -12 quarters of Punjab Agricultural University Campus. The selected women were in the age range of 30-40 years, at least graduate and married. Their family was nuclear and intact having family income between ₹ 15000-25000 per month.

Research Instruments

Presumptive Stressful Life Events Scale by Singh, Kaur and Kaur (1981) was used to assess the level of life stress of the respondents. This scale has been designed to assess the level of life stress of general population that never had sought any psychiatric help and had not suffered from any major physical or psychiatric illness in the past six months. This scale comprised of 51 statements. Events were ranked from high stress to low stress. In this scale two aspects were studied;

- Number of stressful events.
- Amount of stress.

Mental Health Inventory by Jagdish and Srivastava (1993) was used to assess the mental health status of the respondents. This Inventory has been designed to assess the mental health status of normal individuals. It has six dimensions namely–Positive self-evaluation (PSE), Perception of reality (PR), Integration of personality (IP), Autonomy (AUTNY), Group oriented attitudes (GOA) and Environmental mastery (EM). Inventory is comprised of 54 statements well distributed under these six dimensions. Scoring was done as per the instructions given in the Mental Health Inventory manual.

Results and Discussion

Table 12.1 shows that majority of working respondents (70 percent) had average number of stressful events in their lives, followed by 28 percent in high and two percent in low category.

Table 12.1: Percentage Distribution of Respondents across Different Levels of Life Stress

Stress	Level of life stress					
	Working women			Non-working women		
	Less/ Low	Avg/ Med.	More/ High	Less/ Low	Avg/ Med.	More/ High
	N (100)	N (100)	N (100)	N (100)	N (100)	N (100)
Number of stressful events	2 (2)	70 (70)	28 (28)	40 (40)	58 (58)	2 (2)
Amount of stress	14 (14)	58 (58)	28 (28)	8 (8)	90 (90)	2 (2)

* Figures in parentheses indicate percentages.

While in non-working respondents 58 percent of the

subjects had average number of stressful events in their lives followed by 40 percent in low and two percent in high category respectively. Results showed that 58 percent of working subjects had medium level of amount of stress in their lives while 28 percent had high level and only 14 percent had low level. In case of non working subjects majority of the respondents (90 percent) had medium level of amount of stress whereas 8 percent had low level and only two percent had high level of amount of stress. The table clearly shows that nearly one third of working women had high level of life stress while very few of non-working women had high level of stress.

Table 12.2 shows that working women significantly scored higher on level of life stress than non-working women. Working women faced more stressful situations in their lives as compared to non-working women like failure in examination, appearing for examination or interview, trouble at work with colleagues, superiors or subordinates, family conflict, change in working condition or transfer etc. Hence they experience more stress. They also have to perform the dual role of a worker and a home-maker and also share the responsibility of running the house. Many times they may feel guilty for ignoring their children while at work. That further intensifies their stress level.

Table 12.2: Difference between Life Stress (mean score) among Working and Non-working Women

Life Stress	Working		Non-working		t-value
	Mean	S.D.	Mean	S.D.	
Number of stressful events	13.66	3.07	9.7	0.84	8.80**
Amount of Life Stress	21.72	7.27	17.96	1.90	3.53**

**Significant at 1percent.

The results are consistent with the findings of Ojha and Rani (2003) who also found that working women significantly scored higher on number of stressful events and amount of stress. It was found that significant difference existed in the amount of stress among working and non-working women. It was revealed that amount of stress score in working women was more than their counter parts. Nelson and Quick (1985) also found that employed women experience greater stress than both non-employed women and men because of several unique stressors faced by them like interface of marriage and work, sex discrimination and sexual harassment at workplace. Mahtur (2006) pointed out that the balancing work and family is difficult for working women so they experience too much stress.

Table 12.3 shows that majority of the subjects had average status of mental health and this trend was followed in all its dimensions. Majority of subjects had average status of Positive Self Evaluation, Perception of reality, Integration of perception, environmental mastery and nearly half of the subjects had average status of Autonomy and Group oriented attitude. It shows that only few respondents were in poor as well as good status of all the dimensions of mental health. But in case of Autonomy and Group oriented attitude almost 50 percent of the respondents were in good category also.

It reveals that employment provides the women a stable set of internal standards for their action, helps them to be dependent on their own potentialities rather than dependence on other people. They become better able to get along with others, work with others and find recreation. Results are in consistent with the findings of Swanson *et al.* (1997) who found employment has many benefits for women like increased financial resources, a sense of achievement, reduced social isolation which benefit physical and mental health of women. The result is in contrast with the findings of Sinha (1997) who found working women's mental health are hampered because of the tendency to avoid distressful situations, which is inevitable in the working conditions.

Results showed that majority (70 percent) of non-working

women had average status of mental health followed by poor (16 percent) and good (8 percent) status respectively. The overall view of the results reveals that majority of the average status of mental health and this trend was followed in all its dimensions i.e. positive self-evaluation, perception of reality, integration of perception, autonomy, group-oriented attitude and environmental mastery.

Table 12.3: Percentage Distribution of Respondents across Different Status of Mental Health

Dimensions of Mental Health	Working women			Non-working women		
	Poor	Average	Good	Poor	Average	Good
Positive self evaluation (PSE)	10 (10)	82 (82)	8 (8)	10 (10)	76 (76)	14 (14)
Perception of reality (PR)	12 (12)	86 (86)	2 (2)	10 (10)	84 (84)	6 (6)
Integration of personality (IP)	8 (8)	82 (82)	10 (10)	24 (24)	68 (68)	8 (8)
Autonomy (AUTNY)	4 (4)	56 (56)	40 (40)	2 (2)	86 (86)	12 (12)
Group Oriented Attitude (GOA)	4 (4)	58 (58)	38 (38)	16 (16)	82 (82)	2 (2)
Environmental Mastery (EM)	22 (22)	70 (70)	8 (8)	8 (8)	84 (84)	8 (8)
Overall Mental Health	10 (10)	80 (80)	10 (10)	16 (16)	76 (76)	8 (8)

Figures in parentheses indicate percentage.

Table 12.4 illustrates differences in mean scores of various dimensions of mental health among working and non-working women. It depicts non-significant difference in overall mental health among working and non working women.

Significant difference was found in case of Perception of

reality. Non-working women have better Perception of reality than working women. It could be because generally non-working women have limited resources (monetary and social). They spent most of the time in their houses so they are better able to understand the problems of children and home affairs. They are more near to realities and devoid of excessive fantasy.

Table 12.4: Difference between Mental Health (mean score) of Working and Non-working Women

Dimensions of Mental Health	Working Women		Non-working Women		t-value
	Mean	S.D.	Mean	S.D.	
Positive self evaluation (PSE)	24.00	2.40	24.90	2.37	1.24[NS]
Perception of reality (PR)	19.94	1.84	21.98	1.43	2.54*
Integration of personality (IP)	30.78	2.03	29.34	2.88	2.88**
Autonomy (AUTNY)	15.00	1.66	14.88	1.32	0.934[NS]
Group Oriented Attitude (GOA)	25.48	3.05	23.98	1.82	8.79**
Environmental Mastery (EM)	21.44	2.03	20.48	1.89	2.44*
Overall Mental Health	136.64	4.60	135.56	4.3	1.062[NS]

* Significant at 5percent.
** Significant at 1percent.
NS–Non-significant.

Results showed working women had better Integration of personality than non-working women. It could be because working women are more exposed to outer world, they are in contact with more number of people as compared to their counter parts, and they also have to maintain relationship with colleagues, superiors and sub-ordinates. They have to balance household and work activities and are more interested in several other activities than non-working women. This all leads to better integration of personality.

Significant difference was found in Group oriented attitude among working and non-working women. Working group has better group oriented attitude than non-working group. The reason may be that working women have to work with others, maintain relationship with colleagues, superiors and subordinates. They are more able to get along with others and find recreation.

Results showed working women had more Environmental mastery than non-working women. This could be because of financial and social freedom. They have to take responsibilities of household and professional work. They are more capable of working, recreation and adjustment in different situations. The result is in contrast with the findings of Ojha and Rani (2003) who found non-significant difference on all the dimensions of mental health among working and non-working women.

References

Bhatia B.D. (1982) Mental hygiene in education. In B. Kuppuswamy (ed.) *Advanced Educational Psychology*. Sterling Publishers Pvt. Ltd. pp.121-125.

Census of India (2001) Population Tables, Series II, India, Registrar General and Census commissioner, New Delhi.

Dohrenwend B.P and Dohrenwend B.S. (1978). Some issues in research on stressful life events. *J Nervous Mental Dis* 166: 7-15.

Gill S and Kaur G (2005) Moral judgement, intelligence and parental behaviour as correlates of mental health. *Malwa J Edu* 1 (1): 56-62.

Jagdish and Srivastava A.K. (1983) Manual for Mental Health Inventory (MHI) Manovaigyanik Parikchhan Santhan. Varanasi, India.

Nelson D.L. and Quick J.C. (1985) Professional Women; are distress and disease inevitable. Academy of Management Review, 10, 206-213. (Original not seen) cited by Ojha S and Rani U (2003) *Praachi Journal of Psycho-cultural Dimensions* 19 (1): 19-24.

Nelson D.L. and Quick J.C. (1985) Professional Women; are distress and disease inevitable. Academy of Management Review, 10, 206-213. (Original not seen) cited by Ojha S and Rani U (2003) *Praachi Journal of Psycho-cultural Dimensions* 19 (1): 19-24.

Ojha S and Rani U (2003) A comparative study of the level of life stress and various dimensions of mental health among working and non-working women. *Praachi Journal of Psycho-cultural Dimensions* 19 (1): 9-24.

Singh G, Kaur D and Kaur H. (1981) Presumptive stressful life events scale. National Psychological Corporation, Agra.

Spalter-Roth R, Kalleberg A, Rasell E (1997). Managing work and family. Noustandard work Arrangements among Managers and Professionals. Washington DC: *Economic Policy Institute.*

Swanson N, Piotrkowski C, Keita G, Becker A (1997) Occupational stress and women's' health. *American Psychological Association*: 147-159.

13

Micro Finance Institutions and the Economic Empowerment of Women

Dhruvalata D Bhatt

Introduction

Development involves not only economic change but also social and institutional changes. In many developing and underdeveloped countries, developments include new sets of values and new concept of society and Government.

The economic development depends upon a multiplicity of factors like economical, political, social, cultural, technological, etc., efficient devises, effective strategies, co-ordination of all sectors of the economy and involvement of the people.

Social changes achieved through combination of socio-cultural, political, legal, technological, administrative, entrepreneurial and commercial aspects and Financial Laws etc. into economic planning. Economic planning is an instrument of socio-economic transformation in the country. If social motivation is taken care of economic development will begin to take care it self.

The primary objectives of developing countries like India is to achieve rapid, balanced sustained rate of economic growth. The main objective of Indian economic planning is the promotion of agriculture and other allied economic activities through credit intervention for ensuring integrated rural development and securing the prosperity of the rural areas. Rural segment is the dominating segment in our economy, majority of population lives in rural India and they depend upon agriculture for livelihood. Rural India is mainly consisting of two sectors viz. agriculture and non-agriculture.

Indian rural economy has major features like: dependence upon agriculture; unbalanced class structure in the rural India; private ownership and unequal distribution of land; mixture of monetizes and barter economy; predominance of money-lenders; mixture of traditional and modern farm technology; dominance of caste system; poor rural infrastructure; large size of rural population; disguised unemployment; wide disparity in income distribution: low rate of saving and capital accumulation; dependence upon nature; less development of industries.

Credit Needs of the Rural Poor

Financial requirements of farmers vary and depend upon season. They borrow funds for various purposes: for productive use- purchasing of seeds, fertilizers, pesticides, machinery, tractors, land, irrigation facilities, poultry farming, piggery, fisheries, bee-keeping, animal husbandry, etc., for non-productive or household use-family expenses including medical cost, schooling, debt redemption, housing, household purchases, family events like marriage, death etc.

Credit is the basic input needed for the economic development of the country. There are important principles for development through credit: Credit must be used in accordance with the most suitable methods of science and technology; the terms and conditions of the credit (or techno-economic parameters) must be fully respected; work must be done with skill so as to increase productivity and income; A part of the additional income created by credit must be saved; Loan instalments must be repaid in time and regularly so as to recycle credit. Extending credit facilities to the farmers for various economic activities in agriculture and non-agriculture sectors, various sources are: money lenders, friends and relatives, indigenous bankers, co-operative banks, RRBs, NGOs, commercial banks, etc. They may be grouped into institutional, non-institutional and government.

The financial system is diversifying itself to cater to the growing needs of the rural sector and have been experimenting with innovative schemes to meet the needs of the rural sector. This recognition has led to the development of the concept of planning at the grass-root village level and adoption of a service area approach. Thus, rural lending would be more purposive based and at the same time accelerate the process of village development.

With the significant changes in the economic environment and the thrust given by Government of India it is important to increase the farmers' participation in the existing extension system.

Government of India's National Policy for Farmers, 2007 provides greater focus on the economic well being of the farmers, in addition to production and productivity. The policy aims to stimulate attitudes and actions, by assessing agricultural progress, in terms of improvement in the income of the farmers' families, their consumption requirements and capacity to invest in farm related activities. The policy also includes, involvement of co-operative banks, SHGS, agricultural universities, seed companies in providing quality seeds, disease free planting material and soil health enhancement.

The All-India Debt and Investment Surveys (AIDIS) have brought out the crucial role played by institutional agencies in the extension of the credit delivery system in the rural sector. The thrust of rural credit policy has been on the provision of timely and adequate flow of credit, especially to meet the requirements of small and marginal farmers and the weaker sections. The institutional changes in agricultural technology, although there are areas where credit deepening as well as widening is needed.

The main objectives of the institutional credit policy are: To secure an increase in the total volume of institutional credit for agriculture and rural development; To direct a larger share of the credit to the weaker sections; To reduce the regional imbalances in the availability of credit; To bring about greater co-ordination between different credit institutions under the multi agency system; and To improve the recovery of institutional loans.

Micro Finance Institutions (MFIs)

According to Task force on Regulatory and Supervision Frame Work for Micro Finance Institutions set up by NABARD in 1999, a working definition of micro finance is "provision of thrift, credit and other financial services and products of very small amounts to the poor in rural, semi urban or urban area for enabling them to raise their income levels and improve living standards."

As banking services are in the nature of public good, it is essential that availability of banking and payment services is made available to the entire population. They function under a set of regulations that are both self-imposed as well as required by the central bank of the country. These include capital, reserve and liquidity requirements, ceilings on lending and deposits rates, mandatory credit targets and audit and reporting requirements.

Low income households are not obtaining credit from banks and are out of the formal credit delivery network due to low and irregular wages, jobs in the informal sectors, seasonal employment, holding of low valued marketable assets etc. This has led to dependence on informal credit markets to satisfy their credit needs.

Thus, failure of formal credit institutions to address the needs of low-income households, certain important alternatives approaches used to mobilized credit. One important factor that has to be taken into consideration is that there is an existence of informal credit delivery system. Such system needs reorganization, concerted action from authority for necessary resources, training, and support for enhancing activities. Thus people's efforts in mobilizing credit should be seen as a logical complement to banking services.

There have been many significant state initiatives in the institutional and policy spheres, to enable the poor access financial services. Major institutional initiatives includes: the bank linkage program under the overall guidance and supervision of the NABARD, the setting up of Rashtriya Mahila Kosh to re-finance micro finance activities of NGOs and the establishment of SIDBI Foundation for Micro-credit (SFMC) as a financier of micro finance institutions.

International donors and national policy-makers to financial system agents, NGO practitioners and local bureaucrats, everyone is passionately pushing micro-finance as the answer to the worries of the bottom of the development pyramid.

Even the most conservative development practitioners cannot but take note of the rapid pace of expansion in the outreach of microfinance institutions, mostly functioning outside the formal channels of credit delivery. India is home to one of the largest micro credit/micro finance program in the world.

Micro Finance Institutions are an extremely heterogeneous group divisible into two broad categories. One set comprises a basket of institutions incorporated under various legislations such as the Indian Trust Act, Cooperative Societies Act and Section 25 of the Companies Act. Institutions under this category are large in numbers but operate on a limited scale and have a low level of business. The other set comprises a few Micro Finance Institutions, which are registered as (NBFC) Non-Bank Financial Companies and regulated by Reserve Bank of India. Finance Companies and Chit funds offer both savings and credit services. Where local money lenders and pawn brokers offer credit with an option of one-time repayment. Interest rates depend on the amount borrowed and urgency of the situation, (smaller the amount and greater the urgency higher is the interest rate) delay repayment invites compound interest. Friends and relatives are also an important source of credit which is often interest free. Informal financial markets across India offer a wide range of products to meet local demand.

In the evolution of micro finance two different approaches have been identified; The Latin American model that may be called the commercial model has recognized from the outset the significance of allying with formal financial system rather than donors or targeted government program. Focus on social and community development on the poor and marginalized women is conspicuous by its absence in this system. There is an accent instead on enterprise creation and growth. The South Asian model, largely drawing on the strategic and operational features of the Grameen model has its spotlight clearly on women and poverty.

In India the industry has grown under two different systems of patronage. The SHG-bank linkage program by NABARD has the patronage of the state and formal banking institutions. Parallel system promoted by non-state agencies has been depending almost exclusively on subsidized external grants to finance both social mobilization and on lending. Both target the poor and women, predominantly. In the absence of any suitable legal and regulatory framework to carry on with the business of financial service provision, most players in the non-state agencies category have devised strategies to circumvent the government gaze in the most innovative ways.

The policy environment in India has been extremely supportive for the growth of the micro-finance sector in India. The International Year of Micro Credit 2005, significant policy announcements from the Government of India and the Reserve Bank of India for rapid growth. SHGS have spread rapidly due to their ease of replication. The year 1992 marks the formal beginning of the micro finance in India.

Self-help Groups (SHGs)

Self Help Groups is a silent revolutionary concept in the credit delivery system. Micro finance–finance through SHGS offers best form of credit for reaching the unreached and the under reached. The concept is well received in the developing and the under developed countries, as evidenced by the recognition the father of the SHG movement Mr. Mohammed Yunus of Bangladesh received by Nobel Award.

Features: The salient features of the SHG movement are: Groups of homogeneous people from similar economic background living in the neighbourhood; Focus on women; Saving first, credit later; Credit prioritized among the members, which builds pressure for timely repayment; Transparent operations, as decisions are taken collectively in meeting.

The SHG concept has gained momentum due to active participation of banks. In the process, the essentials of financial intermediation including prioritization of needs, setting terms and conditions and keeping financial accounts are imbibed in them. The group, which has learnt this basic process of savings money, lending and recovering it back, are ready to be linked to the bank, thereby having access to the larger resources of the bank. The peer pressure among the group ensures timely repayment. Self-help Group is a small groups of women, have formed voluntary association for poor, formed with the common goal of social and economic empowerment. The formation of common interest groups consisting primarily of women has had a substantial impact on their lives.

Objectives: The main objectives are: To establish a forum where in women can critically analyze their socio – economic situation and act as catalyst to bring about social change; To build up self confidence and spirit of cooperation among women; To eliminate the role of money lender; To establish linkage with the banks, Government and other institutions for social economical development through SHGs; Economic empowerment of women in society aimed at self reliance and self sufficiency.

The members volunteered to organize themselves into a group for the eradication of poverty of the members. They agree to save regularly and convert their savings into a common fund known as the group corpus. They use these savings to make interest-bearing loans to their members. The member of the group agree to use this common fund and such other funds that they may receive as a group through a common management.

Need for SHGs

The rural poor incapacitated due to various reasons, such as; most of them are socially backward, illiterate, with low motivation and a poor economic base.

Individually, a poor is not only weak in a socio-economic term but also lacks access to the knowledge and information which are the most important components of to day's development process. Hence, there are needs of SHGs which in specific terms are as under:

To mobilize the resources of the individual members for their collective economic development; To uplift the living conditions of the poor; To create a habit of savings; Utilization of local resources; To mobilize individual skills for group's interest; To create awareness about rights; To assist the members financially at the time of need; Entrepreneurship development; To identify problems, analyzing and finding solutions in the group; To act as a media for socio-economic development of the village; To develop linkages with institutions of Non-Government Organizations (NGOs); To organize training for skill development; To help in the recovery of loans; To gain mutual understanding, develop trust and self-confidence; To build-up team work; To develop leadership qualities.

Structure and Guidelines for SHGs

The number of members in a group should not exceed 20 otherwise registration becomes compulsory; a SHG may consist of 10 to 20 persons; all members of the group should belong to families below the poverty line; If necessary a maximum of 20 percent and in exceptional cases where essentially required, up to a maximum of 30 percent of the members in a group may be taken from families marginally above the poverty line living continuously with below poverty line families and if they are acceptable to the below poverty line members of the group; The above poverty line members will not be eligible for the subsidy under the scheme; The below poverty line families must actively participate in the management and decision making, which should not ordinarily be entirely in to hands of above poverty line families; Above poverty line family member of the SHG shall not become office bearers like group leader, assistant group leader or treasurer etc. of the group.

The group shall not consist of more than one member from the same family; Person should not be a member of more than one group; The group should devise a code of conduct to bind itself; This should be in the form of regular meetings in a domestic manner allowing for a free exchanges of views, participation by the members in the decision making process; The group should be able to draw up an agenda for each meeting and discussions as per the agenda; The members should build their corpus through regular savings; The group should be able to collect the minimum voluntary saving amount from all the members regularly in the group meetings; The savings so collected will be the group corpus funds; The group corpus fund should be used to advance loans to the members; The group should develop financial management norms covering the loan sanction procedure, repayment schedule and interest rates; The members in the group meeting should take all the loaning decisions through a participatory decision making process;

The group should be able to prioritize the loan applications, fix repayment schedules, fix an appropriate rate of interest for the loans advanced and closely monitor the repayment of the loan instalments from the loanee; The group should operate a account preferably in their service area bank branch to deposit the balance amounts left with groups after disbursing loans to its members; The group should maintain simple basic records such as minutes book, attendance register, loan ledger, general ledger cash book, bank pass book and individual pass books.

SHG Federations

A SHG Federation is a formal group of informal common-interest groups i.e. SHGs. The spread of SHGs led to the formation of SHG Federation which are a more sophisticated form of organization that involve several SHGS forming into village organizations (VOS/cluster Federations and then ultimately into higher level federations. SHG Federations are formal institution and recognized by bankers while the SHG are informal. Many of SHG Federations are registered as a Mutual Benefit Trusts and mutually aided co operative societies.

The SHG Federations are emerging as important players in nurturing of SHGS, increasing the bargaining powers of the group members and livelihood promotion. However, the features and functions of SHG Federation models promoted in the country vary depending on the promoting agencies.

Recognizing the growing role of the SHG Federations and their value addition to SHG functioning. NABARD has formulated the broad norms for deciding grant of financial assistance to SHG Federations. They are: SHG Federation should evolve as per the need of the SHGs where in each SHG is free to join/not join the Federation; the promoting organization to ensure that the Federation is able to sustain it functioning and becomes self-managed over a period of three years; The Federations should be member-owned, member-driven institutions and democratic in its functioning; the SHG Federation may act as business facilitator, business correspondent to the banks; support for SHG Federations should clearly establish value additions to the functioning.

National Bank for Agriculture and Rural Development (NABARD)

It is an apex institution for agriculture sector. It is concerned with all matter relating to policy, planning and operations in the field of credit for agriculture and other economic activities in rural areas. It has taken special attention to strengthening rural financial institutions. It exercises development oriented action plans. It initiated to form farmers clubs under vikas volunteer vahini Program. It co-ordinates the rural financing activities of all the institutions engaged in developmental work at the field level and maintains liaison with Government of India, State Governments, Reserve Bank of India and other national level institutions concerned with policy formulation. It prepares on an annual basis, rural credit plans for all districts in the country; these plans form the base for annual credit plans of all rural financial institutions.

The major objectives of NABARD are: It is an apex organization in respect of all matters relating to policy, planning operational aspects in the field of credit for promotion of agriculture, small-scale industries, cottage and village industries, handicrafts and other rural crafts and other allied economic activities in rural areas; It serve as a refinancing institution for institutional credit such as long-term, short term for the promotion of activities in the rural areas; The bank provide direct lending to any institution as may approved by the Central Government; The bank have organic links with the Reserve Bank of India and maintain a close link with it.

The SHG-Bank Linkage Program of NABARD has emerged as the primary model for providing Micro Finance services in the country. It is a proven tool of extending to the unbaked rural clientele access to formal financial services. Encouraged by the success of the program, NABARD promoted the linkage of Micro Finance Institutions (MFIs) with the banking sectors. The MFI-bank linkage model too has assumed importance on account of credit support extended by banks for on-lending clients by MFIs. NABARD by way of grant assistance continued to support NGOs, Regional Rural Banks, District Central Cooperative Banks, Farmers' Clubs and Individual Rural Volunteers (IRVs) for promoting and nurturing of quality SHGS.

As presented in Table 13.1, during 2007-08, grant assistance of ₹ 1,369.77 lakh was sanctioned to various agencies for promoting 52,877 groups, taking the cumulative assistance sanctioned to ₹ 6,119.37 lakh for 3.62 lakh groups as at end-March 2008. As on March 31, 2008, an amount of ₹ 2,541.04 lakh was released and 1.75 lakh SHGS credit linked to banks.

Table 13.1: Grant Assistance Extended to Various Partners in SHG-Bank Linkage Programme (₹ lakh)

Agency	Sanctions during the year		Cumulative Sanctions		Cumulative Progress	
	Amount	No. of SHGS	Amount	No. of SHGS	Amount Released	SHGS Linked
Cooperative Banks	45.70	3400	426.22	44410	178.49	19388
RRBS	22.35	1750	368.60	43790	173.73	33.850
NGOS	1166.13	40194	4841.41	245276	2093.08	111828
Farmers' Club	-	-	-	-	60.90	7640
IRVS	135.59	7533	483.18	28643	34.84	2655
Total	1369.77	52877	611937	362119	254104	175361

Source: NABARD Annual Report, 2007-08.

NABARD extends support to recognizing the role played by MFIS, in extending Micro Finance services in the unbaked areas, through grant and loan based assistance. It has been selectively supporting MFIS for experimenting with various Micro Finance models like replication of Grameen Model, NGO Networking, credit unions, SHG Federations, etc., to meet credit requirement of the unreached poor.

NABARD provides assistance to commercial banks, Regional Rural Banks for identifying, classifying and to avail services of credit rating agencies (CRISIL, M-CRIL, ICRA,

CARE and Planet Finance) for rating of MFIs. It also provides financial help them for intermediate between lending banks and clients.

The SHG Federations are important players in nurturing of SHGs, increasing the bargaining powers of group members and livelihood. NABARD's support would be extended by way of grant assistance for training, capacity building, exposure visits of SHG members etc.

To assess the suitability of various innovative initiatives and also enhance the sustainability of Micro Finance activities, NABARD continued to extend support for various projects like:

Micro Finance Development fund (MFDF) was established by the NABARD with the corpus of ₹ 80 crore contributed by Reserve Bank of India, NABARD and Commercial banks. This fund is utilized for scaling up of the SHG linkage program and supporting other credit delivery models. The broad objectives of the MFDF are: Support financial services to the rural poor and women, who have less access from the formal financial system; provide capacity building funds to SHG and other grass roots level micro financial institutions; support SHG-Bank linkage program; strengthen expertise in micro finance activities; support regulatory and supervisory mechanisms for micro finance institutions.

SHG-Post Office Program: It was initially launched in five selected Districts of Tamil Nadu to examine the feasibility of utilizing the vast network of post office in rural areas in disbursement of credit to rural poor on agency basis.

Magalia Regional office in partnership with the Department of Posts, Government of India was successful in setting up an Artisan's Product Gallery in General Post Office, Shillong to market the products of SHGs/artisans supported under various developmental program of NABARD. Efforts are on to replicate this model in other states. NABARD extends refinance facilities for two exclusive schemes for women viz. ARWIND (Assistance to Rural Women in Non-Farm Development) and MAHIMA (Marketing of Non-Farm Products of Rural Women).

Women Economic Development Corporation coordinates with NGOs for sponsoring application, conducting sensitization program. It was engaged in formation of SHG and conducts various program through their Anganwadi workers under Swaymsidhya Project. It is implemented through Anganwadi staff under Sakhi Mandal Project.

Social Security System for SHG Members: The pilot project launched during 2004-05 in two villages covering 500 poor households from Betul district of Madhya Pradesh with a view to developing a community based social security system for SHG members in rural areas are being implemented by a NGO. Organization for Awareness of Integrated Social Security (OASIS).The scheme envisages providing a single package covering health and life insurance by paying premium generated through discounts offered by service providers like grocery shops, cloth merchants etc in the project areas.

Financial assistance for developing SOFTWARE-MYRADA: It provides financial assistance to MYRADA for developing a soft ware for NGOS. The software, NABYUKIT is being made available to all NGO partners involved in the promotion and linkage of SHGS.

The Micro-Finance Development and Equity Fund (MFDEF) maintained by NABARD is used for promotion of Micro finance through scaling-up of the SHG-bank linkage program, extending Revolving Fund Assistance (RFA) and capital support to MFIS and under take various promotional initiatives.

The Advisory Board of MFDEF consisting of representatives from RBI, commercial banks, professionals with domain knowledge and NABARD provides guidance in formulation and refinement of policy initiatives.

The State Level Agriculture Development Finance Companies (ADFCs) were established during 1996-97 in

Andhra Pradesh, Karnataka and Tamil Nadu for strengthening credit flow for hi-tech/high value export oriented agriculture, processing, storage, transportation, marketing and infrastructure support systems. During the year Karnataka Agriculture Development Finance Company Ltd. restructured into NABARD Financial Services Limited (NABFINS) as a wholly owned subsidiary of NADARD to facilitate setting-up of benchmarks and standards for the MFI sector. NABFINS will promote and continue providing micro finance, life insurance, general insurance services, etc. to individuals, either directly or through groups/MFIs/Federations in rural and urban areas throughout the country.

Under the NABARD-GTZ Rural Finance Program, a study was undertaken to assess the transaction cost of various agencies, viz. Commercial banks, RRBS, Co-operative banks and MFIs in purveying micro finance through SHGs or other types of groups. Training modules were developed to sensitize bank branch managers and SHG members for monitoring groups so as to minimize risks in lending through early warning. One of the components of the program aims at linking savings and credit SHGs to banks, focusing on improving the quality and viability of financial services under SHG-linkage banking. The NABARD-kfw program (kreditanstalt fur wiederaufbau- German Development Bank) titled Financial Cooperation with India-Capitalization program SEWA Bank to be implemented in Gujarat aims at sustainable improvement in access of poor women to micro credit, both in rural and urban areas.

Programmes for Poverty Alleviation

Swarn Jyanti Gram Swarozgar Yojana (SGSY): Government of India has launched a new programme known as Swarn Jayanti Gram Swarozgar Yojana (SGSY) by restructuring the following existing schemes: Integrated Rural Development Program (IRDP), Training of Rural Youth Self-Employment (TRYSEM), Development of Women and

Children in Rural Areas (DWCRA), Supply of Improved Toolkits to Rural Artisans (SITRA), Ganga Kalyan Yojana (GKY) and Million Wells Scheme (MWS).The SGSY scheme is operative from April 1, 1999 in the rural areas of the country. The scheme is funded by the central and states in the ratio of 75:25 and will be implemented by commercial banks, Regional Rural banks and Co-operative banks. Other financial institutions, Panchayati Raj institutions, District Rural Development Agencies (DRDAs), Non Government organizations (NGOs), technical institutions in the district, would also be involved in the process of planning, implementation and monitoring of the scheme. The scheme aims at establishing a large number of micro enterprises in the rural areas. The list of below poverty line (BPL) households, identified through the BPL census, duly approved by gramsabha, will form the basis for the identification of families for assistance under SGSY.

The objective of SGSY is to bring the assisted poor families (Swarozgaris) above the poverty line by ensuring an appreciable sustained income over a period of time. This objective is to be achieved by inter alia organizing the rural poor into self-help groups (SHGs) through the process of social mobilization, training, capacity building and provision of income generating assets. The rural poor such as those with land, landless labour, educated unemployed, rural artisans and disabled are all covered under the scheme.

The assisted poor families known as Swarozgaris can be either individuals or groups and would be selected from BPL families by a three member team consisting of block development officer (BDO), Banker and Sarpanch. SGSY will focus on the vulnerable sections of the rural poor. Accordingly the SC/ST will account for at least 50 percent, women 40 percent and the disabled 3 percent of those assisted. The SHGs shall be organized by swarozgaris drawn from the BPL list approved by the gramsabha. The scheme provides for the formation of SHG, nurturing and their linkages with banks.

The assistance (loan-cum-subsidy) may be extended to individuals in a group or to all members in the group for taking up income generation activities. Group activities will be given preference and progressively the majority of the funding will be for SHGs. Half of the groups formed at the block level should be exclusively women groups.

As per Economic Survey 2007-08, up to December2007, 27.37 lakh SHGS have been formed and 93.21 lakh Swarozgaris have been assisted with a total outlay of ₹ 19, 340.32 crore. BPL family under the guidelines would be treated as a unit for the purpose of giving income generating assets. The family would consist of members of a household and united by ties of marriage, blood and adoption. The family would consist of husband, wife, dependent parents/sons/daughters/brothers and sisters. The moment a parent /son/daughter/brother/sister is no longer dependent and has a separate household, he will no longer be a member of the same BPL family.

Prime Minister's Rozgar Yojana (PMRY): The Prime Minister's Rozgar Yojana (PMR) has been designed to provide employment to the educated unemployed Youth by setting up of micro enterprises by the educated unemployed poor. It relates to the setting up of the self-employment ventures of industries, services and business. The scheme covers the whole of the country. Reservation: Preference should be given to weaker sections including women. The scheme envisages 22.5 percent reservation for SC/ST and 27 percent for other backward classes (OBCS). Eligibility Norms: All educated unemployed youth between the age of 18 and 35 years on the date of receipt of application by the concerned District Industries Centre (DIC) will be eligible for loan under the scheme in general with a 10 years relaxation for SC/ST/Ex-servicemen/ Physically handicapped and women, up to the age of 45. Qualification: The scheme covers all educated youth with the minimum qualification of VII Standard (passed). Preference will be given to those have been trained for any trade in Government recognized approved institutions for a duration of at least 6 months. Income level: The annual family income should not be more than ₹ 1 lakh p.a. and the beneficiary should be a permanent resident of the area for 3 years.

Eligible Activities: Assistance will be provided for all economically viable activities including agricultural and allied activities but excluding direct agricultural operations like raising crop, purchase of manure etc. The implementing agencies will decide the eligibility and classification of the activity proposed to be financed under industry/service/business sectors.

SHGS could considered for assistance under the PMRY provided: Educated unemployed youth satisfying the eligibility criteria as laid down under the scheme, volunteer to form SHG to set up self-employed ventures (common economic activity); An SHG may consist of 5 to 20 educated unemployed youth; No upper ceiling on loan; Loan provided as per individual eligibility, taking into account the requirement of the project; SHG may undertake a common economic activity for which a loan is sanctioned without resorting to onward lending to its members; Subsidy is provided to the SHG as per the eligibility of the individual members, taking into account the relaxation provided in North-eastern States, Uttarakhand, Himachal Pradesh and Jammu & Kashmir; Required margin money contribution i.e. subsidy and margin to be equal to 20 percent of the project cost should be brought in by the SHG collectively; The exemption limit for obtaining collateral security will be ₹ 5 lakh per borrowing account for projects under the Industry sector. Exemption from collateral will be limited to an amount of ₹ 1 lakh per member of SHG for project under service and business sectors. Enhancement in limit of exemption of collateral may be considered in deserving cases; Implementing agencies may decide the necessity of pre-disbursal training for all the members/ majority of the members in the group.

Small Industrial Development Bank of India (SIDBI)

It is making a concerted effort to bring the micro finance sector into the mainstream financial sector of the economy. It aimed at creating and building a strong and viable network of institutions for promoting financial and non-financial services to the poor in a financially sustainable manner. In addition micro credit program of the bank strives to strengthen the capacities of other entities in the sector such as service providers, training institutions, practitioners etc. with a view to providing professional and technical inputs to the micro finance institutions.

SIDBI (through its SIDBI Foundation for Micro Credit) is the apex institution supporting the growth of MFIS in the country, a few large bilateral funded programs like CASHE (Credit and Savings for Household Enterprises) being implemented by CARE India, to support the incubation of community based micro finance institutions.

Commercial Banks

The banking industry has shown tremendous growth in volume and complexity. However, despite making significant improvements in all the areas relating to financial viability, profitability and competitiveness, there are concerns that banks have not been able to reach and bring vast segment of the population especially the under privileged sections of the society, into the fold of basic banking services.

Reserve Bank of India guide the banking system including foreign, public sector and private sector banks to meet emerging economic challenges, as a banking regulator and supervisor and as the monetary policy authority in India.

A large number of people, especially in rural areas do not have bank account. Banks have been encouraged to make available 'no-frills' bank accounts will nil or very low minimum balances making such accounts accessible to public at large.

The Regional Rural Banks have also been advised to allow

limited overdraft facilities in 'no-frills' accounts without any collateral. Banks are required to make available all the printed material used by retail customers in the regional language concerned. All the State Level Bankers' Committee (SLBC) convener banks have advised to initiate action for identifying at least one district in their state/union Territory for 100 percent financial inclusion. Guidelines have been issued to banks to enhance their outreach by utilizing "business facilitators" and "business correspondents" models.

The guidelines on lending to the priority sector were revised, effective from April 30, 2007 to expand its ambit. The target and sub targets for the sector are being linked to: adjusted net bank credit (ANBC) or, credit equivalent amount of off-balance sheet exposure, as on March 31 of the previous accounting year. The broad categories of the priority sector for Scheduled commercial banks include: Agriculture (direct and indirect finance); Small enterprises (direct and indirect finance); Retail trade; Micro credit; Education loans and Housing loans.

This revised priority sector guidelines envisaged that foreign banks having a short fall in the stipulated priority sector lending target/sub-targets would be required to contribute to the Small Enterprises Development Fund (SEDF) to be set up by the SIBDI or for such other purpose as may be stipulated by the Reserve Bank of India from time to time. As per the Reserve Bank of India stipulation, domestic banks and foreign banks operating in India are required to provide 40 percent and 32 percent, respectively, of their adjusted net bank credit to priority sector.

To improve credit flow to the agriculture sector, the Government initiated a number of policy measures, from time to time, like farm credit package and Special Agricultural Credit Plans (SACP).

Union Budget 2008-09 focus on agriculture and rural sector: Commercial banks to meet the entire credit requirements of SHG members for income generation activities, social needs like housing, education, marriage etc. and debt swapping.

All women SHGS credit linked to banks will be covered under Janashree Bima Yojana operated by LIC, with 50 percent subsidy in premium from the social security fund contribution of ₹ 500 crore for 2008-09.

The Self-help Group (SHG) bank linkage program continued to be the main micro-finance model by which the formal banking system reaches the micro entrepreneurs (including farmers), launched in 1992 as a pilot project. It has since proved its efficacy as a mainstream program for banking by the poor who mainly comprise the marginal farmers, land less labourer, artisans and craftsmen and others are engaged in small business like hawking and vending in the rural areas. The main advantages of the program are timely repayment of loans to banks, reduction in transaction costs both to the poor and the banks, doorstep "saving and credit" facility for poor and exploitation of the untapped business potential of the rural areas.

All 498 banks (50 commercial banks, 96 amalgamated RRBs and 352 co-operative banks) are actively participating in the program.

Table 13.2: Progress under SHG-Bank Linkage

Year	New SHGs Financed by banks		Bank Loan* (₹ crore)	
	During the year No.	Cumulative No.	During the Year Amount	Cumulative Amounts
2002-03	255,882	717,360	1,022.34	2,048.68
2003-04	361,731	1,079,091	1,855.53	3,904.21
2004-05	539,365	1,618,456	2,994.25	6,898.46
2005-06	620,109	2,238,565	4,499.09	11,397.55
2006-07	686,408	2,987,441	6,643.19	18,040.74
2007-08**	126,068	3,051,041	2,072.78	20,113.52

* Includes repeat loans to existing SHGs.

** As on December 31, 2007.

Source: Economic Survey, 2007-08.

As per Table 13.2 as on December 31, 2007, bank loan of ₹ 20,114 crore was availed by 30.51 lakh SHGS. The average bank loan availed of per SHG and per family amounted to ₹ 65,924 and ₹ 4,708 respectively. The outreach of the program has enabled estimated 427 lakh poor households to gain access to micro finance from the formal banking system.

Extension Activities in Rural Areas

Rural development is not only a function of economic factors but socio-psycho cultural factors, knowledge factors and physical input factors also play a dominant role in it supported by strong extension services.

Though credit is a sine qua non for rural development, banks should not be treated as mere lending institutions. The efforts of the bankers should also concentrate around building up awareness in the rural people to bring in the desirable changes in the attitude, knowledge and skill.

Change is a process that occurs over a period of time and consist a series of stages like communication, knowledge, persuasion, decision and confirmation. These stages are largely influenced by a host of factors, such as personality, socio-cultural communication, extension service, etc. An extension agent should realize that it is a continuous process of transmitting knowledge apart from lending to a section of community and the feedback on the problems arising there from for further improvement.

The objective of banks' extension program in rural areas should depend upon the socio-economic conditions of the people in the area and need to transmit the latest developments supported by adequate credit. The main objectives are: To assist people in identifying their problems and needs for the development of the individual; To develop leadership among the various sectors of the rural community; To keep the latest developments in technology for agriculture; To change the outlook and attitude of the farming community and to educate them. For success bankers use the simple methods to fulfil the objectives of extension activities like: Training and visit system, whole farm demonstration approach, problem solving approach, Media method through option leaders etc. With the introduction of service area approach, extension agencies have a vital role to play. The success of the service area approach depends on the right tools, approach that commercial banks as on extension agent will use with the co-ordination of developmental departments of the government.

State Bank of India (SBI)

SBI has taken up SHG movement as a mission to reach those families who were hitherto no access to the credit by any formal financial institution and therefore, were depending on informal sources and money lenders. Micro finance is not new to SBI. Banks' association with NGOS or voluntary agencies in extending financial help can be traced as far bank as 1976 well before NABARD introduced SHG-Bank credit linkage program as a pilot project in 1992. SBI has actively participated in SHG-bank credit linkage program. Since its inception in 1992 as a pilot project of NABARD. Since then the Bank has made a steady progress in financing SHGs. SBI is maintaining its position as a leader among commercial banks in credit linking of SHGs and is a prime driver for the movement. As at the end of March 2006, SBI with a share of approximately 47 percent of total SHG financed by commercial banks is far ahead of others.

Bank has successfully initiated various measures towards widening its SHG network like: Bank's aim is to sensitize the entire staff from Manager to Messenger working in rural and semi-urban branches towards the program; Special training program in SHGS: are being conducted at 54 training centres of the bank in the country apart from state bank institute of rural development Hyderabad; Close liaison with NGOs. Operating functionaries at branch level and region level are in close contact with NGOs in their area to take the movement ahead. For the purpose, regular meetings are arranged with the

NGOS and their support is solicited; Special SHG cells have been opened at major branches;

Lending to credible NGO/Federations of SHG on selective basis for on lending to SHG is being encouraged; SBI has launched its Housing Loan product 'Sahayog Niwas' meant for SHG members. Under the scheme formulated keeping the socio-economic conditions of villages' insight, housing loans are given to the SHG members without any mortgage of house/land. Response to this product is very encouraging; SBI Life-Shakti: SBI Life, insurance subsidiary is the first to introduce a life insurance scheme, especially designed for SHG members. Special features of the scheme is that entire premium amount paid by the member is refunded after maturity, i.e.10 years; Rural Training Institutes: To help the rural youth to stand on their feet, two RUDSETI type training institutes have been established in Karnataka state, to impart training in self employment to youth free of cost; SBI Staff as SHPI:

The main role of formation and nurturing of SHGS have been played by NGOS who, apart from their fundamental role of social service, also aim to make the poor economically self sufficient. SBI's committed work force and number of committed staff members have worked hard to form and nurture SHGS on there own; Bank has sponsored and financially supported NGO 'Samanwita' in collaboration with government of Orissa for supplementing the process of socio-economic upliftment of the Tribal and the downtrodden in the poorest and most backward Kandbamal district of Orissa state where 52 percent of the population is that of Tribal. Core activities performed by `Samanwita' is the empowerment of people through promotion of SHGs, especially women SHGs and development of human resources.

SBI is the first commercial bank to which NABARD has given SHPI status. SBI has set for itself an ambitious target of credit linking one million SHGS up to March 2008. The bank has started to leverage vast SHG network for various services beyond credit delivery.

Social Welfare Activities

The function of the Panchayat was may be classified under the following categories; civic amenities, social welfare activities and Development work. The social welfare activities of the Panchayats encompass the development of women and children, in particular of people who are backward and live below the poverty line. In fact, they form the very core of rural development. Women's empowerment is critical to the socio-economic progress of the community and to bring women into the mainstream of national development has, therefore been a major concern of the government.

The Ministry of Rural development has special components for women in its programs and funds are earmarked as Women's component' to ensure flow of adequate resources for the same. The major schemes having women's component include the Swarnjayanti Gram Swarozgar Yojana (SGSY) Sampoorna Gramen Rozgar Yojana (SGRY), Indira Aawas Yojana (IAY) the Restructured centrally Rural Sanitation Program and the Accelerated Rural water Supply Program. The major provisions are: SGSY: 50 percent of SHGs in each block to be exclusively reserves for women; SGRY: 30 percent of employment opportunities reserved for women; IAY: Dwelling houses to be allotted in the name of women or joint names of husband and wife; Restructured Centrally Rural Sanitation Program: Special Toilet complexes for women; Accelerated Rural Water Supply program: For section of sites for hand pumps and other resources-Active involvement of women, maintaining and proper use of hand pumps, training for women, representation of women in village level committees.

State Governments have actively involved SHG and amend the respective co-operative society's act/bye-laws/rules to have enabling provision for enrolment and financing of SHG by co-operatives. It is envisaged that co-operatives should have a significant role to play in making credit available to the rural poor through SHG linkages. Co-operative society Acts in a few states provide for membership to a co-operative by special order. Therefore, SHG can be legally admitted as member of SHGs within the co-operative fold.

Voluntary Agencies

It covers organizations registered under the various trusts and charitable Acts it includes unregistered groups and organization will to accept the responsibility for some aspect of rural development with or without the aid of a government agency. It covers various youth organizations, Mahila Mandals, civic organizations (like the Lion's clubs, Rotarians etc.) organizations of beneficiaries such as farmers organizations, workers' union, religious organizations, professional bodies, whether they have registered or are informed.

Voluntary agencies have generally been started by an individual or a group of individuals often motivated by the spirit of charity or social work. Voluntary agencies have an important role in informing and motivating people and in carrying out supplemental action for improving incomes by promoting self-employment activity, helping in the identification of eligible households, organizing them for group action, informing them about schemes and official procedures, procedures, preparing application and offering follow-up and liaison services etc. The main responsibility for resources transfer has to remain with official financial institutions. They can help in guiding and project formulation process.

The voluntary agencies may bring supplementary funds to oil and lubricate the movement of projects which often get blocked because of the rigidities in inherent in official program and procedures.

Non-government Organisations (NGOs)

SHG movement in the NGO sector is known as the

linkage-banking model. Linkage-banking is the predominant national model. SHGS are broadly promoted by NGOs, who for the program are called Self-help Promoting Institutions (SHIPS). National Bank for Agriculture and Rural Development (NABARD) provides small grants to SHIPS; the Government also provides grants in case of the purpose of promotion of SHGS is for their participation in the SGSY; or under large multilateral funded program like Swashakti or DPIP or Swayamsiddha or by bilateral donors. The size of the grants for SHG promotion differs from agency to agency.

A few public sector banks like Canara Bank and ICICI Bank too have started providing SHG promoting grants to NGOs. The programme also supported by private sector and multinational banks. A large number of NGOs too have shed their traditional social intermediation. Among these, there are a few like Basix, Spandan, Share, Lashpor, ASA which have established themselves as commercial MFIs (NBFIs)/ Grameen replications.

International Agencies

Micro credit spread to more than fifty countries world wide. The very high and sustained recovery rate attracted many institutions for investment. Foreign Direct Investments are also flowing into this field. The year 2005 was observed as the year of Micro Finance and program were carried out for popularizing the concept. In Delhi, in 2007, a Micro Finance Fair was held to attract the investors and venture capitalists. All this has since attracted the attention of United Nations Capital Development Fund (UNCDF) which has recognized Micro Finance are vital tool for encouraging entrepreneurship, empowering the less fortunate families, a promoter of economic growth and employment and above all the key program for emancipating the down trodden ,word wide.

14

Empowerment of Women in Agriculture

V. Girija Devi

There have been many changes in India since the country gained its Independence from Great Britain in 1947, the most impressive being the rise of the Indian economy. The achievements in Indian agriculture have won national and international appreciation, thereby depicting India as one of the major bread baskets of the world. Agriculture has been termed as "the mother of all industries and the maintainer of human life standing at the need of all sciences and arts, indeed, at the head of civilisation and progress". Besides that agriculture is also the mainstay of a majority of Indian population in the unorganised sector particularly women. But the differences in the health, education and standards of behaviour between the men and women of India, contribute to the impairment of women's ability to improve their economic situation. The economic discrimination that the women of India suffer leads to a cycle of further discrimination in other areas and reinforces their low status.

According to UNDP report [1994], there was not a single country, where women enjoyed equality with men. Women performed US$ 11 trillion worth of unpaid or invisible economic activity world wide. According to study done in 31 countries women worked longer than men do. On an average women put in more time on work than men, 13 percent more in developing countries and 6 percent more in developed countries [Sreekumar et al, 2001]. Another finding is that of the total burden of work, women carry 53 percent and men 47 percent in developing countries and the figures are 51 percent and 49 percent respectively for developed countries [Yadav et al., 1995]

Today, 44 percent of world's food is produced by women which indicates how important their roles is in farming. Women contribute more than half of wealth of a nation, yet they are denied economic, social and even legal rights and privileges that are granted to men.

Farm women of low economic category are found to participate more in farm operations whereas farm women of high and medium economic category participate more in allied farm operations. The position of women has always been an ambivalent one in our culture.

In all farm production, women's average contribution is estimated at 55 percent to 66 percent of the total labour with percentages, much higher in certain regions. In the Indian Himalayas, a pair of bullocks works 1064 hours, a man 1212 hours and a woman 3485 hours in a year on one hectare farm, a figure that illustrates women's significant contribution to agricultural production [WTO Report, 2003].

The feminisation of agriculture has developed with 'feminisation of poverty' according to FAO statistics, showing that more than 550 million women (60 percent of the world's rural population) live below the poverty line in rural India. This represents a 50 percent increase for women over the past two decades compared to 30 percent for men. Factors contributing to feminisation of rural poverty include, among other things, cutbacks in essential services resulting from restructuring policies, environmental and social degradation and increasing male out migration [Nair, K.P.P, 2001].

According to the census reports, there is an increased participation of rural women in economic activities beside doing household duties, though participation of women in agriculture contribute a lot for the economic growth and progress of the country, their problems are shown least concern.

In India, even after Independence, women folk are being supported to repression, marginalisation and exploitation, not withstanding the passage of a plethora of law to protect their rights. In India, employment opportunities for women are shrinking due to modernization and mechanization. Most administrators and policy makers have the tendency to see 'men as farmers' and 'women as farmer's wives' and highlight their 'supportive role'. [Samanta, 1994]

Women in Agriculture

Woman is the moulder and builder of any nation's destiny. They play a significant role in any economy. They are regarded as the backbone of the rural scene. Most of the women perform various types of work for their livelihood and agriculture is considered as the biggest unorganised sector where large number of rural women takes part actively.

About 75 percent of the Indian female population are from rural families, who belonged to the small and marginal farmers and landless agricultural labourers (Census of India, 1991). Though women's primary responsibility is indulging in domestic work, greater emphasis is laid on women's earning in the form of money by working outside the four walls. In India, a significant proportion of the population are below the poverty line and it is a fact that labour force participation increases with poverty, a large proportion of rural women are under pressure to participate in the labour force. These unknown and unacknowledged beings are responsible to keep the economy at a steady pace and helped the nation to occupy a significant place in the world.

India being a predominantly agriculture economy, all the developmental activities are cantered on farming. The traditional notion of confining women to home and hearth has deprived them of adequate health and educational facilities. Women in general are under nourished and mal nourished and have only low expectancy of life. Since most rural women are illiterate, they seek employment in agriculture as casual worker in transporting, harvesting and threshing activities. Rural women cannot aspire to seek jobs outside home because of traditional prejudices, male domination and conservation attitudes.

The trend of distribution of women workers in India from 1951 to 1991 is shown in Table 14.1.

Table 14.1: Distribution of Women Workers in India (1951-1991)
(in thousands)

Year	Total Female Population	Cultivators	Agricultural Labourers	Industry and Service	Total Female Workers
1951	173,543	18,368 (45.3)	12,694 (31.3)	9,477 (23.3)	40,539 (100)
1961	212,467	33,103 (55.7)	14,171 (23.9)	12,128 (20.4)	59,402 (100)
1971	263,900	9,266 (29.6)	15,794 (50.5)	6,238 (19.9)	31,298 (100)
1981	321,357	14,932 (33.2)	20,768 (46.2)	9,273 (20.6)	44,973 (100)
1991	402,813	22,871 (34.5)	28,833 (43.6)	14,485 (21.9)	66,189 (100)

Note: Figures do not include those of Jammu & Kashmir.
Figures within parentheses denote percentage of women workers.
Sources: 1. Towards Equality: Report on the Committee on Status of Women, Government of India, Ministry of Social Welfare, New Delhi 1974,pp.153-158. 2. Census of India, 1981 Series India, Primary Census Abstract, General Population, Part 11B (i), pp.7-8. 3. Census of India, 1991 Series-1; Paper-3; Provisional Population Totals: Workers and their distribution.

The 1991 Census data indicate that 43.6 percent of women are working, as agricultural labourers 34.5 percent are cultivators (Census of India, 1991). Though rural farm labourers work under severe limitations, their contribution towards agricultural production and development is noteworthy. Apart from the job they do outside the household, the unpaid activities in the domestic sphere go unnoticed and unrewarded. Women workforce outside the four walls is larger in rural areas than in urban India. Women in rural areas help to grow at least about 50 percent of the world's food.

The women is the backbone of agricultural workforce but worldwide her hard work has mostly been unpaid. She does the most tedious and back-breaking tasks in agriculture, animal husbandry and homes. Agriculture is the main occupation of Indian economy, since 76 percent of its population is dependent on it, in terms of employment, it is the most important sector. Women play a significant and crucial role not only in agriculture development and allied fields including crop production, live stock production, horticulture, post harvest operations, agro-socio forestry, fishing etc but also in non-farm operations and household activities. The women's contribution in these sectors have either been largely ignored or inadequately acknowledged. Further studies revealed that 50-90 percent of agricultural operations are carried out by women only [Hansra and Dhillion,1995].

For educational rural women, very few employment opportunities exist. Disparity in wages exist between men and women for the same work. Women are concentrated in low paid jobs and sectors. Women worker constitute only 33 percent of the total rural women in India, that is nearly 20 percent of the cultivators, 39 percent of agriculture labours, 32 percent of household industrial workers, 15 percent of other rural work are women, while only 63 percent of economically active men are engaged in agriculture against 78 percent of women.

Historically, Kerala's economy is agro based and a major proportion of women in the labour force work in agro and traditional industries like cashew, coir and handloom. A major proportion of the labour force in agricultural sector comprises women. Men are able to opt out from agriculture and seek new employment avenues elsewhere, when they encountered low prosperity in agriculture.

Gender inequality is reflected in the unequal sharing of benefits and adversities between man and women. It reflects itself in women differential access to employment, education, health care resources and welfare measures.

Despite the facts that Kerala has achieved remarkable development in mass education and civic consciousness, there is growing evidence of disparities across gender, communities and social classes within the state.

Some of the agriculture parameter of Kerala's development are the lower levels of feasibility and higher levels of primary education and politicisation among women. The reason for such development ,vary from better distributed health services, education especially among females, diffusion of reproduction technologies, to social intermediations like health infrastructure, education and attention in and maternal and child health. The improvement in health status of people in Kerala is more related with the political consciousness and organization than the specific medical and technical inputs.

In India until the late eighties the female mortality rate was higher than the male mortality rate. According to the Census 2001, though Kerala has a better female sex ratio [1058], the sex ratio of female children in the age group of 0-6 years had considerably declined when compared to that of the male children of the same age group. The gender discrimination practices are not uncommon. Consequently, it leads to adversities on women. This is often reflected in adverse health outcome including diseases as well as high female mortality and low female sex ratio.

According to Sen [2001], the mortality disadvantage of women workers mainly through a widespread neglect of health ,nutrition and other interest of women that influences survival. In an effort to understand the gravity of the occupation related health problems of women in the country, the national commission on self employed women and women in the informal sector explored a variety of illness found amongst women workers in various unorganized production sector. Most women are employed in low skilled, poorly paid positions, where they are often exposed to health hazards.

Role of Women in Agriculture

The participation of women in agriculture operation varies from carrying out the actual field to supervision, management and decision making. Participation of women headed households is comparatively more in most of the agricultural activities .about 18 percent of the farm families are reported to be headed by women [Hansra and Dhillion, 1995]. They work in all aspects of cultivation including planting, weeding, harvesting, sowing, threshing, etc.

Woman's role has biologically and socially combined to create four distinct functions that of mother, wife, homemaker and worker. The role of worker is equally important as that of the other three roles. But her role as an active worker-producer is rarely acknowledged though it is significant for the family's survival. The women performing agricultural operations have been classified into three categories:

- landless agricultural labourers;
- women cultivating their own piece of land and also working as wage labourers; and
- women working in their own land due to dearth of labourers.

The type and extent of participation by farm women in farm operations vary from state to state. The women has to help the farmer in his traditional tasks of ploughing, interculturing, harvesting, irrigation, after care and post harvest operations. Generally women are hired as extra hand during sowing, dibbling, interculturing, harvesting and threshing periods. Rice planting is considered as entirely women's work, while weeding is exclusively women's work. During harvesting season, utilization of women labour is maximal.

Most of the roles performed by farm women are:

1. Pre-sowing and sowing:-Preparation of land, irrigation for land preparation, puddling /levelling of land, repairing bunds and channels, maintenance of agricultural tools and implements, preparation of compost and manure, seed selection and seed treatment, seed preparation, nursery bed

raising, planting seedlings, application and spreading of fertilizers and insecticides.

2. Post-sowing and weeding: Crop care, fertilizer application, scaring of birds, plant protection measures including procurement, storage, spraying insecticides, plant propagation, hybridination, handpicking of insects, worms etc.
3. Harvesting: Harvesting of yield, unscaling, digging, shelling of pods and picking the products.
4. Post-harvesting: Preparation of threshing floor, hand threshing, threshing through machines, winnowing, grading, processing and vending. Care of storage structure, separating seeds, drying and cleaning of produce, preservation and storage of products.
5. Field labour: Carrying bundles of harvested crop as head load to the spot, where threshing is to be done.
6. Supervision of farm operations: Women supervise at all stages of farming including sale of products, storing of hay etc.
7. Decision making: Women are generally consulted regarding amount of grains to be sold, used and stored, getting credit and repayment of loans, buying new equipments, selling and buying of farms or land.
8. Performing house based activities-preparation of food for labour, carrying food to the farmers, cleaning and maintenance of storage structures, care of equipments and account keeping
9. Performing household activities: Buying of other food articles for the family, cooking and all family related activities.
10. Farm preparations involving drudgery such as physical and mental drudgery, multitasking such as child rearing, farm operations etc., energy expenditure such as bending, walking etc., winnowing in dust, drying in scorching sun, parboiling, dehusking, pounding, and grinding.

Marginalisation of Women in Agriculture

The Green Revolution had set in the process of replacing of traditional farming knowledge and practices of seed saving. The recent economic system giving a free hand to MNCs in agriculture sector has further caused a rapid shrinkage of the traditional practices and replacement of folk crop varieties by high yielding and hybrid varieties, which escalated the cost of agriculture production while stagnating productivity [WTO Report].

Indian agriculture continues to be a gamble on the monsoons in spite of the green revolution and other advancements in agricultural technology [Reddi. P, 2003]. Though green revolution technologies enhanced agricultural productivity, they also widened economic disparities and deepened gender discrimination in community life. The introduction of capital intensive technologies in the agricultural sector has had differential impact on men and women, and women have been adversely affected due to lack of access to technology [Thresia, C.U., 2004].

According to various scholars, the green revolution technologies have enhanced class polarization and deepened gender inequalities in many wages. In no Indian State do men and women earn equal wages in agriculture. Being female in India means being paid less than a man doing the same work. Researchers estimate that women make 40 to 60 percent of the wage earned by a man doing the same work. Often women are employed as a cost cutting measure. Work done by women is seen as unskilled, but in reality is usually much more difficult. For instance, in agriculture, men often do work that is machine aided, such as ploughing, while women do labour intensive work that might include weeding or transplanting. Unfortunately, technological progress seems to have a negative affect of the employment opportunities of women (Dunlop, J.E., 1999). When new machines are introduced, the work is often taken over by men.

Focusing on the impact of mechanization, argue that the

increasing use of new technological devices resulted in an inevitable decline in employment opportunities for women.

Mechanisation has driven out unskilled and semi-skilled workers from gainful employment. Women constitute a large proportion of these groups. In the absence of land reforms, modern agricultural 'revolutions' [green, white etc.] tend to result in falling employment per hectare as land ownership becomes more unequal, farm becomes larger and large scale mechanization take over.

The accelerated shift towards the cash crops associated with the commercialization process in the agriculture sector resulted in reduced employment opportunities for women. Women have remained, in the agricultural sector, accepting the traditional practice of paying wages to women at the half the rate of men.

Increasing casualisation of work, falling income and increasing insecurity of employment are real treats endangering the interests of women in the agricultural sector. These development have had disturbing implications for their health as health is closely linked to a variety of socio-economic, cultural, political, and ecological dimensions.

Retreat from the state especially from the welfare sectors and cutbacks in public sector expenditure accentuated the vulnerability of the poor particularly women, in many of the developing countries. Several studies have questioned the argument that in the process of development, the benefits would 'trickle down' to all sections of society irrespective of gender, class and community.

Women carry the heavier work burden in food production, and because of gender discrimination get lower returns for their work. When WTO rules allow dumping which leads to decline in prices of farm products, it is women already low incomes, which go down further [WTO Report].

Some studies pointed out that with statistical evidence that the expenditure of energy by women on a day to day basis may be higher than that of men. Furthermore, in the rural setting men's work is seasonal ,whereas women perform not only seasonal activities [transplanting, weeding, harvesting],but the perennial life supporting tasks like fetching water and fuel, cooking, looking after children, and old people in the family.

A study among farmers in six villages, 2 each for Kerala, Tamil Nadu and West Bengal found that despite the problems of under employment, women's economic contributions to the household is more than half of the household income and displacement of women without offering adequate other employment opportunities enhanced the pauperisation and marginalization of poor working families.

Impact of Globalization

Globalisation has intensified and heightened the vulnerability of poor women [Goel, 2004]. Globalisation shifts agriculture to capital intensive, chemical intensive system, women bear disproportionate costs of both displacement and health hazards. The livelihood and incomes of farmers in general, and women agriculturists in particular are eroded, they are displaced from productive roles, and their status is further devalued, while the patriarchal power of those who control assets and benefit from asset transfer due to globalisation is increased, other social processes are triggered which result in increased violence against women [WTO Report].

In the past few years ever since the globalisation became the mantra, plantation sector too has been at the receiving end. The unrestricted import and the sharp fall in the international price, whether it is tea, coffee, rubber or palm oil has been negatively impacted. Coffee price dropped from their highs and the producers had to take massive cut in their profit. In coffee plantation, the average working days of the labour largely women have reduced by 30 percent affecting their survival. More women than ever are participating in the market economy, but they do so on terms that are often precarious.

A sharp decline is also witnessed in the tea export from US$ 542 million in 1998 to US$ 209 million in 2003. Tea plantation workers in Kerala, West Bengal and Tamil Nadu are facing starvation, following the closing down of several small and medium tea companies. Starvation deaths among workers of abandoned tea gardens in West Bengal have assumed disastrous proportion.

Planning Projects for Empowering Women in Agriculture

Women also need to be brought to all developmental activities. The basic socio economic units in rural development are not farmers alone but rural households including all activities, income resources and problems of their members. The challenge lies in integrating brain [technology] brawn [physical work] and bank [credit] in a mutually supportive manner so that both men and women can play an active role in improving the productivity, profitability, stability and sustainability of major farming systems.

In one of the world conference of the FAO in Rome emphasized to the importance of consulting and involving women in decision making process.

It is reported that the reason for failure of developmental programme meant for rural women is that the real needs of women have seldom been actively taken into account when projects are planned and implemented.

In India, various forms of the participatory developmental process have come in for experimentation by various voluntary organization. The process has given women in considerable sense of dignity, confidence and economic independence. ICAR pointed out that women are under utilized and that women can significantly contribute to the success of developmental projects.

An important component of empowerment in Third World Countries comprises rural women who play multiple crucial roles in all spheres of development activities. In the recent past added emphasis has been laid on acknowledging and preparing database on multidimensional role sets of women where their roles have become an inbuilt factor for input–output system of empowerment.

In this process, the All India Coordinated Research Project (AICRP) on Home Science aims at developing resource base of rural women for empowering them to become subsistence-generating units for sustaining development and improving quality of life. Food and nutrition component provides a package of instruction regarding what rural women should do to endure health security, food security, economic security and livelihood security. The Human Development component focused attention for empowering rural mothers for optimal development of children through interventions on scientific child care practices, the significance of farm crèche for comprehensive child care facilities in supplementary feeding and development of child through creative play materials.

The ergonomic management of drudgery undertaken by Family Resource Management component aims at introducing women- friendly drudgery reducing technologies related to farm, home and allied activities. The ergonomic cost is being calculated for respective tool/technology as a measure for suggesting improvements in tool/technology that will promote health empowerment. The clothing and textile component since its inception has focussed attention on economic feasibility of use of locally available agro and animal based fibres. Extension component suggests several pathways for empowerment of rural women with reference to their participation and decision making roles in farming and allied activities as per indicators of qualitative data. The pathways have highlighted on empowerment of knowledge, skill, decision making; economic and social empowerment.

The research efforts at the ICAR institutes have been tried to relieve women from the drudgery by providing time and labour saving tools. Vocational trainings are also being conducted, to impart skills to undertake different vocations. In extension activities the women is now the centre point and activities are being planned keeping her in view. Her enlightenment will change the face of rural India. Several programmes started at the National Centre for Women in Agriculture and Krishi Vigyan Kendras, are the right steps in this direction.

According to the study done by Reddi [2003], the socio-economic conditions under which these women live are traditional and exploitative which impede their development and go on lowering their socio-economic status day by day. The socio-economic problems faced by these women rarely attracted the policy makers whose prime interest vaguely appears to be rural development. The impact of technology benefited the rich farmers but the gap between the poor and rich further widened. Women's labour and management roles in agriculture vary from region to region and from crop to crop. The all-round development of agriculture is only possible by the active part of rural women who form a significant part of the working class. Enormous growth in the economic production is witnessed by the orchestrated endeavour of millions of invisible rural working women.

At a time when the world agricultural economy is undergoing important structural changes and those privileged in the industrialised world are beginning to twist the arms of the disadvantaged in the developing world through hither-to unknown concepts, if India's policy-makers do not wake up to the tremendous, yet dormant, potential of what the country's women population can contribute to its advancement on the agriculture front, it will only be at our future peril. Stale ideas such as the "food for work" programme, which is being bandied about to dislodge the embarrassing mountains of food in the godowns of the Food Corporation of India, is but a temporary relief to the backstage manipulation of politicians, in the first place, which resulted in these vast hoarders of food while the super rich farmers of Punjab, Haryana and now Andhra had their bank balance soaring. This food will provide temporary relief to a few million women breaking their backs in the hot sun, but, cannot open up a new chapter in their dimly lit life. For that, a visionary change in the mindset of the powers be is called for, including some of the women, in whose hands the reins of power lie [Nair, K.P.P., 2001].

Researchers have put forward certain suggestions to empower women in agriculture such as:

1. The women participation in agriculture should be recognized and the extension programmes should be planned and executed based on their needs.
2. The women cannot benefit from the new technological developments because of their low literacy level. Evaluation of interactive learning modules and technological needs are necessary in empowering women
3. Most of the technology transfer and training programmes are held in institutions far away from rural areas and it is inconvenient for them to attend such training courses due to heavy family responsibilities and also due to unsuitable timings. Hence the farm labours prefer tailor made training programmes.
4. More farm women should be selected for Lab to Land activities in rural area.
5. There is a need to strengthen and revitalize the channels of communication exclusively for farm women.
6. There is a need for deliberate attempt to identify local farm women leaders by village extension workers in order to make the activities more effective.
7. The constraints that hamper the productivity of women farmers should be identified, appropriate institutional supportive measures should be suggested to overcome those constraints.
8. Establishment of nutrition garden in rural households as cost- effective solution for micronutrient malnutrition and nutritional upliftment of rural population.
9. Organizing stimulation programme in farm crèche for enhancing psycho-motar, mental, social and emotional development of rural children and educational interventions to rural mothers for providing conducive home environment to children.

10. Conducting out-reach programmes through radio and television talks; publication of scientific articles in newspapers, magazines etc.
11. Conducting field trials on drudgery reducing technologies for assessing ergonomic based physiological cost and work efficiency of rural women. To relieve farm women from household drudgeries, guidance and motivational programmes to reduce drudgery should be organized by experts in the field apart from farm based trainings.
12. Sustainability and equity of farm women should be ensured by some new policies.
13. Efforts should be taken to modify the new technology/ machinery/equipments suitable for rural farm women. Development of technology kits and media mixes for promoting knowledge and skill empowerment on various topics related to farming and household practices.

Based on the research study, field surveys and the public hearings, the National Commission for Women and the Government of India has made the recommendations such as:

- Trade and technology policies must protect the livelihood of women in agriculture. The Agreement on Agriculture must be reviewed with a gender perspective.
- Women's work in agro processing is both an important source of livelihood and important source of safe and culturally diverse food. Food safety laws designed to destroy household and community based agro processing need to be changed. The Sanitary and Phyto Sanitary agreement of WTO must be reviewed with women's livelihood and expertise of agro processing in focus.
- The quantitative restrictions must be reintroduced to protect the agriculture from dumping of artificially cheap subsidized products. The right to countries to protect special products and special safe guards, measures must be used to protect the livelihood and income of women.
- Organic farming needs to be promoted to increase women's productive role in agriculture, decrease health

hazards from toxic chemicals and avoid the drain of scarce family income to pay for unnecessary chemicals.

- Use locally procured grain for all public food related programmes and schemes like Integrated Child Development Programme, Food for Work, Jawahar Rozgar Yojana, School Mid Day Meals, as well as in all other public sector institutions such as primary health centre, district health centre and other places.
- Disparity in wages based on sex must be stopped.
- The families of suicide victims should be treated in the same way as victims of natural disasters such as earthquake.
- Minimum support price should be fixed for the plantation sector, like tea, coffee, rubber, jute, arcanut, cardamom, where large number of women are involved.
- Awareness should be created among women involved in agriculture and plantation sector about the impact of globalisation and WTO policies.
- Women should be increasingly involved in the decision making process in agriculture.

Conclusion

Women play different roles as participant in different farm operations as producer, cultivator or as decision maker. Illiteracy, drudgery at home and farm, physical and emotional weaknesses, ill equipped with scientific knowledge and technical know-how, women are facing challenges. It is extremely important that women should be appreciated for their contribution in all roles played in the society while pursing agriculture as a career. If women are considered as backbone of a family, she is also a trend setter in the field of agriculture, but she needs encouragement from the society and policy backing. Change is the need of the hour. To empower women in agriculture, it is necessary to improve their production potential by treating them as an important economic actor than not as a mere dependent member of the family. Men and women have equal access to benefits of development interventions. Extension and institutional support have to be sorted out to decide on a strategy which will enable the women to become equal partners in the process of national development. Thus, it is high time in bringing up policy changes which give equal opportunities and equal status to both men and women. Home science extension and agriculture extension has to play a very crucial role in this regard.

References

Dunlop John, E. and Victoria, A.Velkoff, 1999.Women and the Economy in India. Report by the U.S. Dept. of Commerce, Washington: GPO.

Goel Arun., 2004. Organisation and structure of women's development and empowerment. Deep and Deep Publications, New Delhi.

Hansra, B.S and Dhillion, D.J. 1995. Role of women in Agriculture and other allied areas-The Indian Experience. M.D. Publication Pvt. Ltd., New Delhi, pp. 105-115.

Nair, K.P.P., 2001. Empowering women in agriculture, Business line, Financial Daily, Hindu group Publication. February 15, 2001.

Reddi, P., 2003 Women in Agriculture: A Sociological Study in Southern India Presented at "Women Working to Make a Difference," IWPR's Seventh International Women's Policy Research Conference, June 2003.

Samanta, R.K., 1994. They reap less than they sow, *The Hindu*, April 17, 1994.

Sreekumar. B, Beena. R and Ajithkumar. G. S., 2001. Women in Agriculture-An evaluation of the central scheme in Palakkad District in Kerala. Kerala Research Programme on Local Level Development, Centre for Development Studies. Thiruvananthapuram.

Thresia, C. U., 2004. Women workers in Agriculture: gender discrimination, working conditions and health status. Kerala Research Programme on Local Level Development, Centre for Development Studies. Thiruvananthapuram.

15

Social Security Provisions for Women Workers in the Informal Economy

Kameshwar Pandit, Prabhakar Jha and Randhir Prasad Singh

Introduction

Informal work and informal workers are not a new phenomenon and are in existence since the beginning of the society. The concept of informal sector came into existence for the purpose of tackling the problems of the working poor. The last two decades have witnessed extensive discussions about the meaning of informal sector because of no standard definition. The term 'informal sector' is being increasingly used in various fora in different context. It is mostly referred to or used interchangeably and synonymously with the unorganized sector or with some slight modification thereof. This has given rise to a certain confusion as to whether these are the same and in case they differ only in certain minor details whether there is any need for creating an altogether new nomenclature.

The women workers in the informal sector are amongst those with least access to social protection. Given their vulnerable status at home and at work place, income generation may not improve their socio- conomic status. The economic empowerment needs to go along with political empowerment, which could improve their bargaining power both in the household and at work. The necessary statutory provisions are also needed to safeguard the socio economic condition of informal workers. In the context of growing unorganized components within the country with respect to men and women workers, the workers are suffering a lot of socio-economic problems like poor working and living condition, low wages, ill health, illiteracy, inequality, insecurity and exploitation by the employers.

Government of India and the State Government have enacted a number of legislative measures to regulate the working and living conditions and to provide welfare schemes to the men and women workers and their families. The important among these include, The Factories Act, 1948, Mines Act, 1952, Employees' State Insurance Act, 1948, Maternity Benefits Act, 1961, Equal Remuneration Act, 1976, Beedi and Cigar Workers (Conditions of Employment) Act, 1966, Beedi Workers Welfare cess Act, 1976 and the Beedi Workers Welfare Fund Act, 1976, the Minimum Wages Act, Employees Provident Fund Act, and several other labour laws and women laws. How did the state intervention benefit the workers in informal sectors? When it comes to the state addressing the problems of men and women workers, there is an interesting problem that the part of the workers is organized, while other major part is still unorganized.

The organized part is the one where the companies are registered with the government and workers are provided with legal identity cards enabling them to access the statutory and welfare provisions of the government such as minimum wages, Provident fund, health, education, housing benefits etc. The unorganized part is one where the workers do not have legal identity cards. The unorganized part of the industry is growing at the expense of the organized. This implies that the work contracts are not permanent and certain element of foot-lose nature of work relationship has crept into the industry. One frequently finds the workers shifting their employers (and vice versa) and one worker relating to several employers in a given period of time. One, therefore, witnesses an extreme complexity in the social organization of production in the informal industry. The present paper therefore seeks to address the following questions:

- What is informal sector?
- What is the extent and types of men and women workers in informal sector?
- What are the socio-economic conditions of women workers especially in unorganized sector or informal sector?
- What are the social security(statutory) benefits for the workers for organized or unorganized workers?.
- Whether the workers can access the statutory benefits, and if so, to what extent?
- What has been the role of government in enabling the informal women workers to obtain the benefits?

The present paper keeps some sociological aspects in mind, the changing nature of production relation i.e. from organized to unorganized. Rapid involvement of women and girl children in informal sectors creates great sociological problems in the country as well as state. Due to lack of education, poverty and training, they cannot take up skilled jobs in agriculture as well as in industry. All these factors make them a vulnerable to a lot of exploitations. This study is also based on certain issues of legal, welfare and social security.

India is a welfare state and the Directive Principles of State Policy as given in the preamble of the Indian constitution, clearly mentions that state will provide safety, security and all welfare measures to the vulnerable and deprived section of the society. So some basic questions have been answered by this study.

Do the women workers involve in informal sector are protected by labour laws?

Are they given welfare and safety measures by their employers in the changing production relation?

Has the government been able to provide welfare centres for the informal workers who are in unorganized sector?

How far the social security schemes and legislation formulated by the government central or state are available for women workers who are employed in the informal sector?

What is Informal Sector?

The term 'informal sector 'first appeared in the report of a comprehensive employment mission to Kenya undertaken by ILO in 1972. In the context of employment, one main findings of the mission was that in developing country like Kenya, the main problem was not unemployment but the existence of large numbers of 'working poor' many of whom were working very hard in production of goods and services but whose activities not recognized, protected or regulated by public authorities. This phenomenon was labelled in the report as the 'informal sector' and explained in terms of the inability of the other sectors of the economy-agriculture or other rural activities on the on hand and modern industry and services on the other–to provide adequate incomes or employment opportunities to a rapidly growing labour force. As suggested by ILO, the basic purpose behind identifying the informal sector was to capture the working poor i.e. poor due to visible or invisible under employment.

Banerjee (1998) stated that even after 20 or more years of using the term i.e. informal sector, it was not clear whether it referred to workers or enterprises. This may be one of the reasons why different agencies/research scholars use this term as per their understanding of it. Kundu (1998) had also pointed out that researchers and data producers had failed to standardise the definition and framework for data collection and therefore, studies were being undertaken with widely different concepts and categories. He went on to observe; "... several scholars who agree with each other and appear to be building up one school of thought do not realise that empirically they are articulating quite different thing. Similarly, there are occasions when policy makers disagree vehemently without making the effort to discover that the difference in their perceptions is due to their levels of aggregation or the differences, scope and coverage of concepts."

It is therefore, imperative to examine the concept itself and its relevance in the Indian context. However, The National Commission on Enterprise in the Unorganised Sector (NCEUS), Government of India submitted their report in 2006 and observed as "All unincorporated private enterprise owned by individuals or households engaged in the production and sale of goods and services and operated on a proprietary or a partnership basis and employing less than 10 persons." The Commission has also taken another view that "Unorganised Workers are all those who are working in the unorganized sector defined earlier and the workers in the formal sector without any employment security and social security provided by the employer." Thus, Informal sectors are amongst those who are left out of economic and social protection, legislative protection and are unregulated and unregistered forms of employment and are not fully guided and controlled by any regulatory authorities in the economic system.

Magnitude of Workers in Informal Economy

The informal economy in India employs about more than 90 percent i.e. 90-92 percent of the country's workforce. The National Commission on Enterprises in unorganized Sector (NCEUS) estimated the number of informal workers in the informal sector in India as on January 1, 2000 at 340 million and the total number of informal workers in the economy (i.e. the number of informal workers in the informal sector plus informal workers in formal sector) at 362 million. The latter is referred to as informal employment. The above figure constituted 86 percent and 91 percent, respectively. Many of these women workers are the primary earners in their families-their earnings are necessary for their own and their families' survival.

With growing economic reforms in India, some believe that such informal work, characterized by low earning, irregular employment and unsafe working conditions, is likely to intensify in the coming years. Low-income women workers form one of the most vulnerable groups in Indian society. Their vulnerability arises from their irregular work, their low economic status, their little bargaining power, their lack of control over their earnings, their need to balance work with care of children and homework, and their lack of assets. Unequal gender relations indeed assume a very important role in defining their insecurities. While there are some common experiences amongst women of all race, class and culture, women from poorer income groups in poorer countries are at a grater disadvantage in relation to their men, other men women from higher income groups, and women from richer countries. (Young and Dickerson, 1994)

These poor women's access to institutional credit, training and information is restricted. They are often powerless in the face to forces that rule their lives, social customs and norms, as well as the persons who exercise control over them and their earnings. Their coping strategies in the face of crisis are also few are absent. "The forces which control and sustain the vulnerability of women are institutionalized in society and the economy" (NCL, 2nd, p.168).

In India, Globalization has led to increase in workers' participation in the informal sector. However, workers' opportunities for employment in the manufacturing sector have fallen drastically in all Indian states. On the other hand, workers are increasingly taking self-employment, especially in the informal economy, while some others are engaged in casual wage work. The following elaborates the different types of work status of these workers in the informal economy.

Casual Workers: In rural as well as urban areas in India, women dominate in casual work. Between 1973-74 and 1993-94, the share of women casual work in rural areas increased from 31.4 percent to 38.4 percent. The corresponding rise in share of women in casual work in urban areas over the same time period was from 23.7 percent to 26 percent (Vissaria, 1996). As reported by 57th Round of NSS (2001-2002) this figure increased to 41.2 percent in rural areas and 28.4 percent in urban areas (Bhaumik, 2003).

This rise in casual work amongst women workers is an indication of their increasing insecurity of employment. Studies by the World Bank reveal the strong links between casual work and poverty in both urban and rural areas. In the construction industry which is a large employer of casual workers, women tend to perform the less skilled and less paid casual work. Sometimes when men and women of a family engage in casual construction work, the women workers are not registered as workers. Their output is added to that of their male relative and their earnings are passed on to the male relative as well.

Own Account Workers: Self-employed workers in the informal economy are typically own account workers. Their activities range from agriculture, animal husbandry, fishery and forestry and other agro- based processing and producing work in rural areas, to vending, service work, rag picking, paper recycling, and manufacturing in urban areas. Much of this self-employment requires little capital investment and low level of skills, and low earnings. While their employment is not at the mercy of employer, they little control over market and virtually no access to credit and skills that could ensure their continuous earning and employment or upward mobility within self-employment.

Domestic Workers: A large number of poor workers in India work as domestic workers. These domestic workers work either full time for one employer or part time for many employers. Child labour is quite rampant in domestic service. Domestic work is the least regulated of informal work. Women as domestic workers often work long hours, with no contracts, no protection against job loss and no leave. Those who live in the employers' house are on duty all hours of the day.

Home Workers: Home workers tend to be the most hidden of all informal employees. According to a survey of the National Institute of Urban Affairs (NIUA, 1990) about quarter of all informal work is homework. Amongst the different kinds of work that home workers engage in are making of various food products and pickles, incense sticks, garments, bidi rolling and filling of capsules with medicines etc. There also conceptual confusion between homework and self-employment. Although home workers are often classified as self-employed, some home workers are piece rate workers and some are self-employed workers. Self-employed home workers buy the raw materials from a market, take them their homes and work on them, and finally market their finished products themselves. A businessmen or middleman gives piece rate home workers raw materials which they work on. They then return their produce it to the same person and paid on the basis of their produce. Piece rate home workers are therefore effectively 'disguised' wage workers. According to a directive of the Supreme Court of India, piece rate home workers are employees and the direct hold that the middleman or businessman has over them qualifies as an industrial relation. According to the 57th NSS of India, there are more than 30 millions home workers in India.

The informal workers are mainly engaged in wide variety of occupations such as, Maid servant in domestic services, Hawkers, Cooks, Vendors, Cleaners, Petty traders Construction workers, Paper bags/envelop makers, Tailoring, embroidery work, Handicrafts, Bindi making, cosmetics, Beauty parlour, Beedi rolling, Computer centres, Call centres, Transport, Urban agriculture, Preparing food in roadside, Vegetables/fruit selling, Brick and kiln industry, carpet making etc. Broadly speaking persons in the informal sector can be classified in three categories:

- Women Workers,
- Child Labour, and
- Adults and old people.

Socio-economic Conditions of Women Workers

The women workers in informal sector are suffering a lot

due to their poor socio-economic condition, poor social security provisions, lack of employment condition, lack of statutory provisions of employment and working conditions etc. The low socio-economic status of these informal workers goes hand in hand with their low socio-economic security and statutory benefits, which in turn perpetuates their poverty. According to the Commission, the social security problems of informal workers may be divided into two sets of problems. The first one arises out of deficiency or capability deprivation in terms of inadequate employment, low earnings, low health and educational status and so on, that are related to the general deprivation of poor sections of the population. The second arises out of adversity in the absence of adequate fallback mechanisms (safety nets and statutory provisions) to meet such contingencies as ill health, accident, death, and old age etc.

The women and women workers are the worst sufferer in the home, family, society, as well as work place. There are many evidences which disclose positively the negative observation for the development of women in India. Millions of girls and women throughout the country suffer form discrimination and deprivation of their human rights based on their gender. Throughout the country, women and girls often face systematic discrimination in legal, political, social, economic and cultural settings. In many societies violence against women is an everyday occurrence and sometimes even considered "normal." The incidence of crimes against women has increased from 135771 in 1999 to 140601 in 2003. However, the proportion to the total crimes has marginally declined from 2.76 percent in 1999 to 2.56 percent in 2003. According to police report;

- Every 26 minutes a woman is molested.
- Every 34 minutes a rape takes place.
- Every 42 minutes a sexual harassment incident occurs.
- Every 43 minutes a woman is kidnapped.
- Every 93 minutes a woman is burnt to death over dowry.

Although the penalty is severe, the convictions are rare

(Kurukshetra, September, 2008).

The Indian women are suffering a lot in the society event then the empowerment of is growing day by day. The basic problems before women are poor health, sexual harassment, dowry, female infanticides and sex selective abortions, domestic violence, trafficking and over burdened work load. Table 15.1 depicts the real status of women in society.

Table 15.1: Status of Women in Society

S.N	Crime	Incidence			Variation in
		1998	2000	2003	1998-03
1	Rape	15151	16496	15847	4.6
2	Kidnapping and Abduction	16351	15023	13296	-18.7
3	Dowry Death	6975	6995	6208	-11.0
4	Torture	1376	45778	50703	22.5
5	Mole Station	30959	32940	32939	6.4
6	Sexual Harassment	8054	11024	12325	53.0
7	Importation of Girls	146	64	46	-68.5
8	Sati Prevention Act	0	0	0	0
9	Immoral Traffic Act	8695	9515	5510	-36.6
10	Indecent Representation of Women Act	190	662	1043	448.9
11	Dowry Prohibition Act	3578	2876	2684	-25.9
	Total	131475	141373	140601	0.9

Source: National Crimes Record Bureau, "Report on the Elimination of All Forms of Discrimination against women" 22nd Session at Meetings on 24th and 31st January 2005, CEDAW Periodic Report GOI.

The Commission believes that the absence of a meaningful social security arrangements and lack of proper statutory provisions of regulated employment and living condition is merely a problem of individual workers and their families. It also has wider implications for the economy and the society. From the economic point of view, it adversely affects the worker's ability to meaningfully use his/her efficiency for increasing production and productivity. Low earning power coupled with vulnerabilities lead to poverty that reduces the aggregate demand in the economy. Socially, it leads to dissatisfaction and disaffection, especially when small segment of the society is well endowed and seen to be prospering. The indirect costs of the absence of social security might well be the increasing social costs resulting from the need for policing and management of crimes and illegal activities, widespread ill health and a variety of related social problems.

After independence the feminist activism picked up momentum during later 1970s and women participate in all activities such as education, politics, media, art and culture, service sectors, science and technology, etc. The Constitution of India guarantees to all Indian women equality by (Article 14), no discrimination against women by [Article 15(1)], equality of opportunity by (Article 16), and equal pay for equal work by (Article 39(d). Further, the self-help groups and NGOs such as Self Employment Women's Association (SEWA) have played a major role in Women's rights in India now a days. The government of India during planned growth of the country has adopted various policies and programmes for women's development. The gist of the government efforts during five year plans may be summarized as under:

Five Year Plans on Women Development in India

- **First Five Year Plan (1951-1956)** set up the Central Social Welfare Board in 1953 to promote welfare work through voluntary organizations, charitable trusts etc.
- **Second Five Year Plan (1956-1961)** supported the

development of mahila mandals to work at the grassroots.

- **Third, Fourth and Interim Five Year Plans (1961-74)** had provisions for women's education, pre-natal and child health services, supplementary feeding for children, nursing and expectant mothers.
- **Fifth Five Year Plan (1974-1978)** saw a major shift in the approach towards women, from welfare to development.
- **Sixth Five Year Plan (1980-85)** accepted women's development as a separate economic agenda. Took a multi-disciplinary approach with a three-pronged thrust on health, education and employment.
- **Seventh Five Year Plan (1985-1990)** had the objective of bringing women into the mainstream of national development.
- **Eighth Five Year Plan (1992-1997)** saw a paradigm shift from development to empowerment and benefits to women in the core sectors of education, health and employment. Outlay for women rose from Rs 4 crore in the first plan to RS. 2000 crore in the eighth.
- **Ninth Five Year Plan (1997-2002)** had empowerment of women as its strategic objective. Accepted the concept of a women's component plan to assure that at least 30 percent of funds/benefits from all development sectors flow to women.
- **Tenth Five Year Plan (2002-2007)** suggests specific strategies, policies and programmes for the empowerment of women.
- **Eleventh Five Year Plan (2007-2012)** has focused on promoting gender equality and more inclusive growth. The government will constitute 'Feminist' Economists to advice on Eleventh Plan.

The need for women's empowerment was felt in India long back. Women's empowerment is a global issue; UNO has also expressed concern in the matter. The charter of United Nations declares equal dignity and worth of human person-all types of human rights, civil, political economic and cultural.

The Government of India has been implementing various schemes and programmes for welfare and empowerment of women in the areas of poverty alleviation, skill up-gradation, micro credit, development and sustainable income generation, science and technology, education, health services, awareness generation, legal literacy and support services. The details are as under:

- Awareness Generation Projects for Rural and Poor Women;
- Condensed Course of Education for Adult Women;
- Crèche Programme;
- Border Area Projects;
- Welfare Extension Project;
- Welfare Extension Projects;
- Mahila Mandal Programme;
- Kishori Shakti Yojana;
- Rastriya Mahila Kosh;
- Support to Training and Employment programme for women(STEP);
- Swawalamban Programme;
- Swashakti Project; and
- Swayamsidha Scheme etc.

National Policy for Empowerment of Women

The National Policy of Empowerment of Women, 2001 has set certain clear cut goals and objectives. The goal of this Policy is to bring about the advancement, development and empowerment of women. The policy will be widely disseminated so as to encourage active participation of all stakeholders for achieving its goals. Specially, the objectives of this Policy include:

- Creating an environment through positive economic and social policies for full development of women to enable them to realize their full potential.
- The de jure and de facto enjoyment of all human rights and fundamental freedom by women on equal basis with men

in all spheres-political, economic, social, cultural and civil.

- Equal access to participation and decision making of women in social, political and economic life of the nation.
- Equal access to women to healthcare, quality education at all levels, career and vocational guidance, employment, equal remuneration, occupational heath and safety, social security and public office etc.
- Strengthening legal systems aimed at elimination of all forms of discrimination against women.
- Changing societal attitudes and community practices by active participation and development of both men and women.
- Mainstreaming a gender perspective in the development process.
- Elimination of discrimination and all forms of violence against women and the girl child.
- Building and strengthening partnerships with civil society, particularly women's organizations.

Legislative Support for Women

Apart from the Constitutional provisions, a large number of laws have been enacted to protect the Human Rights and eliminate discrimination for women. The women specific legislations and women-related acts are as under:

Women-specific Legislations:

- Immoral Traffic (Prevention) Act, 1956;
- Dowry Prohibition Act, 1961;
- Indecent Representation of Women (Prohibition) Act, 1986;
- Commission of Sati (Prevention) Act, 1987; and
- Domestic Violence Act, 2005.

Women-related Legislations:

- Guardians and wards Act, 1860;
- Indian Penal Code, 1860;
- Christian Marriage Act, 1872;

- Indian Evidence Act, 1872;
- Married Women's Property Act, 1874;
- Workmen's Compensation Act, 1923;
- Legal Practitioners (Women) Act, 1923;
- Indian Succession Act, 1925;
- Child Marriage Restraint Act, 1998;
- Payments of Wages Act, 1936;
- Muslim Personal Law (Shariat) Application Act, 1937;
- Factories Act, 1948;
- Minimum Wages Act, 1948;
- Employees' State Insurance Act, 1948;
- Plantation Labour Act, 1951;
- Cinematograph Act, 1952;
- Special marriage Act, 1954;
- Hindu Marriage Act, 1955;
- Hindu Adoptions and Maintenance Act, 1956;
- Hindu Succession Act, 1956;
- Maternity Benefit Act, 1961;
- Beedi and Cigar Workers (Conditions of Employment) Act, 1966;
- Foreign Marriage Act, 1969;
- Indian Divorce Act, 1969;
- Medical Termination of Pregnancy Act, 1971;
- Code of Criminal Procedure, 1973;
- Bonded Labour System (Abolition) Act, 1976;
- Equal Remuneration Act, 1976;
- Contract Labour (Regulation and Abolition) Act, 1976;
- Inter-State Migrant Workmen (Regulation of Employment and Conditions of Service) Act, 1979;
- Family Courts Act, 1984;
- Juvenile Justice Act, 1986;
- Child Labour (Prohibition & Regulation) Act, 1986;
- National Commission for Women Act, 1990 (20 of 1990);
- Infant Milk Substitutes, Feeding Bottles and Infant Foods

(Regulation of Production, Supply and Distribution Act, 1992; and

- Pre-Natal Diagnostic Technique (Regulation and Prevention of Misuse) Act, 1994.

In the context of poor women workers in the informal economy, however economic empowerment through income generation and work force participation alone may not improve their socio-economic status. This is because this redistribution of resources cannot be complete unless the women control over their earnings, and control over materials and methods of production. An equally important issue is therefore how best to overcome those forces which perpetuate the subordination and oppression of these women workers in their families, in their work place and in their society. In this context although the country does not have a formal social policy, it has along standing and universal social development aged arising out of directive principles of state policy enshrined in the constitution. In addition, it has also several targets oriented and long – standing programmes with the objective of eradication of poverty and deprivation.

There is need to locate the evolving/proposed national social security system and statutory provisions within the framework of the existing (and also evolving) national social protection/social development programmes, human development programmes for the poor men and poor women and the larger framework of universals social/human development programmes. The I.L.O. has passed several Conventions and Recommendations for employment, working and living condition apply equally to men and women workers, which has been ratified by the Govt. of India by providing labour laws.

Some of the existing important labour laws which are operative in the informal sector are as under:

1. Minimum Wages Act, 1948.
2. Beedi and Cigar Workers (Conditions of Employment) Act,1966.

3. Maternity Benefit Act, 1961.
4. Equal Remuneration Act, 1976.
5. Beedi Workers Welfare Cess Act, 1976.
6. Beedi Workers Welfare Fund Act, 1976.
7. National Rural Employment Guarantee Act, 2005.
8. Workmen's Compensation Act, 1923.
9. Bonded Labour System (Abolition) Act, 1976.
10. Inter-State Labour Migration Act.

Social Security Net

Presently, the social security framework in the country is operating at three levels as suggested by commission (NCEUS). At the first level, the universal programmes and schemes for basic social/human development such as the mission of literacy, schooling, healthcare services, drinking water, and sanitation, technical training, etc. that should be viewed as being foundational to any sound social and economic development policy. These programmes address the issue of the creation and enhancement of human capabilities through the provision of entitlements to all citizens funded by the public exchequer. The effectiveness and advancement of these functions of the state are often a prerequisite for the effectiveness of specific protective social security policies and schemes.

At the second level, the social/human development scheme that is intended to provide a measure of socio-economic security to the poorer citizen, irrespective of their status as working or non- working poor. The underlying idea here is to meet both the promotional and protective needs of some sections of the population in their basic social security needs. Over time, a number of programmes have come to stay in the country like the Integrated Child Development Scheme (ICDS), Development of Women and Children in Rural Areas (DWCRA), Mid-Day Meal Scheme for Schooling Children, Public Distribution system, Housing for the Poor, The National Social Assistance Programme (NSAP) and the recently introduced National Rural Employment Guarantee (NREG) programme. In order to address the social security concerns of specific groups, sub-targeting is often resorted to as in the case of the old aged poor, widows, child labourers, the physically and mentally challenged etc.

At the third level, according to commission, constitute a social security system for unorganized/informal workers as well as especially for women workers. This should address both deficiency and adversity. The social security concerns arising out of deficiency relate to access to credit/finance (especially for the self-employed), loans for upgrading skills, loans for housing, children's education, etc. The adversity arises out of various contingencies such as absence of social security cover for ill health, accidents, death, and old age.

The Second National Commission on Labour (2002) gave some notable recommendations for the unorganised labour for regulating the employment and working condition and social security provisions are as under:

1. The commission is strongly of the opinion that our laws and systems of social security should prevent and eliminate discriminatory attitudes and practices.
2. The Commission recommends that the government formulate a national policy on Home based work in conformity with the provisions of ILO Convention.
3. To deal with the shrinkage of employment that results from mechanization and introduction of new technology, the commission recommends skill training and up gradation of skills for women on widespread and continuous scale.
4. The Commission's concern is to assure minimum level of income and security to all women workers regardless of where and under what employment relations they work.
5. There should be a provision for crèches where 20 or more workers are employed irrespective of gender of workers.
6. A feasible, autonomous Childcare fund may be set up at the state level. The fund can be drawn upon to provide

childcare facilities to all women, regardless of income, number of children or other considerations.

7. A statutory scheme for the implementation of maternity entitlement should cover all women under income criteria. The scheme should provide financial support for childbirth, childcare and breast-feeding in the first few months of the child's life. The funds to support such a scheme should be raised from basket of services.
8. There is need to extend maternity benefits measures to women workers in the unorganized sector.
9. The Commission recommends that governments should allow widespread registration of Mutual Benefit Organizations (MBOs) of women workers under the Trade Unions Act.
10. To achieve recognition as a worker, each person who is actually working should be given an official identity card. The identity card gives the worker a definite legal identity and recognition.
11. The law should be capable of being implemented and monitors easily. It should, therefore include machinery for the disposal of claims and complaints at a place that is not too distant from the place of work, with expedition.
12. The employer employing more than 5 workers shall insure that the workers engaged by them are registered with Board and issued identity cards by Board and those employing less than 5 workers shall help the workers in securing the registration and identity cards.

The Commission was also in view of an "Umbrella Legislation" for the workers in the unorganized sector to ensure at least a minimum protection, social security, employment conditions, job guarantee, proper health and safety provisions, protection against the exploitations of their poverty, minimum wage protection and mechanism of welfare etc. to the worker.

Role of the Government

The informal workers who, as mentioned earlier, constitute

more than 91 percent of the workforce have limited or no formal social security cover which increases their vulnerability during times of illness, old age, unemployment and untimely death. The absence of social security mechanism constitutes a critical factor in the worsening of the condition of these households, many of which are already poor. A number of social security programmes are being implemented by both Central and State governments for the benefits of unorganized workers. In general, the model that has been adopted in most of these programmes has been that of welfare funds. A few schemes have also been implemented by central government either directly or through insurance companies. Separate legislations have been enacted by parliament to set up five welfare Funds to be administered by ministry of Labour for providing housing, medical care, social security, education and recreational facilities to workers in selected mining operations, beedi-making and the production of feature films (called cine workers). All these funds are financed out of the proceeds of the Cess levied under respective Cess/Funds Act on manufactured beedi, feature films, export of mica, consumption of limestone and dolomite, and consumption and export of iron ore, manganese ore and chrome ore etc.

The National Social Assistance Programme (NSAP) is a programme of a cash-transfer nature in the country, which was launched with the objective of protecting the poor and destitute persons (men and women) in the events of insecurities during old age, death of the breadwinner and maternity. The scheme is 100 percent centrally funded to ensure that a measure of social protection, albeit limited, is available to the poor and old persons throughout the country. The NSAP, by its very character, has made it possible to extend a scheme of social assistance to states, which did not have one so far. The gram panchayat and municipalities play an important role in the identification of beneficiaries, monitoring of the NSAP and disbursement of funds. The programme currently covers two benefits:

- National Old Age Pension Scheme (NOAPS), and
- National Family Benefit Scheme (NFBS).

By launching this scheme, the government has expressed its recognition of the fact that a social security measures of this nature demands national attention and initiative. Apart from the NSAP, a number of central government schemes for social security have been in operation over a period of time. These have been targeted at the poorer section of the society and selected occupational groups, and are mostly contributory in nature. Some of these schemes discussed in the report are the Varishta Pension Bima, Group Health Insurance Scheme (GHIS), Janshree Bima Yojana, Universal Health Insurance scheme and Krishi Samajik Suraksha Yojana. In the union budget 2007-2008, the union Finance Minister P. Chidambaram has introduced Aam Admi Bima Yojana (AABY) for the unorganized sector workers.

Mr. Chidambaram termed it a "beginning and effort to cover the unorganized sector under death and disability insurance through the Life Insurance Corporation of India." He also stated that "Under AABY, I propose to cover the rural landless households which enjoy no cover and a number may actually be more than what is indicated in the NSS report. Under the proposal, the head of the family or one earning member will be insured."

At the state level, there a number of social security initiatives. However those are found to be uneven, in terms of coverage of both men as well women worker. With the exception of a few, most social security initiatives do not cover sickness. They mostly cover such requirements as accidental death and injury, maternity and more financial assistance for the education of children. One of the major insecurities of workers stems from frequent incidences of illness and need for medical care and hospitalization of the workers and other family members.

Conclusion

The women workers in informal sector are suffering a lot

due to their poor socio-economic condition, poor social security provisions, lack of employment condition, lack of statutory provisions of employment and working conditions etc. The low socio- economic status of these informal workers goes hand in hand with their low socio-economic security and statutory benefits, which in turn perpetuates their poverty.

Much has been done to protect the workers employed in the formal or organised sector but nothing more attention has been paid to regulate the employment and working conditions of workers in the informal economy. The Government central and state are trying to empower the men and women and eager to provide legislative base to promote healthy employment and working conditions and to protect from the exploitation and deprivation in the society with sound base of protective social security legislation and scheme.

The major schemes have undertaken by the Govt. of India for the empowerment of women such as Kishori Shakti Yojana, Nutrition Programme for Adolescent Girls, Swaym Siddha, Support to Training and Employment Programme for Women, Swadhar for Distressed Women, Short Stay Homes, Family Counselling Centres and Working Women Hostel. The Govt. has also enacted some important Laws and Legislation for protection of women such as Protection of Women from Domestic Violence Act, Dory Prohibition Act, Indecent Representation of Women Act, The Commission of Sati (prevention) Act and Rules, Sexual Harassment Act of Women at the Work Place Bill, The Immoral Traffic (Prevention) Act, The National Rural Employment Guarantee Act etc.

The Government has formulated major policies for establishment of National Commission for Women, Rashtriya Mahila Kosh, National Policy on Empowerment of women, Integrated Women's Empowerment Programmes through Self Help Group. These all schemes, provisions and policies undoubtedly will improve the socio-economic status of the women but issues so far as concerned with employment and working condition of women workers in informal economy, will not be provide a sound base to regulate the employment and working conditions. The nature of employment and working conditions in informal sector are different and women are not in a position to access the provisions and benefits of such legislations, schemes and policies.

Thus, there is a need for separate legislation and Social security provisions to regulate the employment and working conditions for workers (men and women) in the unorganized sector. The recommendations of the second National commission on Labour should be followed by the government and for "Umbrella Legislation" Unorganised Sector Workers (Employment and Welfare) Bill should be passed to growth of the economy, to improve the quality of employment, to provide decent life to workers and to integrate them with the growing opportunities in the country.

The basic purpose for the legislation will be removal of poverty of the working population of the country through improving their productivity, quality of work, enhancing income earning abilities, and increasing bargaining power. The obligation of the government, employment providers and the society towards the country's working population include, minimum wage, social security like health and old age insurance, welfare like childcare and prospects for skill and technical advancement so that they could lead decent life in the society. Ex-President A.P.J. Abdul Kalam, said empowering women was a perquisite for creating a good Nation, "When women are empowered, society with stability is assured. Empowerment of women is essential as their thoughts and their value system lead the development of a good family, good society and ultimately a good nation."

References

Banerjee, Nirmala (1998), "A Note on Conceptualising the Informal Sector, The Indian Journal of Labour Economics, Vol. 41.

Dasgupta, Sukti, 2003, "Women Organising for Socio-economic Security," The Indian Journal of Labour Economics, Vol. 46,

No. 1.

Deepali Singh and Nafees A. Ansari, "The Empowerment of Indian Women with reference to Five Year Plans, Kurukshetra, September, 2008 Government of India, (2002), Second National Commission on Labour.

Devaki Jain, "Women and Development: 150 Years", Yojana, August, 2007.

Documentation, (2006), "Social Security for Unorganised Workers", The Indian Journal of Labour Economics, Vol. 49, No. 2.

Girija Vyas, Women's Empowerment: Remedy for Social Elevation, Yojana, October, 2008.

Indira Rajaraman, "Women in the Eleventh Plan" Yojana, May, 2007.

K Muthalagu, "Indian Women in Development Perspective?", Kurukshetra, September, 2008.

Kundu, Amitabh (1998), "Introduction," The Indian Journal of Labour Economics, Vol. 41, No. 3.

16

Women Workers in Beedi Manufacturing Sector

Ravi Prakash Yadav, Kumar Chandradeep and Barsa

Introduction

Indian economy is an 'unorganised sector' based economy. About 93 percent (India, 2007) of the total work force of the Indian economy is working in the unorganised sector. This sector contributes about 60 percent of GNP (Chauhan, 2001:3). Despite of this contribution, a large chunk of workers of unorganised (Informal) sector is still 'exploited and deprived' from many basic welfare and social security benefits. Majority of them are far from legislative protections. Beedi manufacturing is an unorganised 'home-based' sector. The Beedi industry in India is one of the largest employers of workforce, after agriculture, handloom and construction (ILO, 2001:1). This industry is one of the largest informal sector industries in India. The tobacco and beedi industries are now about 300 and 100 years old respectively (Verma and Rehman, 2005: v). Tobacco was routed into India in the medieval times when it was presented to 'Emperor Akbar' as a medicine for some illness by some European doctors (not documented). The poor mostly used crude forms of tobacco, whereas the rich could afford more refined tobacco products.

The earliest evidence of 'beedi smoking' in India is the 'Bombay Gazette',1879 which mentions that the inhabitants of Kheda and Panchampae district of Gujarat used to consume tobacco in ASTRA LEAVES, But it were 'Rajasthani families' who started the process of beedi making in the 19th century and named their product as 'Beedi' (Chauhan, 2001:9).

Beedi is made by rolling about 0.2 gram of tobacco flakes in 'Tend Leaf' (Scientifically known as Diosyros Melanoxylon) (ILO, 2003:1). Beedi is a 'common man's smoke' mostly popular among 'rural people' and lower class of urban areas.

During last 40 years, there has been a shift (Spe. from 1966) away from the 'factory-based' production to the 'homes' of the workers. This shift has also been accompanied by growing 'Feminization' (ILO, 2003:1) of the workforce. The Beedi industry in India employs over 5 million (Ministry of Labour, 2001:109) workers consisting of males, females and children. The industry spreads over, 13 states and 3 unions territories. Out of total beedi workers, about 90 percent (ILO, 2001:1) workers are 'home based' women workers. According to trade union, this industry provides employment of nearly 75 lakh (Chauhan, 2001:3) people of whom approximately 90 percent are women. Majority of beedi women workers live and work in extremely 'vulnerable' conditions. Various studies have been conducted on working and living conditions of the women workers in the beedi industry. The general conclusion reached by most of these is that 'piece-rated' women workers are working under most 'exploitative conditions' in India. Still they are struggling for their survival. They are facing so many problems like low wages, irregular employment, lack of credit, lack of basic facilities, exploitation by the middlemen and owner and so on. Despite of a number of legislation and welfare schemes as well as trade unions' efforts, the conditions of women beedi workers have not improved remarkably. In addition to the economic exploitation of the beedi worker, they are also exposed the occupational health hazards. In this context, a multi-faceted effort is needed to improve their working conditions, living conditions and levels of income security. The entire discussion of the paper is dived into following sections:

1. Introduction;

2. Origin and growth of Beedi Industry;
3. Systems of Beedi Production;
4. Women workers in Beedi Manufacturing Sector and
5. Conclusions.

Origin and Growth of Beedi Industry

The history of Beedi smoking is closely associated with the history of 'Tobacco'. It is believed that tobacco began growing in the America about 6000 B.C. As early as I B.C. 'American Indians' began using tobacco in many different ways, such as in religious and medicinal practices. Tobacco was believed to be a care for all, and was used as painkiller as well as to dress wounds (Goodman, 2005). In Europe tobacco cultivation is reported to have started in 15th century. As per one record, on an October 15, 1492, Christopher Columbus was offered dried tobacco leaves as a gift from the American Indians that he encountered. Soon after, sailors brought tobacco back to Europe, and the plant was being grown all over Europe (Goodman, 2005). By the end of the reign of Queen Elizabeth I (1603) smoking was common in classes in England. By the end of the 17th century, tobacco had reached most pants of the world (Chauhan, 2001:12).

In India, tobacco cultivation had already during 17th century. It is commonly known that the British introduced the tobacco cultivation in India, but some believe that Portuguese introduced it. As per another sources, tobacco began to be cultivated in Andhra Pradesh (Deccan-South India) during the reign of Krishna Dev Rai (Chauhan, 2001). Smoking, enjoyed by the rich and the poor, the young and the old of both sexes and considered as a solace in moments of depression, was first advocated by the ancient physicians of India as one of the means of curing certain disease (GOI, 1967). But there is no clear evidence about when the beedi rolling industry began to operate in India. As per Ratnakar records, the earliest evidence of 'Beedi smoking' in India is the Bombay Gazette, 1879 which mentions that the inhabitants of Kheda and Panchamal district of Gujarat uses to consume tobacco in astra leaves.

As per another records, the Rajasthani families started the 'process of beedi making' in the 19th century, and named their product as 'Beedi'. According to the some related study, the beedi industry is 100 years old in the Poona, Konkan and Vidarbha regions of the Maharashtra state. In the case of Bihar and Madhya Pradesh, it came in the first decade of the present century. As per official report, the manufacturing of Beedi was introduced by the merchants who hailed from Gujarat (Labour Investigation Report, GOI, 1946). The oldest beedi making formal firm was established as early 1887 (Report of the Count of Inquiry into Labour Conditions in Beedi, Government of Madras, 1947).

The traditional smoke of the Indians was the Hookah and Chillum. Hookah, a magnificent and elaborate device, was a pride of 'Royal Palaces' of the great Mugal Emperors. It was a symbol of wealth and status and the 'Rajas and Amirs' uses to enjoy smoking with the help of the hookah. The 'tribal people' of ancient India uses to smoke tobacco in a 'pipe' made from leaves of trees and the idea of making beedis by rolling tobacco in a piece of wrapper leaf probably originated from that (Marketing of Beedi Tobacco, Tendu leaf and Beedi in India, GOI, 1967). It is clear from above discussion that beedi is a 'Common man's Smoke'. The raw material was easily available in the rural areas. Beedi production spread very fast as a 'local activity' after the invention of the art of 'beedi rolling' (Chauhan: 9).

Initially, people knowing this art first started producing beedi for their own consumption and then for others who did not have the 'required skill' could afford to buy them. Very soon beedi smoking became the 'permanent habit' of the poor rural people. This habit created a vast 'rural market' for beedi. This growing demand for beedi paved the way for its production on a much larger scale. Thus, the 'beedi-manufacturing units' towards the end of the 19th century gradually replaced beedi making as a 'local activity' in the rural areas. The beedis were manufactured by firm level (on large scale) during the beginning of the 21th century, which are as follows:

- P.V.S. Beedi (P) Limited Mangalore, established by Puttu Vainkult Shet in 1904;
- Beedi manufacturing in Jabalpur (M.P.) by two brothers- Mohanlal Patel and Hargovinddas Patel. It is also important to note that they were the first to discover that 'tends leaves' found in the forest of Madhya Pradesh were better suited for beedi making them astra leaves (Chauhan: 10);
- Messes Haribhai Desai were first to register their 'Brand' in 1901 and Messes Mohanlal Hargovinddas registered their brand in 1902; and
- Bharat Beeti Works Ltd.

Over a period of time the industry had spread over the length and breadth of the century. Today there are about '300 major manufacturers' of branded beedis apart from thousands of small-scale manufactures cum contractors who account for the bulk of the beedi production in India (S.K. Das). But there is a drastic change in beedi sector. Specially after 1966, there has been a fast shift-away from the factory based production to the homes of the workers. This shift has also been accompanied by growing 'feminization' of the workforce (ILO, 2003:1). Today the bulk of beedi rolling takes place in the 'unorganised', 'home based sector' and largely through the 'sub-contracting system' (ILO, 2001:1). Today it is undertaken on a large scale in 12 states.

Systems of Beedi Production

There are no single or uniform methods of production system in Beedi sector. The medhod of Production of beedi used by the manufacturers varies from state to state, district to district and sometimes block to block, depending on local conditions and also on the business exigencies of the manufacturer. But three main systems (Chauhan, 2001:15-16) are adopted in the manufacturing of beedies, which are given below:

- **Factory System:** The entire process of beedi manufacturing taking place in factory premises. Under this system beddi rolling and other work is carried out under the direct control and supervision of owner or Manager/Supervisor. Workers work for a fixed time and are paid fix wages for their work. Since 1887 this system was more prevalent. Especially after 1970, due to many reasons, owners are shifting to other systems. Now a day very few examples of this so called 'factory system' are existing;
- **Home-Based Work System:** Under this system factories/branches issue fixed quantities of raw materials (tobacco, thread and tendu patta) directly to the individual workers (who are mostly women). Who roll beedis at their homes and after rolling (Kaccha Beedi) deliver it back to the factory. The roasting, labelling and packing process performed by the factory's workers. Then factory owner/manager is sold it directly in the market. No middleman is involved in this system. This system is 'home-based work system';
- **Contract System:** Under this system factory owner/manager distributes the raw material to intermediaries like sattedar/contractor/Agent who in turn employs worker and get the beedi rolled either the shed maintained by him (first) or through 'out workers' (second). This system is the widely prevalent system where by contractor get the beedis rolled and the company does the checking, roasting, labelling and packing in its premises. In this system the second sub-system (beedi rolling by workers in their own homes) is most prevalent in the beedi industry; and
- **Sale-Purchase System:** Under this system the raw material is sold to the workers (in most cases on credit basis) who roll beedis at their own homes. Then the beedi

rolled by the worker (initially buyer of Raw Material) are brought from them by the same contractor/trades/company (but using different name). This system has been adopted by the factory owner to avoid the 'employer-employee relationship and obligations' under the beedi workers laws. Under this system the factory owner registers different companies for the purpose. The details are given below:

1. One company is responsible for buying the raw material from the market and sells it to the second company;
2. Second company then sells the raw material to the contractor or directly to the worker;
3. The worker is required to prepare the beedis which are then 'sold' back by them to third company. This company is responsible for only 'buying' the finished beedis from the workers; and
4. The fourth company is for 'sell out' the finished beedi in the market.

The most interesting fact is that all there companies are owned usually by one family. The worker has no choice and no control over the entire process. They are the mute spectators of the 'play'. Under this system workers are exploited most and their wages are very low.

Home based beedi rolling is the most widely prevalent and within the home based system there can be three work systems through which the beedi is made, namely—the direct system, contract system and the sale purchase system. In the direct system women directly take raw materials from the owner/managers and return the rolled beedis. Under contract system women take raw materials from contractors. Under this system process exhaust as mentioned above. According to different studies, earlier when the work was direct, men used to be equally active in the beedi rolling but since most factories and work units have close down. Now the beedi rolling work has become 'home-based' and thereby dominated by women (non-factory work). Men workers are involved mainly in warming, labelling, packing, dispatching, marketing and selling the finished product.

As per WHO report, there were about 110 crore smokers (Table 16.1) in the world. Out of them, 30 crore were (27 percent) in the developed countries, while 80 crore (73 percent) were in the developing countries. Out of total smokers, 90 crore (82 percent) were males and 20 crore (18 percent) were female (Verma and Rehman, 2005: 8).

Table 16.1: Number of Smokers in the World

Countries	No. (crore)			Percent			Total percent
	M	F	T	M	F	T	
Developed	20	10	30	67	33	100	27
Developing	70	10	80	87	13	100	73
World	90	20	110	72	18	100	100

Source: Prepared from Verma and Rehman, 2005, p. 8.

Virtually smokers consume tobacco in a variety of forms like-cigarettes, beedi, snuff, chewing and so on. As far as the matter of Indian smokers is concerned, the most popular forms are beedi and chewing tobacco. However, the maximum employment is generated in beedi manufacturing.

Women Workers in the Beedi Manufacturing Sector

Beedi manufacturing is a traditional 'agro-forest' based and 'home-based' industry in India. It is highly 'labour-intensive' and predominantly unorganised (ILO, 2003). There are varying estimates of the numbers of beedi workers in India. Most of the 'Statistical Agencies' arc unable to capture the complete picture of beedi' workers. Official estimate of the total number of beedi workers in India is about 44 lakh (Ministry of Labour, A.R. 1999-2000: 109). Unofficially however, the trade unions and NGOs tell the actual number of 'beedi rollers' could be much higher than official estimate. But the trade unions estimate that the figure would be close to 70 lakh (Rajashekher and Sreedhar, 2002). As per the estimate of AITUC, about 75 workers are engaged in this industry (K.L.

Mahendra, G.S., 2001). They argue that since most of the home based beedi workers do not have 'identity cards'. In terms of Employment the share of beedi industry is about 46.16 percent (Table 16.2). Beedi tobacco is the most important 'non-Virginia tobacco' produced in India. As per the report of Tobacco Institute of India, beedis account for over 50 percent of tobacco consumed in India.

Table 16.2: Segment-wise Employment in Tobacco Industry in India

S.N		Employment	
		No. (in lakh)	Percent
1.	Beedi	55.23	46.16
2.	Cigarette	9.43	8.39
3.	Tendu Leaves	19.66	17.50
4.	Non-Smoking Tobacco Processing Sector	27.59	24.56
5.	Match	0.44	0.39
Total		112.34	100.00

Source: Computed from Varma and Rehman, 2005, p. 14.

In terms of employment, Beedi manufacturing sector occupies an important place in the country next only to agriculture, handloom and construction sectors (Rajashekhar and Sreedhar, 2002: 1). If we taking into account those engaged in the beedi trade, including tendu leaf collection, the actual numbers of people involved in beedi sector as a whole would be at least twice as high. That is the beedi sector in known as 'largest employers' of the workers.

In the beginning employment in the industry was mostly concentrated in small and big factories. But now a day most of the beedi workers are 'home-based'. Presently, the great majority of the workers are constituted by women and child labourers. Out of total beedi workers about 90 percent are 'home-based' women workers (ILO, 2001). Over the years, there has been a shift away from the 'factory based production' to the homes of the workers. This shift has also been accompanied by 'feminization' of the workforce (ILO, 2003). This sector is predominated by women virtually beedi rolling sector is female intensive sector.

Two important features are co-related with each other in beedi sector. First, home-based work and second, female intensity. Where the beedi and cigar workers (Conditions of Employment) Act, 1966 came into existence in the year of 1966, this work (Mainly Beedi Rolling work) shifted from factories to workers' house due to certain reasons from employer side (Demand Side). Many scholars accept it. According to Jhabvala (1985), over the years, beedi rolling has increasingly moved from 'factory premises to workers homes' thus enabling the employer to avoid (his) 'legal obligations' under various social security acts. This way work travelled from factory to workers' house. This selfish desire of employers was mainly behind this move. If workers work in their own homes, then no direct 'employee-employer relations' stand between them. In this situation, employers should be free from such legal obligation provided in Beedi and Cigar Workers Act, 1966 and other social securities acts. This new home-based system is serving the desires of factory owners. That's why this new system was introduced by the factories owners.

When this work of beedi rolling came into the home from factory, women of family shared this responsibility. After some time they became a trained beedi workers. She can not take away from the work, which is stand at her home. The fact is that women are the sole performer of the work at home. We all know about that women have the responsibility for reproductive work of all kinds, including childcare, husband care, elder care, kitchen care, home maintenance and other duties, which can discharge at house level. In many communities 'cultural traditions' require that women observe 'seclusion' and 'pardah'. Women's mobility is very restricted. The work out of home is generally not permitted for women.

The only kind of work 'socially acceptable' for women in many communities is home-based work. As per on study in Muslim household, beedi manufacturing in homes offers the best opportunity to optimize labour utilization. In its absence, and given the continuing restrictions on women working outside their home, the average income of the households would fall by nearly half (Bhatty, 1980). The study further emphasized that the utilization of household female labour depends on the 'availability or remunerative opportunities' of work whose acceptance does not conflict with established customs; if such opportunities are available, households are likely to respond to them.

As we think this is good thing to limited extend because 'economic compulsions' are breaking the 'painful customs'. If they go with the painful custom, they have no option expect their families far-far away from bread. This work is harmful for them. When women accept this work, they loss sleep, rest, leisure and some time even missing of meals (Gopal, 1988). Under economic and other compulsions, women accept the work of beedi rolling. In this situation, we can imagine the 'deplorable condition' of beedi workers.

Another study (Dharmalingam, 1993), Beedi manufacturing involves 'certain skill' that needs to be imparted gradually. Girls are introduced to beedi manufacturing when they are as young as four years old. Out of 100, 50 percent beedi assistants were introduced to work between 5-10 years of age and another 50 percent between 11-15 years of age. It took around 5 years to learn the full beedi manufacturing process. It is clear from different study that such 'apprenticeship' makes it easy for mothers to pass on their skill to their daughters. It also affects the 'Inter-Generational occupational mobility'. We think that there are following reasons behind this low mobility or downward mobility:

- Mobility of women is restricted in that community, where the tradition of Pardah and seclusion is strictly observed.

- Now it is being largely home based work especially after 1966.
- Under economic pressure, they have no option but to accept this hazardous work, which is easily available to their homes.
- They have no alternative options regarding employment.
- In many cases, their male partners are in under-employment. They are lacking availability of work for the whole month.
- Male partners are not getting even the notified minimum wages from the employers.
- In many studies, the size of families is too big in comparison to their earning capacities.

There are three important things regarding the numbers of beedi workers:

- There are not sufficient number estimates prepared by the governmental agencies;
- The related estimates are too old; and
- The official estimate is too small in comparison to the actual size of the workers.

So we can say the official estimate is not giving us a 'real picture' about the number of women workers engaged in beedi manufacturing sector. Due to underestimation, no one can reach nearer to the 'actual condition' of beedi women workers. Underestimation of the numbers of people employed in beedi making results in their 'invisibility' to policy makers and in the allocation of resources, and as such, contributes directly to their vulnerability (Sudarshan and Kaur, et al. 1999:678). The Government of India estimates that there are close to 5 million (50 lakh) workers involved in the rolling of beedis, 90 percent of whom are home-based women workers. Unofficially however, the trade union, NGOs and academician say the actual number of beedi rollers could be much higher since most of the home based beedi workers do not have identity cards (ILO, 2003:1).

As per one trade union estimates, 75 lakh or more workers

are employed in Beedi industry of which 90-95 percent are women (Ratnakar, the president of the All India Beedi, Cigar and Tobacco Workers Federation, 2001).

The extent of under counting can be guessed also at from micro studies. As per the official estimate about the number of beedi workers in Tirunelveli district of Tamilnadu was around 1.8 lakh. But as per unofficial survey, the total number of beedi workers was 5.5 lakh (Gopal, 1999). Similarly in the case of West Bengal, the official estimate was 4.5 lakh beedi workers, whereas in another study only on Murshidabad district of West Bengal found that workers and middlemen engaged in home based put-out beedi rolling system were about 3 lakh (Bagchi and Mukhopadhayay, 1996:27). The 90 percent presence of home workers in one of the important factors to arrive at 'reliable estimates' of employment of women beedi workers.

This shows that there is a considerable difference between the estimates of the workforce in beedi work made by government and non-government sources. The necessity of having a 'proper assessment' of the workforce employed in beedi industry is important.

The identification and the provision of ID card is a major issued for the beedi workers. According to the provision of the Beedi and Cigar Workers (Conditions of Employment) Act, 1966, the beedi sector 'employers' are responsible for issuing the 'identity card' to the beedi workers. Since many employers do not fulfill this responsibility, the labour welfare organization under the Ministry of Labour also issues ID cards to the beedi workers through the welfare commissioners (ILO, 2003:2). According to Ministry of Labour, nearly 86.86 percent of beedi workers in India hold ID cards. It means about 14 percent identified workers are waiting for their ID cards. When we see the state-wise and sex-wise breakup, a very unsatisfactory picture come before our eyes. Uttar Pradesh and Bihar are the state, where more than 40 percent beedi workers not get their ID cards out of them majority chunk are women.

In the case of Murshidabad, only 9 percent workers have been issued ID cards (Sudarshan and Kaur, 1999:679). The trade unions also claim that majority of the beedi workers (mostly women) still do not have the ID cards. The Labour Welfare Fund (Amendment) Act, 1987 provides for a fine up to ₹ 200 to every employer/contractor engaged in beedi manufacturing for non-issuance of ID cards. One vital problem is identification of unidentified women beedi workers.

Socio-economic Conditions

Various studies on the socio-economic conditions of beedi workers in different parts of the country reflect that beedi workers come from lower socio-economic strata. Socially and economically backward communities have been the main source of labour in beedi industry (Report of the Committee on Co-operatisation of Beedi Industry: 1-2). Among Hindus, the beedi sector is dominated by other backward caste (43 percent) and scheduled caste (15.2 percent). The other major religious category the Muslims (20 percent) who are primarily located in Kerala and Andhra Pradesh (S.K. Das, 2000 and MOL, 1995). Even today the beedi workers are found to be either Muslims or from the backward castes. We can testify the things from different studies. In Ahmedabad, most of the women beedi workers come from three communities/castes (Chauhan: 21) viz.:

- Padmashali (migrants from Andhra Pradesh);
- Kosthi community (backward caste migrated from Madhya Pradesh); and
- Muslim community (local to Ahmedabad).

In Ahmednagar, most of the women workers belonged to backward 'Telugu' communities (migrated from Telangana region). In Gudiuttam and Vellore the female workers belonged to backward and lower caste of 'Tamil' Communities (Chauhan: 21). The unions also point out that beedi workers constitute a major share of the workforce under the poverty line (ILO, 2001:11). Majority (60 percent) of the women beedi workers are illiterates. Bihar had the highest percentage (91 percent) of illiterate women workers. But the over all literally rate among the Beedi workers was 39 percent (socio-economic conditions of women workers in selected beedi units of the country, 1994-95, MOL, 1995). So it is clear that the incidence of illiteracy is very high among women beedi workers.

Wages and Earnings

The earning of beedi workers tend to be much lower than in other industries. Workers do not get the 'minimum wages' due to various practices in this industry such as rejections of rolled beedis on grounds of quality or making the worker pay for extra leaves, making the workers pay for short falls in the beedis rolled are some ways of cutting payments (ILO, 2001:12). Not only this, minimum wages for beedi making are different in different places. Different states have fixed different minimum wages for beedi workers. Sometimes within states there are differences in minimum wages for different districts. We can take the examples of West Bengal, where minimum wages in 24 Paraganas and Calcutta are ₹ 71.16, in Howrah and Hoogly ₹ 62.15 and in Purulia only ₹ 39.90 (Chauhan: 21). This 'wide discrepancy' in wage affects the earning and standard of living of women beedi workers.

Minimum wages are generally fixed on a daily or monthly rate. After the enactment of Beedi and Cigar Workers Act, 1966, the minimum wage in beedi sector began to be fixed on a 'piece rate' basis (per 1000 beedi rolled). The Regional Labour Ministers' conference in 1994-95 recommended that the minimum basic wages for beedi workers should not be less than ₹ 25 a day for 1,000 beedis based on the estimate that an average worker could roll 800 beedis per day. It was also recommended that minimum wages in the adjoining states should not vary by more than ₹ 3 (Bhattacharya and Bhattacharya, 2000). One-study reveals that the official minimum wages fixed for the beedi workers range from as low as ₹ 29 per thousand beedis rolled in Tripura to about 65 per thousand beedis rolled in Gujarat (S.K. Das, 2000).

This industry is also an important example of 'Gender based discrimination'. It is clear from many studies that men generally earned more than women. Employers and contractors attitudes towards men and women workers differ. As per one study, it is found that women's earning is 'additional' or 'marginal' to the total household income. Women workers rarely get minimum wages prescribed by the state governments. According to one study, the actual average earning of the Beedi Workers are about 20 percent less than the minimum wage (Jhabvala et al., 1885). The average weekly wage per thousands is between 55 and 60 percent of what they are entitled to. The minimum wage of beedi workers is too low compared to many types of work. Even 'agricultural labourers' get more wages than beedi workers.

In M.P. beedi rollers earn ₹ 700-₹ 900 per month and the minimum wages are ₹ 32 (Ajit Jain); in Munger (Bihar) minimum wages are ₹ 41 but average income of beedi workers is ₹ 200-₹ 500 (Virendra Vikal). They spend more than 12 hours in a day and not get the minimum amount notified by the government. The situation of 'under-employment' also affects the earning of beedi workers. As per various studies, the majority of beedi workers of India are in under employment. The income is critical to the survival of the households, who are mainly dependent on beedi work.

Unionisation of Beedi Workers

The 'bargaining capacity' of the women beedi workers is very weak. Neither the employer non trade union recognize women as an important segment of the labour force (Prasad and Akhtar, 1984 and Sudarshan and Kaur, 1999). Out of 75 lakh beedi workers, hardly 15 percent are organized in the unions (Ratnakar, President, T.U., 2001). The All India Beedi, Cigar and Tobacco Workers Federation (AIBCTWF) affiliated to the AITUC still has a fairly large membership of nearly 2.5

lakh members among beedi workers (Ratnakar). According to another calculation, the total number of organized workers in this sector will be nearly 5.55 lakh. So hardly 8-10 percent of the workers are affiliated with recognized trade unions (Chauhan: 20). The rage of unionization is very low among the women beedi workers. The rate of membership is not satisfactory.

Health Conditions

The health hazards connected with tobacco use have been well documented, and have resulted in a worldwide campaign against tobacco. We know that those persons, who are in close contact with tobacco, as rollers or processors, would face some ill effects. According to the study of National Institute of occupational health, there is a 50 percent reduction in the 'Lung capacity' of the workers after a period of five years (Jhabvala, Gupta and Mishra). The presence of 'Nicotine' in tobacco causes various health problems both for tobacco users and those who work with tobacco.

The continuous contact of beedi women workers with tobacco (Nicotine) and the inhalation of 'tobacco dust', it creates some health hazards for them. Ultimately, they are suffered from occupational disease like abdominal pains, bronchitis, anemia, asthma, tuberculosis, cancer, arthritis, spondilitis, swelling of lower limbs, indigestion, constipation and so on. As per Rao (1992, Jabalpur), most women workers complained of backache and joint-pains. About 50-60 percent women reported gynaecological problems, whereas 36 percent had eye problems like watering, burning and about 60 percent reported giddiness and headache, of which the main cause could be the exposure to tobacco dust. Respiratory problems seemed to be quite common. Women tend to suffer a number of problems relating to menstruation and pregnancy. Many of women workers reported in various studies about their heavy bleeding during menstruation and pain in lower abdomens. They also have a high degree of leuchorrea. There have been a large number of miscarriages, which the women connect with their postures (ILO, 2001). In this study most of these problems have been confirmed by the doctors to the researchers. According to one gynaecologist, the 'UKARY' position which the women sat in while rolling beedis created a pressure on their 'Abdominal Region' leading to 'pregnancy complications' and occasional miscarriages.

Legal Protection

The beedi industry comes under the unorganized sector. There are so many legislations enacted for the protection and welfare of the beedi workers. In 1948, after the passing of the Factories Act, the beedi factories began to close down and work began to move into the homes, to be done both by men and women. By the early sixties, homework was more the rule than expectation. The degree of exploitation was very high. Over the years, many efforts have been made by the trade unions and government (social partners) to improve the working and living conditions of workers and their families engaged in the beedi industry.

In order to protect the interest of the beedi workers and their families, the Government of India has taken two types of measurers- legislative and welfare measurers. The Government has enacted labour laws specifically for the beedi sector workers, which are given below:

1. **Beedi and Cigar (Conditions of Employment) Act, 1996:** To regulate the working and service conditions of the beedi workers. But this act does not address the problem of social security coverage for the beedi workers, especially the home based work and
2. **Beedi Workers Welfare Fund Act, 1976:** The main objective of this act is to provide welfare facilities related to health, educations, maternity, group insurance, recreation and housing to beedi workers and their families.
3. **Beedi Workers Welfare Cess Act, 1976:** The second one is important legislation meant for the welfare of beedi

workers. The BWWF is financed through a levy of cess (@₹ 2/- per 1000 beedis) by ways of 'excise duty' on manufactured beedi. About 39 lakh workers are currently covered under the BWWF (ILO, 2003). Out of 44 lakh beedi workers, 36.57 lakh workers were issued ID cards by the year 1999-2000. Further 44 static dispensaries, 11 mobile units, 1 chest clinic, 1 ten bedded hospital and 20 fifty-bedded hospitals were being operated by the fund by the years 1999-2000 (Chauhan: 81). The welfare fund spends about ₹ 300 million per year on the above mentioned schemes.

Beside this, in April, 1992, the Ministry of Labour has introduced a 'Group Insurance Scheme' under the social security scheme of LIC of India for those beedi workers who not covered under the Provident Fund. This insurance scheme provides insurance cover or ₹ 10,000 in the case of nature death, ₹ 25000 in case of accidental death or permanent total disability (PTD) and ₹ 12500 in case of partial disability to those beedi workers who have ID cards (ILO, 2003:2).

Conclusions

Despite many acts, they are being exploited by the employers, contractors and government officials. More than 50 percent beedi workers are still far from the welfare facilities provided by the government. Majority beedi workers do not enjoy the legal protection provided under different act due to the prevalence of 'contract system' and 'gharkhata system'. There is lack of awareness among the workers about the act and its benefits. They were benefited only in those areas where unions are strong like in Ahmednagar, Ahmedabad and Guddiuttam (Chauhan : 85). Trade Union also claim that out of 36 lakh ID card holders, only small portions of them are getting the benefits and welfare and other social security schemes. The identification and the provision of ID cards is still a major issue for the beedi workers. Apart from this, related acts are not being implemented strictly. These efforts have led to the revision of minimum wages and coverage of many beedi workers for social security under the BWWF in several states. In this context, few co-operatives of beedi workers are doing best from their parts. They are protecting the interests of the beedi workers in true sense. In this regard, we can quote the example of 'Kerala Dinesh Beedi Workers Co-operative society Ltd. This co-operative at one time was providing employment and other benefits to more than 32,000 workers such type of efforts should be rewarded and promoted. In this light women beedi workers should be brought under the co-operative system at the village level so that every worker could be reckoned with and avoid different form of exploitation. There is also a need of 'Uniform National' or 'Zonal minimum wage' for the work in the beedi industry. In view of bleak future of the beedi industry, there is a need to prevent increase in the number of beedi workers by promoting 'alternative employment opportunities' for women workers and their families. This would require a programme for 'capacity building' of women beedi workers, skills diversification, micro-credit and marketing support.

References

Bhattacharya, Sharma and Bhattacharya, Manas (2000), "A study on the Beedi Industry in India: Employment Diversification for the New Millennium, ILO, New Delhi.

Bhatty, Zaina (1980), Economic Role and Status of Women: A case study of women in the Beedi Industry in Allahabad, ILO, Geneva.

Dharmalingam (1993), 'Female Beedi Workers in a South Indian Village', Economic and Political Weekly, July 3-10, pp. 1461-1468.

Das, S. K. (2000), A Better Deal for Beedi Workers: An Investigation into the impact of the Beedi workers welfare Fund and social Security Workers, a Report prepared for the ILO.

Gopal, Meena (1999), Disempowered Despite Wage, Work: Women Workers in Beedi Industry, EPW, April 17-23/24-30, pp. WS 12-20.

ILO (2001), Losing Work: A study of Beedi Workers in India,

Renana Jhabvala, Neelam Gupta and Nitu Mishra, a report prepared for ILO, pp. 1-5.

ILO (2003), Beedi Sector in India: A note, Improving working conditions and employment opportunities for women Beedi Workers, pp. 1-2.

ILO (2001), The Beedi Industry in India: An overview, improving conditions and employment opportunities for women workers in Beedi Industry, pp.1-12.

Rajashekhar and Sreedhar (2002), "Changing Face of Beedi Industry: A Study in Karnataka", Economic and Political Weekly, Vol. XXXVII, No. 34, pp. 4023-4028.

Verma, Uday Kumar and Rehman, M.M. (2005), Tobacco, Tendu Leaf and Beedi Workers in India: Problems and prospects, Shipra Publications, Delhi, p. 8.

Index

Index